T0367864

The Revelation of the Sealed Book

ANÍBAL VÉLEZ

WESTBOW®
PRESS
A DIVISION OF THOMAS NELSON
& ZONDERVAN

Cover design by Diane Sheats and Ariel Vélez.
Original cover image of John on Patmos by Gustave Doré (1832–1883).

WestBow Press books may be ordered through booksellers or by contacting:

WestBow Press
A Division of Thomas Nelson & Zondervan
1663 Liberty Drive
Bloomington, IN 47403
www.westbowpress.com
1 (866) 928-1240

ISBN: 978-1-4908-2417-8 (sc)
ISBN: 978-1-4908-2418-5 (hc)
ISBN: 978-1-4908-2416-1 (e)

Library of Congress Control Number: 2014901593

Printed in the United States of America.

WestBow Press rev. date: 5/12/2014

Who is worthy to open the scroll
and to loose its seals?
Behold, the Lion of the tribe of Judah,
the Root of David, has prevailed to open
the scroll and to loose its seven seals.
Then He came and took the scroll out of the
right hand of Him who sat on the throne.

Contents

List of Figures

About the Author

Aníbal Vélez, author of this book, was born on the island of Puerto Rico, where he also began his walk and life in the Lord Jesus. His first encounter with God occurred in 1974, when he was completing his university studies in chemical engineering. Since then, he has been a fervent servant of the Lord Jesus Christ, with great zeal for God's word, which is powerful to open the eyes of those who with sincere heart surrender to Him.

During his fruitful career, together with his beloved wife and six children (four sons and two daughters), he has experienced the goodness and grace of God in all the aspects of his life. He has travelled to several countries to share the word of God, including several times to remote places in Philippines, Nigeria, and Kenya in Africa, where his stay lasted two months for each visit.

His deep interest in the topic of prophecy began when, at the time of his first steps in the Lord, he had a dream where several related end-time events were shown to him. This brother saw an Elder with white garments and hair as snow, and as He approached him, his body was trembling. The Old Man tenderly took him to a cleft of a rock which was on the side, and then said: "Look beyond, at what I show you."

As he looked at a large valley, from the hill where he was, he saw several apocalyptic events which caused him great shock. Upon waking from sleep, the brother was amazed, and although it was still night, he proceeded to write the dream on a paper and save it. At that time he had not yet read or heard about those events to happen in the future; so he did not understand anything he had seen in the dream.

Over time, while he was reading the Book of Revelation in the Bible, he found various passages which described some events he remembered from his dream. He looked for the paper with the dream and could see that they were the same events described in the Scriptures.

Although Aníbal does not depend on dreams to walk in the Lord, this dream sparked his interest to study end-time prophecies more deeply. He dedicated more than fifteen years to complete this book, considered as a fascinating and comprehensive research of end times.

Preface

The Great Tribulation is a long period of sufferings that will be experienced by all inhabitants living on the earth during the latter times. In the past, many catastrophic events and terrible wars have been registered in the history of humanity, such as the First and Second World Wars, where millions of human beings died.

Although these conflicts were disastrous, none of them is to be compared to the events prophesied to start soon. Jesus said, "For then there will be great tribulation, such as has not been since the beginning of the world until this time, no, nor ever shall be" (Matt. 24:21). The word of God is real and true to point out the specific events that will happen and the scope that these will have in the entire world.

This book is the product of more than thirty-nine years of contact with the Scriptures, and has been written under the teaching and inspiration of the Holy Spirit. After feeling a deep yearning in my heart to share with others what God has let me see by His grace and kindness, I have completed this book, which I hope in the Lord will be of great blessing to everyone who reads it. I spent more than fifteen years completing this job.

An interesting note is that when I felt I had almost all the information to start writing, I decided to read the whole Bible again with only one thought in my mind: the end times. This offered me an excellent opportunity to see again a fresh panorama of God's plan for the church, the people of Israel, and all the other nations. It was the most wonderful reading I have experienced in my years serving the Lord Jesus. I could see the plan and goal of God from a macro point of view—from Genesis to Revelation.

There is relevant and fascinating information in this book, in such a way that the reader will enjoy it very much. You will find the most complete information about the end times in only one book. The book includes historical issues, detailed and deep explanation of the most relevant scriptures (some chapters of Daniel and Ezekiel, Matthew 24, the whole Book of Revelation, and others), as well as an explanation of one of the last prophecies to be fulfilled before the judgment of God commences—Russia's attack on Israel.

I pray before the Lord that He may light up our lives and guide us, in this time we live in, to a place where we can please and serve Him with all our minds and hearts. Oh Lord, we pray that we may know You and be part of what You are doing at this time in the body of Christ, Your church, which You will keep from the hour of trial that will come over the whole world, to test those who live on the earth! Father, blessed are You forever, for Your great mercy and love to Your children, those who love You and obey Your word with a sincere heart. Amen.

Acknowledgments

I am very thankful to God for allowing me to complete this writing, which after many years of study and work, I know will be of great benefit and blessing for many.

I thank Sister Diane for her contribution in the cover development and design, and for her great job in editing and some other related jobs. I thank also my son Ariel for his help with the cover design and the interior figures. I thank all of those who through their prayers have also partaken in the completion of this book.

Original cover image of John on Patmos by Gustave Doré (1832–1883).

Notes

Unless otherwise noted, all Scripture references in this book are taken from the New King James Bible version, copyright © 1982 by Thomas Nelson, Inc. (Used by permission. All rights reserved.) This bible was used through the online version: http://bible.gospelcom.net or http://www.biblegateway.com.

Translations to English are made when references from other languages Bible versions are used. The abbreviations of Bible versions are used for some quotations, according to *References*.

When a Bible reference is quoted and it is written between parentheses, the abbreviation *v.* or *vv.* may be used to replace the word *verse* or *verses*, respectively. When a comment, word, or phrase is inserted within a Bible reference, it will be written in square brackets. To give more emphasis to some words or phrases in Bible references, boldface or italic types are used by the author.

In many cases, the referenced passage is too long and not included in the book. I suggest that all biblical references be read to obtain the greatest benefit.

Dedication

Although I have written this small book with all my heart, all inspiration and revelation to produce it are from God. It has not been conceived by means of human reasoning or private interpretation. Therefore, I believe that there is no person to whom I can dedicate this writing, but only to our Lord Jesus Christ. He is worthy of all honor and glory. He paid the great price for our salvation; therefore, it is He who deserves to be recognized and honored.

I only feel I am His servant, grateful for the work He has done. Oh Lord Jesus, receive this writing with pleasure, that You may use it for the blessing and edification of those who with sincere heart come close to You, our only God and Savior! Blessed are You, Lord, blessed be Your holy name forever.

Introduction

Much has been written and preached about the future events that await humanity and the entire earth. For many this is a worn-out subject, for others it is a frightening subject, and others view it with indifference. But for those who believe by faith in the Lord Jesus Christ, and seek and live each day a life closer to God, this is a subject of great edification.

What we hear today more and more from the leaders of the nations is related to the so-called *New World Order,* the *New Global Community,* or *Globalization.* In February 2009, the members of the seven greatest nations of the world, the so-called G-7, met and in a unanimous voice declared that it is necessary to develop a *New Economic World Order* to deal with the economic problems being experienced worldwide.

Through these leaders, the foundations are being set, so that the direction or government of a single leader will be widely accepted—a "wise" and charismatic one capable to accept this great responsibility.

While I was searching for certain information, I encountered some articles mentioning a famous historian, who apparently has stated that the nations of the world are ready to give their governments to a man who offers a solution to the current problems that they are experiencing.

In an article about another leader, who was in the highest positions of the United Nations Organization (UNO) and North Atlantic Treaty Organization (NATO), who once apparently said that what they wanted was a man that had enough maturity and influence to gain the support of the people, and bring the world out of the economic morass in which it is sinking, and when this man appears, no matter where he comes from, he would be welcomed.

The nations of the world are under the effects of a "convulsion" and do not know where the end of the tunnel is. They do not even understand the alternatives or processes they can implement to solve the many complex problems that distress society. That is why they are allowing themselves to be led by leaders with revolutionary ideas with great cost consequences. Those who have no knowledge of biblical prophecies, whose lives are not given to God, are the ones who will be deceived by this stream of ideas—many of which reflect a lack of value of human life.

But you, beloved reader, may open your eyes in time, and come in and live an abundant life in the Lord Jesus, because "if God is for us, who can be against us?"

Through this book, I have wanted to present what I understand is clear according to the word of God. I have not wanted to echo interpretations that have no clearness and foundation in the Scriptures. I have searched out these apocalyptic topics with all sincerity of heart for many years, in order to write with the most biblical foundation possible.

This book has not been prepared to criticize other authors or expositors, who understand these topics in a different way, but to encourage and edify, specifically those who with sincere hearts walk close to God.

To have more understanding of apocalyptic subjects, it is necessary to consider certain topics related to the purpose that God had in the past and continues having for the people of Israel. There are prophecies directly related to the nation of Israel which have not been fulfilled yet. Many people think that Israel is already out of the focus or purpose of God, but this is not so; God has not yet finished His dealing with His chosen people.

To understand more clearly what will happen in the world in latter times, I believe it is necessary to touch these areas. To accomplish this purpose, I have included in this book those events that the ancient prophets saw and those that they did not see: events related to issues that in some way changed the history of the whole world.

Also, some prophecies of the Book of Daniel have been included, such as what I call the "prophetic clock," which describe the fulfillment time of apocalyptic events. Chapter 24 of the Gospel of Matthew is included too, since the message contained in it, along with the Book of Revelation, describes what God has purposed to happen by the end of this generation.

I included in chapter 6 some interesting information related to a battle where Russia will attack Israel soon. This battle is prophesied by the prophet Ezekiel. The destruction of Russia and its coalition military forces by a direct intervention of God will produce such a great spiritual awakening in the people of Israel that many of them will believe in God.

This book presents a great amount of information related to catastrophic events prophesied to happen soon. It will be of great relief for our souls to see that God is great in mercy and yes, He has remembered those who love and serve Him with a sincere heart. For this reason, the last two topics included in this book are related to the church that the Lord designed and the "catching up" of the faithful believers by Jesus. I believe it is indispensable to clearly understand what kind of church the Lord will take up when He delivers her from the hour of trial which shall come upon the whole world.

I do not pretend to include in this writing all the biblical references related to this topic; neither will I present myself as one with special wisdom to teach others. All published writings may have points of view which sometimes at first look strange or different from others, and I think this writing will not be exempt from that.

However, before the reader rejects something written here, I invite him to have a little patience, and consider each part in the light of a mind and heart enlightened and directed by God. It is my intention to share these riches in Jesus Christ manifested by the Holy Spirit and made known to those who get nearer to God, who recognize His word and the revelation of the eternal purpose of God for mankind.

The Scriptures tell us in Romans 16:25–26 that since ancient times, the prophets (the men through whom God chose to declare His word) spoke the word of God "in mysteries."

> Now to Him who is able to establish you according to my gospel and the preaching of Jesus Christ, according to the revelation of the mystery kept secret since the world began but now made manifest, and by the prophetic Scriptures made known to all nations, according to the commandment of the everlasting God, for obedience to the faith.

Nevertheless, the "fuller" revelation has been brought through Jesus Christ, the Messiah, our Savior. The ancient prophets did not understand many things of which they spoke. We might say that they saw through the "prophetic eye," so that even in seeing the things to come, they could not discover their meaning. Daniel 12:4 says, "But you, Daniel, shut up the words, and seal the book until the time of the end." Daniel 12:8–9 also says,

> Although I heard, I did not understand. Then I said, "My Lord, what shall be the end of these things?"
> And he said, "Go your way, Daniel, for the words are closed up and sealed till the time of the end.

But glory to God, who sent Jesus Christ to give us understanding! Hallelujah, to Him be the glory and honor forever! God did not leave us orphans and lacking understanding. He sent His Spirit who, among many other things, teaches and directs us to green pastures and waters of rest.

The end time has come, the time to open the book which Daniel was commanded to seal. For this, God raised another prophet, the apostle John. This man was chosen by God to open the book that the prophet Daniel had closed and sealed. In Revelation 22:10 we read, "And he said to me, 'Do not seal the words of the prophecy of this book, for the time is at hand.'"

As it says in the above-mentioned scripture of Romans chapter 16, "made known to all nations … for obedience to the faith," God reveals His purpose and will to those who are capable of obeying and experiencing the riches of His glory. The simple knowledge of facts and the experiences of others do not make us partakers of His promises. The "law of the Spirit of life in Christ Jesus" has to be experienced by each of us in an individual way.

Each one must know the Lord and must have the capability to live in Him and experience Him in a real and continuous way. We are property of the Lord, and in this way we must walk, expressing His true image in this world. "He who says he abides in Him ought himself also to walk just as He walked" (1 John 2:6). Therefore, when God reveals His purpose and will, He does it so that we can obey Him.

Why is this word of the end times for the church, if she will not go through the trials of the Great Tribulation? God chose the church for a great mission: to spread the gospel and to bring understanding of His purpose and will to all people. Ephesians 3:9–11 says,

> and to make all see what is the fellowship of the mystery, which from the beginning of the ages has been hidden in God who created all things through Jesus Christ; to the intent that now the manifold wisdom of God might be made known by the church to the principalities and powers in the heavenly places, according to the eternal purpose which He accomplished in Christ Jesus our Lord.

Therefore, it is the church which must have a full understanding of all future events, in order to teach and proclaim them in a sound and clear way. He who loves God and walks in His will can know and understand the mysteries of God, since they are understood not through human intelligence or ability, but by the revelation of God through the Holy Spirit. Jesus said, "If anyone wills to do His will, he shall know concerning the doctrine, whether it is from God or whether I speak on My own authority" (John 7:17).

The Book of Revelation was written for the church.

> John, to the seven churches which are in Asia: Grace to you and peace from Him who is and who was and who is to come.
> What you see, write in a book and send it to the seven churches which are in Asia.
> He who has an ear, let him hear what the Spirit says to the churches.
>
> Revelation 1:4, 11; 2:7

Therefore, all members of the church have the responsibility to understand and keep this word of God. "Blessed is he who reads and those who hear the words of this prophecy, and keep those things which are written in it; for the time is near" (Rev. 1:3).

> Then he said to me, 'These words are faithful and true.' And the Lord God of the holy prophets sent His angel to show His servants the things which must shortly take place.
> 'Behold, I am coming quickly! Blessed is he who keeps the words of the prophecy of this book.'
>
> Revelation 22:6–7

In addition to this, in the last two chapters of Revelation we find one of the most wonderful and glorious pictures of God's final purpose—the full union (wedding) of the Lord Jesus with His bride, the church. With this final event, God fulfills His goal for mankind as He states it in Ephesians 1:9–12,

> having made known to us the mystery of His will, according to His good pleasure which He purposed in Himself, that in the dispensation of the fullness of the times He might gather together in one all things in Christ, both which are in heaven and which are on earth—in Him. In Him also we have obtained an inheritance, being predestined according to the purpose of Him who works all things according to the counsel of His will, that we who first trusted in Christ should be to the praise of His glory.

How great and wonderful is the plan of God for us! Amen.

CHAPTER 1

What the Old Prophet Saw

P rior to Christ, God selected servants and prophets to be torches shining the way of men. These were faithful people given to the will of God, who heard the voice of the Lord and immediately obeyed Him. Part of the plan of God for future generations was revealed through them. I say that "part" was revealed, because not the entire plan of God for all times was revealed to them. The revelation of God to the ancient people before Christ was a "shadow of things to come" (Col. 2:17).

Then what did the ancient prophets see in relation to God's promises? They saw what I call the revealed mystery through the *prophetic eye*, which did not provide a total understanding of its meaning. Many of the events they foretold were experienced in their age, while others were to be fulfilled in the future. Still other prophecies were fulfilled more than once. God is a supreme God who does things in a way that sometimes we do not understand with total clarity. But this is what is marvelous about Him.

This is like many of the parables told by the Lord Jesus in the gospels. Many people did not understand His words. On the other hand, Jesus told His disciples that He would not speak in parables to them but would speak clearly to them.

He who loves God and walks in His will shall understand and know the mysteries of God, since they will be understood and known not by human intelligence or ability but by the same revelation of God through the Holy Spirit. Jesus said, "If anyone wills to do His will, he shall know concerning the doctrine, whether it is from God or whether I speak on My own authority" (John 7:17).

The ancient prophets who lived before the Lord Jesus and prophesied about future events on earth did not see all the coming events, especially those related to the church of the Lord.

Of this salvation the prophets have inquired and searched
carefully, who prophesied of the grace that would come to you,
searching what, or what manner of time, the Spirit of Christ
who was in them was indicating when He testified beforehand
the sufferings of Christ and the glories that would follow.
To them it was revealed that, not to themselves, but to us
they were ministering the things which now have been
reported to you through those who have preached the
gospel to you by the Holy Spirit sent from heaven—things
which angels desire to look into.

1 Peter 1:10–12

In order to give the clearest possible expression of what I am saying,
let us consider the diagram in figure 1: The Prophetic Eye. (This figure
was conceived using an idea or example of one chart found in the book
Dispensational Truth by Clarence Larkin—Ref. 1.)

In this diagram, each "peak" represents an important event that
affected or will affect the earth and its inhabitants. The ancient prophet
saw the peaks presented in this diagram, but he did not see what I call the
"valley," nor did he see the short peak that represents the "catching up"
(rapture) of the church.

Let me mention some examples of events that the ancient prophets saw,
which are represented by the peaks of the diagram in figure 1.

- The great flood, prophesied by Noah, was to be fulfilled in the time
  of the prophet Noah.
- The prophets saw the birth of Christ (Isa. 7:14; 9:6–7; Mic. 5:2), His
  sufferings and death (Isa. 53:1–12, Num. 9:12, Ps. 34:20), His resurrection
  (Ps. 16:10), and the pouring out of the Holy Spirit (Joel 2:28–29).
- After the death of the Messiah Jesus Christ and the coming of the
  Holy Spirit, something happened in Israel that was also prophesied.
  This event was of great importance, since it was the last event to
  happen before the coming of the final judgment over Israel and all
  the other nations. Daniel 9:26 says,

  And after the sixty-two weeks Messiah shall be cut off,
  but not for Himself; and the people of the prince who is to
  come shall destroy the city and the sanctuary. The end of it
  shall be with a flood, and till the end of the war desolations
  are determined.

2

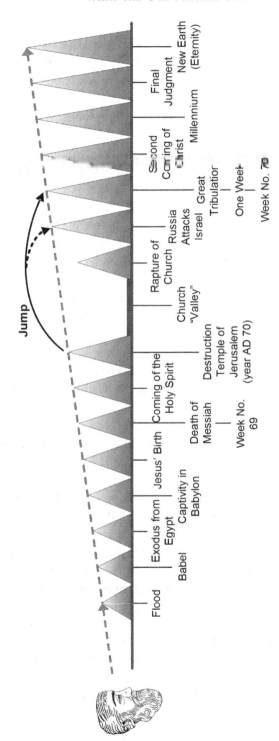

Figure 1: The Prophetic Eye

In year AD 70, this prophecy was totally fulfilled, when a Roman general named Titus Flavius Vespasianus destroyed the city of Jerusalem and the temple. At that time, thousands of Jews lost their lives and other thousands were scattered far.

According to history, when the temple was burned, the gold over the walls melted and spread over the stones. Trying to recover the gold, the Roman soldiers took away stone by stone, fulfilling in this way the prophecy of Jesus, who said, "Not one stone shall be left here upon another, that shall not be thrown down" (Matt. 24:2).

- The battle in which Russia attacks Israel is another surprising event prophesied by Ezekiel (Ezek. 38—39). This prophecy will have its fulfillment *in the latter days* before the Great Tribulation starts. The Lord will suppress all of Russia and its allies' military forces with "flooding rain, great hailstones, fire, and brimstone" (Ezek. 38:22).

- Another event that the prophets saw was the so-called Great Tribulation. The Great Tribulation will happen in the second half of a seven year period, during which all of the earth and its inhabitants will experience some events never seen before (Jer. 30:7; Dan. 7:19–25; 9:24–27; 12:1; Zech. 14:1–2).

- The Great Tribulation ends with the visible second coming of Christ to the earth. This event was also seen by the prophetic eye (Rev. 1:7; Zech. 12:10–14; 14:3–4; Matt. 24:30; Dan 7:13–14; 26–27). For the Jews, this will be like the first coming of Christ, since they did not believe in Jesus as the Messiah when He came the first time.

- The Millennium is another event prophesied by the ancient prophets (Zech. 14:16–19; Mic. 4:1–4). It consists of a period of one thousand years, which will take place after the Great Tribulation.

- One of the last events that the ancient prophets saw was the creation of the new heaven and a new earth: in other words, a new world (Isa. 65:17–25; 66:22)—which will happen after the Millennium.

God had a purpose in each event prophesied by the ancient prophets. Although this topic will be touched on later, it is very important to understand the place that the nation of Israel and the church occupy in the promises of God. The fulfillment of God's promises for Israel is not the same as that for the church. This is why the ancient prophets saw future events in a limited way.

CHAPTER 2

What the Old Prophet Did Not See

A s you see in figure 1: The Prophetic Eye, the ancient prophet did not see what is represented by the "valley," the church age, and the peak of the rapture of the church. This valley represents the period between the coming of the Holy Spirit, after the ascent of Jesus to heaven, and the beginning of the Great Tribulation. In this period, very important events have happened, and others will continue to happen up to the beginning of the Great Tribulation.

The most outstanding event was the origin of the church of the Lord. The ancient prophet did not have any idea what the church could be, according to the hidden purpose of God. He could see what was related to his own nation of Israel, even without much understanding, but could not see what was related to the new covenant in Christ Jesus, which is the church as the dwelling place of the Holy Spirit. Ephesians and Colossians talk about this mystery:

> … which in other ages was not made known to the sons of men, as it has now been revealed by the Spirit to His holy apostles and prophets: that the Gentiles should be fellow heirs, of the same body, and partakers of His promise in Christ through the gospel.
>
> Ephesians 3:5–6

> … the mystery which has been hidden from ages and from generations, but now has been revealed to His saints.
> To them God willed to make known what are the riches of the glory of this mystery among the Gentiles: which is Christ in you, the hope of glory.
>
> Colossians 1:26–27

The church, as the body of Christ and the habitation of the Holy Spirit, was hidden from the forefathers in the time before Christ until the coming of the disciples and apostles of Jesus. However, from the day of Pentecost, the purpose of God related to the design of His church has been available to those who love the Lord and live in obedience to His word.

Although there were men of God (prophets and kings) who loved God and had a relationship with Him (speaking in general terms), the Jewish people did not see the intimate spiritual communion that man could have with God. In ancient times, man communicated with God through other men (priests and prophets) and through sacrifices and rites. It was a very different relationship from the one established by Christ.

After the establishment of the church, man can now have a close relationship with God, in which he does not need sacrifices of animals or the intervention of other men. God has now made man capable of having direct communion with Him through the Holy Spirit.

> Likewise the Spirit also helps in our weaknesses. For we do not know what we should pray for as we ought, but the Spirit Himself makes intercession for us with groanings which cannot be uttered.
> Now He who searches the hearts knows what the mind of the Spirit is, because He makes intercession for the saints according to the will of God.
>
> Romans 8:26–27

The ancient prophet did not see the valley or "parentheses" of the church. The church is not only a people; it is more than a people—it will be the "bride" prepared by God for His Son. These are believers from all nations that will be saved, who are part of an organism (not an organization or system) which expresses the image and purpose of the Lord Jesus. The church waits for her **Lord** and **Husband**; on the other hand, Israel awaits the **Messiah** and **King**.

Another event the ancient prophets did not see was the catching up (rapture) of the church by Christ to dwell in heaven. The rapture will occur before the Great Tribulation, and it is not identified as the second coming of the Lord. This subject is discussed in more detail in the last chapter of this book.

There are many scriptures that clearly show the skip from Jesus and the outpouring of the Holy Spirit to the Great Tribulation events, without reference to the church time. Therefore, according to the old prophetic eye (mainly Daniel and Joel's prophecies), the next event to be fulfilled for Israel is the Great Tribulation (see figure 1); although Ezekiel prophesied of the closest event before the Great Tribulation—this is, the attack of Russia against Israel.

As we will expand later on Daniel chapter 9, the prophets saw what God designed for the people of Israel, but they did not see the new covenant with the church, so the ancient prophet overlooked the time of the church. For example, let us take Joel 2:28–32, which mentions three events that seem to occur in a continuous way:

- The pouring out of the Holy Spirit (Joel 2:28–29)

  > And it shall come to pass afterward that I will pour out my Spirit on all flesh; your sons and your daughters shall prophesy, your old men shall dream dreams, your young men shall see visions.
  > And also on my menservants and on my maidservants I will pour out my Spirit in those days.

- Great Tribulation events (Joel 2:30–31)

  > And I will show wonders in the heavens and in the earth: blood and fire and pillars of smoke.
  > The sun shall be turned into darkness, and the moon into blood, before the coming of the great and awesome day of the Lord.

- Millennium events (Joel 2:32)

  > And it shall come to pass that whoever calls on the name of the Lord shall be saved. For in Mount Zion and in Jerusalem there shall be deliverance, as the Lord has said, among the remnant whom the Lord calls.

It is well known by believers that the prophecy about the pouring out of the Holy Spirit took place fifty days after Jesus' death, as we see in Acts 2:1–4, confirmed by the apostle Peter when he accurately cites the Joel prophecy in Acts 2:16–21. After the pouring out of the Holy Spirit, there is no record in human history of the fulfillment of the other parts of Joel's prophecy.

7

According to Matthew 24:29 ("Immediately after the tribulation of those days the sun will be darkened, and the moon will not give its light; the stars will fall from heaven, and the powers of the heavens will be shaken."), and Revelation 6:12 ("I looked when He opened the sixth seal, and behold, there was a great earthquake; and the sun became black as sackcloth of hair, and the moon became like blood."), the events of Joel 2:30–31 will take place in the Great Tribulation.

Finally, Joel 2:32 will be fulfilled in the Millennium, after the second coming of Christ, at the end of the Great Tribulation. It is in this time that the remnant of Israel will be saved. There are other passages (prophecies) that show this same message, such as Zechariah 8:20–23, Micah 4:1–2, and others.

What happened between the pouring out of the Holy Spirit (vv. 2:28–29) and the events of the Great Tribulation (vv. 2:30–31)? In this period of time, the church arose, which, again, the old prophet did not see; this is why the prophets "jumped over" that period of time. There are other examples similar to the one in Joel that are presented in the section on Matthew in this book.

At this point, I would like to note two things: the dealing and covenant of God with Israel are not the same as with the church, and second, the church will not be present in the Great Tribulation. These items will be developed in more detail in this book.

As a summary, the following is stated:

- Israel is the people of God which will be shepherded. God promised them a land from the river of Egypt to the River Euphrates in Babylon—modern-day Iraq (Gen. 15:18). This will be Christ's kingdom (in the Millennium) on this earth.
- The church is the bride of the Son of God, Jesus, and co-heir with Him in the Father's kingdom in the new earth. God promised the church the New Jerusalem, the habitation of God the Father, to be established in the new earth (Revelation 21—22). The church is not "the spiritual Israel," as some teach.

CHAPTER 3

Book of Daniel

T he Book of Daniel is a very special book of the Scriptures which contains several prophecies of extreme importance for our understanding of the events that are to take place soon. We have included some chapters of the Book of Daniel which will contribute to a better understanding of the prophecy related to apocalyptic events.

In the first letter of the apostle Peter we find that,

> Of this salvation the prophets have inquired and searched carefully, who prophesied of the grace that would come to you, searching what, or what manner of time, the Spirit of Christ who was in them was indicating when He testified beforehand the sufferings of Christ and the glories that would follow.
> To them it was revealed that, not to themselves, but to us they were ministering the things which now have been reported to you through those who have preached the gospel to you by the Holy Spirit sent from heaven—things which angels desire to look into.
> 1 Peter 1:10–12

As we have mentioned, the ancient prophets saw certain events related to the nation of Israel, but did not understand them entirely. "And I, Daniel, fainted and was sick for days ... I was astonished by the vision, but no one understood it" (Dan. 8:27). They prophesied for our benefit. Through their prophecies, we have been able to receive understanding to see with clarity the future events related to Israel and other nations, as well as those related to the church.

I am only including here a few chapters of the Book of Daniel which have a direct relation with the end-time prophecies.

The Image of Nebuchadnezzar's Dream

Daniel Chapter 2

Chapter two of the Book of Daniel relates the prophet Daniel's interpretation of a dream that Nebuchadnezzar, king of Babylon, had. Daniel 2:31–35 describes an image that the king saw in his dream.

> You, O king, were watching; and behold, a great image! This great image, whose splendor was excellent, stood before you; and its form was awesome.
> This image's head was of fine gold, its chest and arms of silver, its belly and thighs of bronze, its legs of iron, its feet partly of iron and partly of clay.
> You watched while a stone was cut out without hands, which struck the image on its feet of iron and clay, and broke them in pieces.
> Then the iron, the clay, the bronze, the silver, and the gold were crushed together, and became like chaff from the summer threshing floors; the wind carried them away so that no trace of them was found. And the stone that struck the image became a great mountain and filled the whole earth.

Figure 2 shows the image of Nebuchadnezzar's dream. God, in His great mercy, reveals through this dream "what will be in the latter days" (Dan. 2:28). Daniel 2:45 also says, "the great God has made known to the king what will come to pass after this."

The interpretation of the Nebuchadnezzar dream, which the prophet Daniel received from God, says that each piece of the image represents a kingdom that will govern the earth, beginning from the days of Nebuchadnezzar, which would greatly affect the territory of Israel.

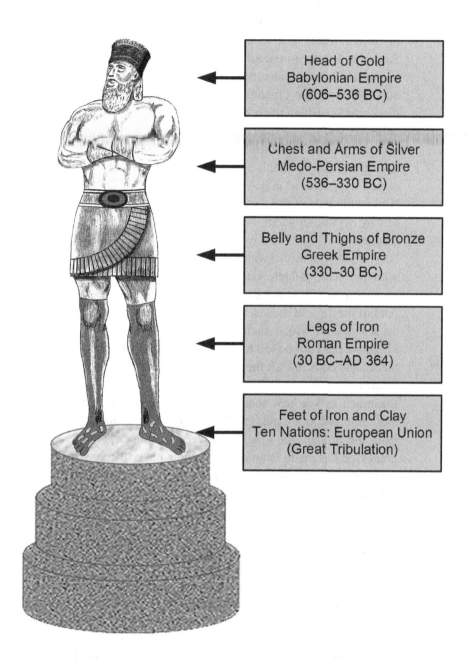

Head of Gold
Babylonian Empire
(606–536 BC)

Chest and Arms of Silver
Medo-Persian Empire
(536–330 BC)

Belly and Thighs of Bronze
Greek Empire
(330–30 BC)

Legs of Iron
Roman Empire
(30 BC–AD 364)

Feet of Iron and Clay
Ten Nations: European Union
(Great Tribulation)

Figure 2: Image of Nebuchadnezzar's Dream

You are this head of gold. But after you shall arise another kingdom inferior to yours; then another, a third kingdom of bronze, which shall rule over all the earth.

And the fourth kingdom shall be as strong as iron, inasmuch as iron breaks in pieces and shatters everything; and like iron that crushes, that kingdom will break in pieces and crush all the others.

Whereas you saw the feet and toes, partly of potter's clay and partly of iron, the kingdom shall be divided; yet the strength of the iron shall be in it, just as you saw the iron mixed with ceramic clay.

And as the toes of the feet were partly of iron and partly of clay, so the kingdom shall be partly strong and partly fragile.

As you saw iron mixed with ceramic clay, they will mingle with the seed of men; but they will not adhere to one another, just as iron does not mix with clay.

And in the days of these kings the God of heaven will set up a kingdom which shall never be destroyed; and the kingdom shall not be left to other people; it shall break in pieces and consume all these kingdoms, and it shall stand forever.

Inasmuch as you saw that the stone was cut out of the mountain without hands, and that it broke in pieces the iron, the bronze, the clay, the silver, and the gold—the great God has made known to the king what will come to pass after this. The dream is certain, and its interpretation is sure.

Daniel 2:38–45

Following, each part of the image is briefly described:

- The golden head represents the Babylonian kingdom, and being of gold, we understand that this kingdom was one of majesty and greatness. The kingdom of Babylon extended approximately from 606 BC to 536 BC.
- The chest and arms of silver represent the Medo-Persian kingdom, and being of silver, as Daniel says, this kingdom was inferior to the Babylonian one. This Medo-Persian kingdom extended approximately from 536 BC to 330 BC.

- The belly and thighs of bronze represent the kingdom of Greece, which extended approximately from 330 BC to 323 BC. After 323 BC, the Greek kingdom was divided into four kingdoms, which we will see in Daniel chapter 8. These four kingdoms lasted approximately until year 30 BC.
- Finally, we have the legs of iron and the feet, partly of iron and partly of potter's clay. The iron legs represent the Roman Empire, which invaded and conquered the previous Greek kingdom. The feet, partly of iron and partly of potter's clay, represent the future political Roman Empire (since there will also be a religious Roman Empire), that will manifest and receive authority together with the Antichrist in the period of the Great Tribulation.

    As we will see later, the ten toes represent ten nations or kingdoms that will be united by means of human agreements, which will come out of the territory occupied by the old Roman Empire. The old Roman Empire kingdom existed approximately from 30 BC to AD 364.

From the golden head to the feet of iron and clay, we can observe the decay or deterioration of the kingdoms.

> But after you shall arise another kingdom *inferior* to yours; then another, a third kingdom of bronze, which shall rule over all the earth.
> And the fourth kingdom shall be as strong as iron, inasmuch as iron breaks in pieces and shatters everything; and like iron that crushes, that kingdom will break in pieces and crush all the others.
>
> Daniel 2:39–40

Let us see in more detail the last kingdom that will also go into effect at the latter time. The old Roman kingdom arose before the Greek kingdom, but it was not until the Greek empire fell that Rome reigned as a powerful empire. This fourth and **last kingdom** extended approximately until AD 364. It is important to consider this last Roman kingdom a little while, because this one has certain peculiarities very different from the three previous kingdoms.

The fact that this kingdom is represented by feet and toes of iron mixed with clay signifies that it will be a divided kingdom, partly strong and partly fragile.

Whereas you saw the feet and toes, partly of potter's clay and partly of iron, the kingdom shall be divided; yet the strength of the iron shall be in it, just as you saw the iron mixed with ceramic clay.

And as the toes of the feet were partly of iron and partly of clay, so the kingdom shall be partly strong and partly fragile.

Daniel 2:41–42

The old Roman Empire was the one that reigned at the time that Jesus lived in Israel. It was the last one of the prophesied kingdoms, and we will see it at greater length when we enter the Book of Revelation.

Although we touch this subject later in Daniel chapter 9, we will make several comments here, so we can see with more clarity the message related to the ten toes in the dream of the image. As per the prophecy, it would seem that the reign of the Roman Empire would stop after the destruction of the temple in Jerusalem in AD 70.

However, after many years, in the latter days, according to the Nebuchadnezzar dream, the Roman Empire will return again to reign, but this time through ten nations. These ten nations will arise from the same territory that was occupied by the old Roman Empire.

Daniel 7:24 tells us about this fact that will happen soon, "The ten horns are ten kings who shall arise from this kingdom ..." This will happen by the time of the Great Tribulation. The ten toes of the image represent these ten nations which will reign together, where "they will mingle with the seed of men; but they will not adhere to one another, just as iron does not mix with clay" (Dan. 2:43). Although these ten nations will reign together, the relationship among them will be fragile.

These ten nations are also represented by the ten horns of the beast in Revelation 13:1—"Then I stood on the sand of the sea. And I saw a beast rising up out of the sea, having seven heads and ten horns, and on his horns ten crowns, and on his heads a blasphemous name." Revelation 17:12–13 gives us the key to the interpretation,

The ten horns which you saw are ten kings who have received no kingdom as yet, but they receive authority for one hour as kings with the beast.

These are of one mind, and they will give their power and authority to the beast.

This beast of Revelation is the Antichrist, who will receive honor and authority from the Roman Empire, represented in that time by the ten nations or kings.

It should not surprise us that the majority of the territory occupied in the past by the Roman Empire is now occupied by the nations that compose the European Union (EU). These nations of Europe have been entering into many agreements or alliances to form an "empire" among them.

The EU has already formed a solid basis to have a common government. It is well known that they already have a common currency, the Euro, and plan to have a common army. Commercial and political activities are also elements of alliances among them. The EU is strengthening so much that it is currently considered a great power at worldwide levels.

There is something very interesting about the origin of the EU that is related to the image of Nebuchadnezzar's dream. Let us begin with the period of the dominion of the old Roman Empire. This kingdom integrated, in a single political and economic system, the majority of the territory of what today we know as Europe, along with a good part of North Africa and the Middle East.

Seeing it in a little more detail, this empire ruled the lands around the Mediterranean Sea, the regions to the south and west of the Rhine and the Danube Rivers, Macedonia, Greece, Asia Minor (Turkey), Syria, Lebanon, Judea, and the eastern zone of Mesopotamia (Ref. 2). The citizens of that empire had freedom to dedicate themselves to their businesses and the practice of their professions anywhere in the territory that composed it.

After the collapse of the Roman Empire, kings and emperors arose trying to bring back the glory of that empire. One of those was the Roman emperor Charlemagne (AD 742–814), who tried to establish an imperial government related to so-called Christianity, under the Roman popes. Napoleon Bonaparte (AD 1769–1821) was another one who crowned himself emperor of the French and tried to conquer all Europe. This emperor achieved many successes as he was trying to unite Europe by force, including the "Napoleonic code," a single code of law adopted by all the lands he conquered.

There were many reasons to try to unite all European nations into a single kingdom. One of these reasons was the existence of many varied natural resources in these nations. Union would provide the advantage of sharing these natural resources.

After World War II, the European nations began to think with more seriousness about the possibility of union. Many speeches in favor of the European union were given by Winston Churchill of Great Britain. It was not until the year 1950 that France and Germany proposed to begin a "Common Market," related to the coal and steel industry.

After signing a treaty, other nations of Europe also joined the initially named "European Coal and Steel Community" (ECSC), denominated the "Community." The Community was responsible to assure the production of enough coal and steel at an advantageous price for all its members. In March of 1957, six European nations (France, Germany, Belgium, Italy, Holland, and Luxembourg) signed in Rome the treaty that officially established the "European Common Market." Some years later, six more nations were added: Denmark, Great Britain, Ireland, Portugal, Greece, and Spain.

Actually, the European Common Market is known as the European Union (EU), and groups many more nations of all Europe (Ref. 3— information about the European Common Market). The interesting thing here is that Rome was chosen to formalize this powerful organization of nations! All these nations are located in the territory that in the past was occupied by the Roman Empire. In addition, as a special note to be expanded later, Rome is the seat of the Vatican, source of the Catholic Church.

I believe that all these previously mentioned historic events are not a coincidence. As we see, the efforts to establish the European Union date from the time of the old Roman Empire itself. This EU will be the organization of nations instrumental in the latter times and is represented by the ten toes in the image of Nebuchadnezzar's dream (Dan. 2:41–43). It is equally represented by the ten horns of the fourth beast in Daniel's prophecy (Dan. 7:7–8, 24), and the ten horns of the beast in the apostle John's prophecy (Rev. 13:1).

The EU will have a great leader who will rule all the nations; this is the Antichrist, of whom we will speak in more detail later.

Some may ask how the EU, which actually groups more than ten nations, can be represented by the ten toes and the ten horns in the prophecies. I believe that this question is not difficult to answer. Many of the actual nations in Europe are the result of divisions or unions with other nations. The ten nations of the prophecy must be considered from the point of view of the division of European territory in the time of the old Roman Empire. Therefore, today there can be two or more nations that belong to the EU, that in the past they were only one nation.

It is important to stress that these ten nations emerge from the territory occupied by the ancient Roman Empire; in this way the Roman Empire will be present in the last times through the European Union. It is not a coincidence that the territory occupied by the EU coincides with the territory occupied by the old Roman Empire.

Today the EU is strengthening as a worldwide power; however, it will be strengthened even more in the Great Tribulation, when authority is granted to it to govern the world, not just Europe, together with the Antichrist. Revelation 17:12 says, "The ten horns which you saw are ten kings who have received no kingdom as yet, but they [will] receive authority for one hour as kings with the beast."

As a matter of fact, there are some strange things that happened during the period of the middle of the twentieth century to the early twenty-first century, which show the political-religious relationship between the European Union and the Catholic Church. When the new EU Constitution was signed in October 2004, the heads of state and government took it in turn to sign it in the same room where the Treaty of Rome was signed to found the EU in 1957.

The EU leaders signed the document in the Orazi and Curiazi hall at the Campidoglio, the political and religious center of ancient Rome, today the home of Rome's city hall, located on the Capitoline hill. The background of the document signing table had a bronze statue of Catholic Pope Innocent X with his right arm extended in a position of "blessing" the signers (Ref. 4). The Capitoline hill is one of the seven hills on which Rome is seated, as mentioned in Revelation 17:9 (see comments on Revelation 17 in chapter 5 of this book).

Another interesting thing is that the EU official flag shows twelve stars in a circle on a blue background. This is strikingly similar to the halo of twelve stars that appear around the Madonna in Catholic pictures of her. A former secretary-general of the Council of Europe has affirmed that the stars are those of "the woman of the Apocalypse" (Rev. 12:1), which the Catholic Church has always claimed represents the "virgin Mary, the mother of God."

Another amazing thing is the symbol of a woman riding a beast (Revelation 17), used as the official picture by the EU, as stated by a former Northern Ireland-Protestant minister and member of the European Parliament. A large sculpture of a woman riding a beast was built outside the new Brussels headquarters of the Council of Europe, while inside, there is a dome with a colossal painting (three times life-size) of that same symbol.

The woman riding a beast's symbol is used Europe-wide, like some of the following examples: a mural of a naked woman riding a beast in the European Parliament in Strasbourg, France, the 2002—2 and 1996—5 Euro coins, the

1992 German-Ecu coin, 1948 German-5 mark, a 1984 European stamp, the cover of May 2000 Der Spiegel magazine, and other U.S. magazines.

One of the buildings of the European Parliament in Strasbourg, France, includes a tower that appears to be unfinished. The design of this "unfinished" building, inspired by a painting done in 1563 of the Tower of Babel, has the expressed purpose of resembling the Tower of Babel as described in the Book of Genesis. This French structure was labeled "The Tower of Eurobabel," and was named by a member of the parliament as "the temple of a bold new empire."

Considering the above-described account, I may conclude that the European Union, together with the Catholic Church, represents the revival of the ancient Roman Empire, to have its full accomplishment in the Great Tribulation time.

In the Nebuchadnezzar dream, the Roman Empire is the last earthly kingdom. Daniel 2:44–45 says that after this fourth and last kingdom,

> the God of heaven will set up a kingdom which shall never be destroyed; and the kingdom shall not be left to other people; it shall break in pieces and consume all these kingdoms, and it shall stand forever.
> Inasmuch as you saw that the stone was cut out of the mountain without hands, and that it broke in pieces the iron, the bronze, the clay, the silver, and the gold ...

Christ will appear in His second coming at the end of the Great Tribulation, and "shall break in pieces and consume all these kingdoms," then He will establish a new kingdom which will remain forever. This is the kingdom of Christ in the Millennium. Christ is the stone that will crumble all these kingdoms, as Matthew 21:42 and 44 say:

> Jesus said to them, "Have you never read in the Scriptures: 'The stone which the builders rejected has become the chief cornerstone. This was the Lord's doing, and it is marvelous in our eyes'?
> Whoever falls on this stone will be broken; but on whomever it falls, it will grind him to powder.

Revelation 11:15 says, "Then the seventh angel sounded: And there were loud voices in heaven, saying, "The kingdoms of this world have become the kingdoms of our Lord and of His Christ, and He shall reign forever and ever!" Chapters 7 and 8 of Daniel (to be discussed) also mention the event when the Lord comes and defeats the Antichrist, the leader who will rule the world in the last days.

Vision of the Four Beasts, the Ram, and the Male Goat

Daniel Chapter 7, 8, and 11

Because these three chapters deal with the same subjects, and have many passages that mean the same thing, they will be considered at the same time. Inclusively, these chapters coincide with the image of Nebuchadnezzar's dream.

Something interesting that we can notice is that the kingdoms that King Nebuchadnezzar saw in his dream do not express the savagery and fierceness of the same kingdoms that Daniel saw in his visions. It is to His servant Daniel that God reveals the reality of what those kingdoms are and the way they work. When seeing them as monstrous beasts, we can understand the impious and savage character of these kingdoms, especially the fourth and last kingdom, which is described as a dreadful and terrible beast that devoured and crumbled.

This prophecy of the beasts, just as the Nebuchadnezzar dream, began to be fulfilled in the time of the Babylonian kingdom, and it extends into the future, until the Great Tribulation and the millennial kingdom. Daniel 2:28 shows that these prophecies will have their final fulfillment in the latter days. "But there is a God in heaven who reveals secrets, and He has made known to king Nebuchadnezzar what will be in the latter days." See also Daniel 2:45; 8:17, 19, 26.

According to Daniel 7:1, the prophet did not disclose all what he saw in his dreams and visions, for it says, "Then he wrote down the dream, telling the main facts." It seems that the Lord showed much more to Daniel, but He did not allow him to disclose all of it. What Daniel saw in his visions was so strong that "As for me, Daniel, my thoughts greatly troubled me, and my countenance changed; but I kept the matter in my heart" (Dan. 7:28).

Then in Daniel 8:27 he says, "And I, Daniel, fainted and was sick for days; afterward I arose and went about the king's business. I was astonished by the vision, but no one understood it." Also, in Daniel 10:8 we find, "Therefore I was left alone when I saw this great vision, and no strength remained in me; for my vigor was turned to frailty in me, and I retained no strength."

All this shows us that what was prophesied to happen in the near future is truly terrible and dreadful. Who will be able to endure it? Dear reader, you can be freed from that hour, because it is written, "Because you have kept My command to persevere, I also will keep you from the hour of trial which shall come upon the whole world, to test those who dwell on the earth" (Rev. 3:10).

We have already mentioned the correlation between chapters 7 and 8 and chapter 2 of Daniel. You can refer to figure 3: Correlation of the Prophecies in the Book of Daniel, where a description of each kingdom and the chronology of the time of their reign are provided.

In God's revelation, Daniel sees four beasts different from each other. "Those great beasts, which are four, are four kings which arise out of the earth" (Dan. 7:17). These four kingdoms will succeed one another, according to the chronology shown in the prophecy. This is confirmed by the history of the last 2,600 years.

"The first was like a lion, and had eagle's wings. I watched till its wings were plucked off; and it was lifted up from the earth and made to stand on two feet like a man, and a man's heart was given to it" (Dan. 7:4). The first beast the prophet Daniel saw was a lion, which represents the Babylonian kingdom (see figure 4: First Beast–The Lion). The Babylonian kingdom was a very strong kingdom which subdued a large territory, and was used by God to give faithful fulfillment to the prophet Jeremiah's prophecies.

These prophecies were related to the deportation of the Judean people to Babylon, where they spent seventy years in captivity. This first beast, the lion, rose as a man after its wings were plucked off, and a man's heart was given to it.

This portion of the prophecy signifies the king Nebuchadnezzar, when at the end of his reign he recognized the greatness of God and exalted Him as the Highest God. From this first experience with God, the life of this king changed, and from the "beast" that was, he was transformed into a man with all his senses under complete control. Daniel 4:34 and 37 say,

> And at the end of the time I, Nebuchadnezzar, lifted my eyes to heaven, and my understanding returned to me; and I blessed the Most High and praised and honored Him who lives forever: for His dominion is an everlasting dominion and His kingdom is from generation to generation.
> Now I, Nebuchadnezzar, praise and extol and honor the King of heaven, all of whose works are truth, and His ways justice. And those who walk in pride He is able to put down.

FIGURE 3: CORRELATION OF PROPHECIES IN THE BOOK OF DANIEL

King or Kingdom	Image of Nebuchadnezzar Dream Daniel Chapter 2	Four Beasts: Daniel Chapter 7 "Those great beasts, which are four, are four kings which arise out of the earth"	Ram and Male Goat Daniel Chapter 8
Babylon (606–536 BC)	Head of gold	Lion with eagle's wings. After its wings were plucked off, it was lifted up and stood on its feet like a man, and a man's heart was given to it.	
Media-Persia (536–330 BC)	Chest and arms of silver	Bear with one side raised up and three ribs in its mouth.	Ram with two horns. One of the horns was higher than the other one.
Greece (330–323 BC) (Four Kingdoms) (323–30 BC)	Belly and thighs of bronze	Leopard with four wings and four heads.	Male goat with a notable horn between his eyes. Notable horn was broken and four others came up.
Rome (30 BC–AD 364)	Legs of iron	Dreadful and terrible beast, with huge iron teeth, nails of bronze and ten horns.	
Rome (10 Kingdoms or Nations) (Great Tribulation Period)	Feet, partly of iron and partly of clay	Dreadful and terrible beast, with huge iron teeth, nails of bronze and ten horns.	
Antichrist		Little horn coming up among the ten of the Rome kingdom, with eyes like a man and a mouth speaking pompous words.	Little horn came up among the four of the Greece kingdom, which grew toward the south, east, and the glorious land.

Figure 3: Correlation of the Prophecies in the Book of Daniel

Figure 4: First Beast–The Lion
(Babylonian Kingdom)

God transformed that haughty king to one with a *heart of man*.

"And suddenly another beast, a second, like a bear. It was raised up on one side, and had three ribs in its mouth between its teeth. And they said thus to it: 'Arise, devour much flesh!'" (Dan. 7:5).

This second beast represents the Medo-Persian kingdom (see figure 5: Second Beast–The Bear). The raised side of the bear represents the stronger kingdom, Persia; and the three ribs are three nations or kingdoms (Lydia, Babylon, and Egypt), which united in agreements to fight against this new kingdom. The Medo-Persian army did not waste time in devouring the three.

On the other hand, in Daniel chapter 8, the Medo-Persian kingdom is represented by a ram with two horns—one horn higher than the other, a symbol of the greater force that was Persia (see figure 6: The Ram).

> Then I lifted my eyes and saw, and there, standing beside the river, was a ram which had two horns, and the two horns were high; but one was higher than the other, and the higher one came up last.
> I saw the ram pushing westward, northward, and southward, so that no animal could withstand him; nor was there any that could deliver from his hand, but he did according to his will and became great.
>
> Daniel 8:3–4

The same chapter 8 provides the meaning of this beast: "The ram which you saw, having the two horns—they are the kings of Media and Persia" (Dan. 8:20).

"After this I looked, and there was another, like a leopard, which had on its back four wings of a bird. The beast also had four heads, and dominion was given to it" (Dan. 7:6). The beast that the prophet Daniel sees now represents the Greek kingdom (see figure 7: Third Beast–The Leopard). In chapter 8, the kingdom of Greece is represented by a male goat with a "notable horn" between his eyes. The large horn was broken, and in place of it four horns came up (see figure 8: The Male Goat).

> And as I was considering, suddenly a male goat came from the west, across the surface of the whole earth, without touching the ground; and the goat had a notable horn between his eyes.

Figure 5: Second Beast–The Bear
(Medo-Persian Kingdom)

Figure 6: The Ram
(Medo-Persian Kingdom)

Figure 7: Third Beast–The Leopard
(Greek Kingdom)

Figure 8: The Male Goat
(Greek Kingdom)

> Then he came to the ram that had two horns, which I had seen standing beside the river, and ran at him with furious power. And I saw him confronting the ram; he was moved with rage against him, attacked the ram, and broke his two horns. There was no power in the ram to withstand him, but he cast him down to the ground and trampled him; and there was no one that could deliver the ram from his hand. Therefore the male goat grew very great; but when he became strong, the large horn was broken, and in place of it four notable ones came up toward the four winds of heaven.
>
> Daniel 8:5–8

Daniel reveals the interpretation of these beasts:

> And the male goat is the kingdom of Greece. The large horn that is between its eyes is the first king.
> As for the broken horn and the four that stood up in its place, four kingdoms shall arise out of that nation, but not with its power.
>
> Daniel 8:21–22

The four horns represent the division of the Greek Empire after the death of the first king, Alexander the Great, who is represented by the large horn between the eyes. After the death of Alexander, the four generals of the Greek army divided the Greek Empire into four nations or kingdoms: Syria, Egypt, Macedonia (South of Greece and Turkey), and Asia Minor or Phrygia (Bulgaria and Romania). The division of the Greek kingdom into four kingdoms is represented in chapter 7 by the four wings and four heads of the leopard.

"After this I saw in the night visions, and behold, a fourth beast, dreadful and terrible, exceedingly strong. It had huge iron teeth; it was devouring, breaking in pieces, and trampling the residue with its feet. It was different from all the beasts that were before it, and it had ten horns" (Dan. 7:7).

The prophet Daniel had great curiosity to know more about the fourth beast, "which was different from all the others, exceedingly dreadful, with its teeth of iron and its nails of bronze, which devoured, broke in pieces, and trampled the residue with its feet" (Dan. 7:19). Daniel 7:23 says, "The fourth beast shall be a fourth kingdom on earth, which shall be different from all other kingdoms, and shall devour the whole earth, trample it and break it in pieces" (see figure 9: Fourth-Dreadful Beast).

Figure 9: Fourth-Dreadful Beast
(Roman Kingdom)

It is clear that this dreadful and terrible beast symbolizes the Roman Empire, from which also will emerge the most terrible, cruel, perverse, and tyrannous king of all time, known as the Antichrist or "the beast," according to the Book of Revelation.

Daniel says that this kingdom "will be different from all the other kingdoms," because in the latter days, it will extend not only over Europe and the Middle East region, but throughout the entire world. Under the leadership of the Antichrist, this kingdom "shall devour the whole earth, trample it and break it in pieces." The Antichrist will have no mercy, even on his own people.

Daniel 7:8 says that when the small horn, the Antichrist, was coming up among the other ten, three horns were subdued: "I was considering the horns, and there was another horn, a little one, coming up among them, before whom three of the first horns were plucked out by the roots. And there, in this horn, were eyes like the eyes of a man, and a mouth speaking pompous words."

Verse 7:24 says, "The ten horns are ten kings who shall arise from this kingdom [Roman Kingdom]. And another shall rise after them; he shall be different from the first ones, and shall subdue three kings." In order to understand the meaning of this scripture, it is necessary to see what will be happening in Europe and the Middle East at the time of the Antichrist's appearance.

As we will see in the next section, the Antichrist will first appear as a great political leader. He will arise at the most critical time that the Middle East and the entire world have ever gone through. This time will be when the members of the church of the Lord have disappeared, and Israel is attacked by the armies of many nations led by Russia (see chapter 6 of this book). After this attack, where Russia will be totally defeated by God's intervention, the Israelites will insist on constructing their temple.

The Antichrist will take advantage of this initiative, interceding so that the Hebrews can construct their temple. This action will bring great controversies between three nations of the European Union, which will not be in agreement with the decision of the Antichrist. The Antichrist will lash out against the leaders of those three nations, destroying them without any mercy ("before whom three of the first horns were plucked out by the roots"). This act will enhance his relationship with Israel, giving more strength to the agreement or covenant carried out between this great leader and Israel, as we will see in more detail in the section on the seventy weeks (Daniel chapter 9).

The events to happen during the last period of the fourth kingdom cannot compare with any other period. Matthew 24:7 says, "For nation will rise against nation, and kingdom against kingdom. And there will be famines, pestilences, and earthquakes in various places." Matthew 24:21 also says, "For then there will be great tribulation, such as has not been since the beginning of the world until this time, no, nor ever shall be." God is love, but also consuming fire. All these prophecies will be entirely fulfilled.

At the end of the Great Tribulation, the Messiah Jesus Christ will appear with all His angels, and will overcome that iniquitous and evil leader. In Daniel 7:11, we find that the Antichrist will be killed and given to be burned in the fire that is never extinguished, the lake of fire and brimstone. The expected day is coming, the day of great victory over the kingdom of darkness, and its destruction will be forever and ever—by the hand of God himself: "but he shall be broken without human means" (Dan. 8:25).

After victory over the Antichrist, Jesus Christ, the King of kings, will establish His kingdom (Millennium) on the earth. This is the promise given many centuries ago, a time in which His people, faithful believers who come through the Great Tribulation, will live with Jesus for a thousand years. In Daniel chapter 7 we find several passages related to this kingdom which the believers will inherit.

Verse 7:10 says that "the court [Judge] was seated, and the books were opened." Beloved reader, do these words not give you fear? What are these books? These are books containing the descriptions of works and names, names of the people who were faithful and kept the testimony of Christ. What great sadness and suffering for those who are not found in those books in the Judge's hands! The hour of truth has arrived, when the goats will be separated from the sheep.

> When the Son of Man comes in His glory, and all the holy angels with Him, then He will sit on the throne of His glory.
> All the nations will be gathered before Him, and He will separate them one from another, as a shepherd divides his sheep from the goats.
> And He will set the sheep on His right hand, but the goats on the left.
> Then the King will say to those on His right hand, 'Come, you blessed of My Father, inherit the kingdom [Millennium] prepared for you from the foundation of the world.
> Matthew 25:31–34

There is no doubt, God will fulfill His promises to the people He chose and to all those who love His truth; "until the Ancient of Days came, and a judgment was made in favor of the saints of the Most High, and the time came for the saints to possess the kingdom" (Dan. 7:22).

The Antichrist: His Ancestry

In this section, a description of the Antichrist is presented, including his origin, as revealed through the prophet Daniel. This subject will also be discussed in chapter 5, *Book of Revelation*, showing how the apostle John saw it.

There are many who wonder who the Antichrist will be and where he will come from. The Scriptures are wonderful, and in them are all the treasures of God, revealed to those who love the truth and approach Him with a sincere heart. "All things have been delivered to Me by My Father, and no one knows the Son except the Father. Nor does anyone know the Father except the Son, and the one to whom the Son wills to reveal Him" (Matt. 11:27).

Let us see firstly what the Scriptures say about the origin of the Antichrist. According to the prophet Daniel, the Antichrist, symbolized by a small horn, comes out from the ten horns, which as we have mentioned previously, represent ten kings or nations which will arise from the territory of the Roman Empire. "I was considering the horns, and there was another horn, a little one, coming up among them ... And there, in this horn, were eyes like the eyes of a man, and a mouth speaking pompous words" (Dan. 7:8).

These ten nations (European Union) will be the political representation of the Roman Empire at the time of the fulfillment of the prophecy. The Antichrist will emerge from a nation located in the old Roman kingdom. The Roman Empire ruled the lands around the Mediterranean Sea, the regions to the south and west of the Rhine and the Danube Rivers, Macedonia, Greece, and Asia Minor (including Turkey), up to Syria, Lebanon, Judea, and the eastern zone of Mesopotamia. Therefore, it is clear that the Antichrist will come from a nation that is somewhere in these territories.

We find the key of the specific Antichrist's lineage in Daniel 8:8–9:

32

> Therefore the male goat grew very great; but when he
> became strong, the large horn was broken, and in place
> of it four notable ones came up toward the four winds of
> heaven.
> And out of one of them came a little horn which grew
> exceedingly great toward the south, toward the east, and
> toward the Glorious Land.

This small horn that came out of one of the four horns of the male goat represents the very despicable Syrian King Antiochus Epiphanes (168 BC). This king tried to exterminate all the Jews and their religion. He destroyed the city of Jerusalem and profaned the temple, sacrificing a pig on the altar, which was very abominable according to the Jews' law.

Antiochus acted in so worthless and cruel way that he even placed an image of the Greek god Zeus in the area of the altar. Many Jews were sold as slaves and others were tortured to force them to relinquish their religion. This king has been the leader with the most similar characteristics to the Antichrist, and for this reason he was a true type of the Antichrist himself.

However, by the characteristics and descriptions found in the prophecies, we can clearly establish that this small horn also represents the "great leader" to come, the real Antichrist. By this we can see that this prophecy has double fulfillment, in the King Antiochus Epiphanes and in the Antichrist. It is not rare to see a double fulfillment of prophecies in the Scriptures.

Matthew 24:15–16 says,

> Therefore when you see the 'abomination of desolation,'
> spoken of by Daniel the prophet, standing in the holy place
> (whoever reads, let him understand), then let those who are
> in Judea flee to the mountains.

Jesus is speaking in this passage in future terms. This passage, which coincides with the Daniel prophecy and was fulfilled in the time of Antiochus Epiphanes, will also have its fulfillment in the future under the reign of the Antichrist, who will also erect an image to be adored. The first Book of Maccabees (considered a historical book, but apocryphal) confirms these facts related to the King Epiphanes (BJ, Ref. 5).

Therefore, the Antichrist will come from one of the four kingdoms which divided from the Greek kingdom: Syria, Egypt, Macedonia (south of Greece and Turkey), and Asia Minor or Phrygia (Bulgaria and Romania).

The Antichrist will come from one of these four nations or regions, which also were part of the territory of the old Roman Empire.

When we consider these four nations or regions, we can infer that Syria is the one with the most probability to be chosen for the Antichrist's birth. This is because, as we will mention more ahead, the Antichrist will arise as a leader who has a great influence on the Jewish people, but also on the Arab or Muslim people.

By the actual events we see in the Middle East region, it is clear that the role of that charismatic leader fits a Syrian man very well, and not one of the other three remaining nations. In addition, Antiochus Epiphanes, the wicked king who caused great suffering to the Jewish people, who was also a type of the Antichrist, was of Syrian ancestry, which is not a coincidence.

On the other hand, the Antichrist could also be of Jewish roots, that is, a Syrian-Jewish citizen. In this manner, as a Syrian, he could influence the Muslim and Arab people, and as a Jew, his influence on the Israelites would be much more effective. Ezekiel 21:25–27 provides a word that seems to be related to the Antichrist:

> 'Now to you, o profane, wicked prince of Israel, whose day has come, whose iniquity shall end, 'thus says the Lord God: "Remove the turban, and take off the crown; nothing shall remain the same. Exalt the humble, and humble the exalted.
> Overthrown, overthrown, I will make it overthrown! It shall be no longer, until He comes whose right it is, and I will give it to Him."'

This scripture seems to describe the Antichrist as the "profane and wicked prince of Israel."

Daniel chapter 11 relates certain events which happened with the Syrian King Antiochus Epiphanes, which also point to the Antichrist. Daniel 11:24, talking about the Antichrist, says that "he shall do what his fathers have not done, nor his forefathers." Then, in verses 11:37–38 he says, "He shall regard neither the God of his fathers ... But in their place he shall honor a god of fortresses; and a god which his fathers did not know ..."

These verses throw light on the possibility that the Antichrist has Jewish ancestry. It is clearly known that Israel is the only nation that the Scriptures mention as having patriarchs and many kings who served

God. The phrase "he shall regard neither the God of his fathers" clearly establishes a connection of this man, the *prince* Antichrist, with the Jews.

There are some other interesting scriptures that can enlighten us a little more on this subject, related to the tribe of Dan. If we study Dan, son of Jacob, we find firstly that his name means "He judged" (Gen. 30:6). When Jacob was on the verge of dying, he called all his children and prayed for all of them. His prayer was prophecies for all of them. In Genesis 49:1 we read that the patriarch Jacob called all his children to declare to them "what shall befall you in the last days." Prophesying to Dan, Jacob said:

> Dan shall judge his people as one of the tribes of Israel.
> Dan shall be a serpent by the way, a viper by the path, that
> bites the horse's heels so that its rider shall fall backward.
>
> Genesis 49:16–17

I ask myself, when did Dan judge his people? We have never seen the tribe of Dan governing Israel. In Jacob's prophecy, Dan is called a serpent and a viper that makes a man fall. I believe that these are not worthy names for people of honor. I realize the malevolent future of Dan when I see how Jacob was so affected that he finished praying for Dan with this exclamation: "I have waited for your salvation, O Lord!" (Gen. 49:18). This exclamation is a sigh of relief, as if something harmful was going to come from Dan.

Jacob's feeling is confirmed in Revelation 7:3–8, where it is shown that the tribe of Dan was not included in the list of 144,000 Jews (12,000 of each tribe of Israel) chosen by God to serve and preach His word in the time of the Great Tribulation. Manasseh, son of Joseph, replaces Dan in these selected.

There are several passages that present Dan in a precarious situation before God, in such a way that he was rejected by the Lord. Deuteronomy 29:18–21 describes what can happen to those people given to idolatry:

> So that there may not be among you man or woman or
> family or tribe, whose heart turns away today from the
> Lord our God, to go and serve the gods of these nations,
> and that there may not be among you a root bearing
> bitterness or wormwood; and so it may not happen, when
> he hears the words of this curse, that he blesses himself in
> his heart, saying, 'I shall have peace, even though I follow

the dictates of my heart'—as though the drunkard could
be included with the sober.
The Lord would not spare him; for then the anger of the
Lord and His jealousy would burn against that man, and
every curse that is written in this book would settle on
him, and the Lord would blot out his name from under
heaven.
And the Lord would separate him from all the tribes of
Israel for adversity, according to all the curses of the
covenant that are written in this Book of the Law.

Judges 18 and 1 Kings 12:28–31 describe the degree of great idolatry
reached by the tribe of Dan. It seems that the curse fell on Dan. For all
these reasons, I believe there is a possibility that the tribe of Dan is the one
chosen to engender the Antichrist.

After considering in the Scriptures the actions of the Antichrist from
the beginning of the Great Tribulation, I believe that this man will deceive
the Israelites and the Arabs, so he will be recognized by both people as a
great political leader. However, I do not see that Israel will recognize him
as the Messiah.

Israel will be impressed by the great leadership and power that the
Antichrist will demonstrate by the signs he performs. So the Antichrist will
make agreements with Israel (and also with the Arabs and other nations),
but he will do them as a political leader with great knowledge of their
religious beliefs, not identifying himself at the beginning as the hoped-for
Messiah.

To be able to impersonate the Messiah before the nation of Israel,
the Antichrist would have to fulfill many requirements of the Scriptures,
such as being born in Bethlehem of Judea and being a true Israelite, of
the descendants of King David. According to the information mentioned
above, the Antichrist will not be able to fulfill these requirements.

We will see in chapter 12 of Revelation that the people of Israel, as soon
as they realize definitively that this leader is the Antichrist, they will fly
"into the wilderness, where she [remnant of Israel] has a place prepared by
God, that they should feed her there one thousand two hundred and sixty
days,"—three and a half years.

On the other hand, many other non-Israelite people and nations will
be deceived, thinking that this leader is the true Messiah, due to the signs
he will do, together with the False Prophet (whom we will see described
in Revelation 13:11–18). In the middle of the Great Tribulation, this leader

will be self-proclaimed publicly as the "Christ." At that time, the Antichrist will no longer deceive the entire world only as a charismatic leader, but also as the "savior" of the world.

The Antichrist: His Traits and Actions

We have already clearly seen that the Scriptures, talking about the Antichrist as king, say that "another shall rise after them; he shall be different from the first ones." The small horn, representing the Antichrist, will be different because he will be much more cruel and despicable than the others, and will have greater extent in his reign. He will govern, not only the region of Europe and the Middle East, but the entire world. Let us see what Daniel says about this worldwide leader, the Antichrist.

The prophecy says that the small horn which grew had "eyes like the eyes of a man, and a mouth speaking pompous words" (Dan. 7:8). The Antichrist will be a great and eloquent speaker; "I watched then because of the sound of the pompous words which the horn was speaking" (Dan. 7:11). Then it says, "He shall speak pompous words against the Most High, shall persecute the saints of the Most High, and shall intend to change times and law." (Dan. 7:25).

It is well known in history that many leaders have risen and even deceived whole nations. They have appeared initially as charismatic men with a capacity to solve the problems of the nations, but after a time, they take off their masks and show their true personality and intentions. Then they carry out their malevolent plans, and there are no longer any who can stop them, because by means of deceit they have already deeply dug into the minds and hearts of the people. This is an effective tactic of the devil, tested and proven; therefore, he will use it again in the person of the Antichrist.

Who is the Antichrist and from where will he get his power? If we take a look at the end of Jesus' lifetime on earth, when He was partaking of the last supper with His disciples, we see something very interesting that is similar to what shall come to pass with the Antichrist at the beginning of the Great Tribulation. John 13:21 and 26–27 say,

> When Jesus had said these things, He was troubled in spirit, and testified and said, 'Most assuredly, I say to you, one of you will betray Me.'

> Jesus answered, 'It is he to whom I shall give a piece
> of bread when I have dipped it.' And having dipped the
> bread, He gave it to Judas Iscariot, the son of Simon.
> Now after the piece of bread, Satan entered him. Then
> Jesus said to him, 'What you do, do quickly.'

Judas had been with Jesus for about three years, and behold, he betrays Him now. At a given time, demons representing Satan (because Satan is an angel who has a body and is not spirit, so he cannot possess a person) entered into Judas, and then Judas went to fulfill what already had deeply penetrated his mind and heart. I think this is a clear example of what shall come to pass in the Antichrist: demons shall possess this man, and in this way he will receive special characteristics that will enable him to be the leader expected by all nations. Daniel 8:23–25 confirms this matter when it says that

> in the latter time of their kingdom, when the transgressors
> have reached their fullness, a king shall arise, having
> fierce features, who understands sinister schemes.
> His power shall be mighty, *but not by his own power*; he
> shall destroy fearfully, and shall prosper and thrive; he
> shall destroy the mighty, and also the holy people.
> Through his cunning he shall cause deceit to prosper
> under his rule; and he shall exalt himself in his heart …

We see that the Antichrist will be a haughty man, shrewd and able to deceive, and very wise and knowledgeable, who will receive all these gifts from Satan (*not by his own power*). The Antichrist will be nourished by the same devil to whom has been granted all the kingdoms of the world, and the devil may give those kingdoms to whomever he wants—as he tried to do when he tempted the Lord Jesus, related in Luke 4:5–7,

> Then the devil, taking Him up on a high mountain, showed
> Him all the kingdoms of the world in a moment of time.
> And the devil said to Him, "All this authority I will give
> You, and their glory; for this has been delivered to me, and
> I give it to whomever I wish.
> Therefore, if You will worship before me, all will be
> Yours."

Revelation 13:2 and 16:13–14 show how Satan will give the Antichrist power and authority through the demons:

> Now the beast [Antichrist] which I saw was like a leopard, his feet were like the feet of a bear, and his mouth like the mouth of a lion. The dragon [Satan] gave him his power, his throne, and great authority.
> And I saw three unclean spirits like frogs coming out of the mouth of the dragon, out of the mouth of the beast, and out of the mouth of the false prophet.
> For they are spirits of demons, performing signs ...

Satan always desires to be worshiped and exalted as God. For this fact he was expelled from the presence of God. This is why Satan will induce the Antichrist ("his son," which will be explained later) to be worshiped by the inhabitants of the earth; even an image in his honor will be made, so that all the people prostrate themselves and worship it.

The Antichrist will be a nasty figure who will use everything at his disposal to highly blaspheme the name of God. His blasphemy will reach such a height that he will possibly be a homosexual. Daniel 11:37, referring to the Antichrist, says, "He shall regard neither the God of his fathers *nor the desire of women*, nor regard any god; for he shall exalt himself above them all." Saying that he shall not regard "the desire of women" suggests that perhaps this wicked leader will also add homosexuality to his corrupt attributes, which is very abominable before God, being a relationship against the nature created by God. In this way, he would come as a "gay messiah" to try to offend the Lord as much as he can.

Daniel 7:25 says that the Antichrist "shall intend to change times and law. Then the saints shall be given into his hand for a time and times and half a time." Here does not say that the Antichrist will succeed in changing times and the law, but that he shall try to do it. I understand this passage to refer to specific times and dates of celebrations of different solemn Jewish feasts and many commandments of the law provided by God in the old covenant.

As mentioned before, the King Antiochus Epiphanes profaned the temple, sacrificing animals on the altar that were identified as unclean under Jewish law, and even placing an idol in the temple. The Antichrist will do the same. He will have all sorts of malicious strategies in his agenda, particularly against the Jewish people, because they are the "people of God;" they are the people of the promises.

At the beginning, the Antichrist shows himself as a great leader, and will speak about peace as his primary tactic: "He shall enter peaceably, even into the richest places of the province" (Dan. 11:24). This is well-represented in the first horse that appears when Jesus opens the first seal, described in Revelation chapter 6. The white horse represents the peace strategy.

The Antichrist will negotiate a treaty of peace between Jews and Arabs, which will also include the transfer or barter of the territory of the present Muslim temple to the Jews, for the construction of the new Jewish temple. This agreement will also include freedom for the Jewish people to perform their religious rites in the temple, such as sacrifices and offerings. However, three and a half years later, after the agreement is confirmed on the ground of peace, the Antichrist will break it, removing his disguise of peacemaker and imposing his strength with war. Here begins the fulfillment of the Scriptures related to the real Great Tribulation.

There are several biblical passages that describe this subject, such as Daniel 8:11–13; 9:27, and 11:30–31. In these passages we can see how the Antichrist could mislead the Jews, permitting them to establish their religious rites, as part of his strategy, and then go against them with all his power and malice. So as the prophecy says, this wicked one stops the sacrifice and the offering. This is the time when the Antichrist will sit in the Jewish temple in Jerusalem proclaiming himself as "God" or divine.

Let no one deceive you by any means; for that Day will not come unless the falling away [apostasy] comes first, and the man of sin is revealed, the son of perdition, who opposes and exalts himself above all that is called God or that is worshiped, so that he sits as God in the temple of God, showing himself that he is God.

2 Thessalonians 2:3–4

Mark 13:14 also warns us about this: "So when you see the 'abomination of desolation,' spoken of by Daniel the prophet, standing where it ought not (let the reader understand), then let those who are in Judea flee to the mountains."

Daniel 11:21–24 says that this new leader will remove the peace and make great spoils:

And in his place shall arise a vile person, to whom they will not give the honor of royalty; but he shall come in peaceably, and seize the kingdom by intrigue.

With the force of a flood they shall be swept away from before him and be broken, and also the prince of the covenant.

And after the league is made with him he shall act deceitfully, for he shall come up and become strong with a small number of people.

He shall enter peaceably, even into the richest places of the province; and he shall do what his fathers have not done, nor his forefathers: he shall disperse among them the plunder, spoil, and riches; and he shall devise his plans against the strongholds, but only for a time.

From that moment, the so-called peace will end, "for when they say, "Peace and safety!" then sudden destruction comes upon them, as labor pains upon a pregnant woman. And they shall not escape" (1 Thess. 5:3). The Antichrist will have many strategies to deceive the largest number of people possible. As we have seen, he will begin by bringing peace in the most difficult and tumultuous region of all time, the Middle East.

We will see this in more detail in Revelation 6:2–8, where the first strategy of this worldwide leader will be the establishment of peace (white horse). Then, he will present himself as the Antichrist, to sweep the nations with wars (red horse), hunger (black horse), and other kinds of tortures and killings (yellow horse). This is the true nature of this leader: "The coming of the lawless [iniquitous] one is according to the working of Satan, with all power, signs, and lying wonders" (2 Thess. 2:9).

But the end of this evil leader will come at the end of the days, because the Lord himself "shall take away his dominion, to consume and destroy it forever" (Dan. 7:26). Daniel 8:25 says, "He shall even rise against the Prince of princes; but he shall be broken without human means."

The Seventy Weeks and the Prophetic Clock

Daniel Chapter 9

Before proceeding with the prophecy of this chapter, let us consider the length of time between the following events—the death of Christ, the coming of the Holy Spirit, and the destruction of the city of Jerusalem with its temple (sanctuary)—and the Great Tribulation. As we have already mentioned, the ancient prophet saw the Great Tribulation as an event that **immediately follows** the three events previously mentioned.

In other words, the *prophetic clock* stopped with the completion of those three events, as mentioned in the example of Joel 2:28–32, showing clearly how the outpouring of the Holy Spirit (occurring in the first century of the Christian era) was united with the events of the Great Tribulation (see chapter 2, *What the Old Prophet Did Not See*). The prophet Joel made a parenthesis between the pouring out of the Spirit and the events of the Great Tribulation.

We see here how the ancient prophet did not see the time of the church; it is as if it was overlooked. Indeed, the ancient prophet only saw the peaks showed in figure 1, and for him they were something continuous. He only sees the prophecies related to his people Israel ("… for your people and for your holy city"—Daniel 9:24). The revelation of the mystery of the church was hidden from the ancient prophet.

Revelation 12:1–6 describes a woman who gave birth to a son, and "her Child was caught up to God and His throne." Then it says that "the woman fled into the wilderness, where she has a place prepared by God, that they should feed her there one thousand two hundred and sixty days." That Son caught up to God is Jesus when He ascended to heaven. The woman, who represents Israel (not Mary, Jesus' mother), flees to the wilderness, where she is nourished for 1,260 days (three and a half years).

In this passage, the apostle John connects Jesus' ascension with events of the Great Tribulation (this subject will be discussed in more detail in chapter 5, *Book of Revelation*). He does not include here the period of the church. Remember that God, before the first coming of Jesus Christ to the earth, was dealing with the people of Israel as a nation. After the Jews rejected and killed Jesus Christ, this treatment from the national point of view stopped. The time of the church then began, in which God's relationship is now personal with everyone who believes, no matter his origin.

God no longer deals primarily with nations, but with individuals. He incorporates individuals into the "body of Christ," the church, through the Holy Spirit. It is important to understand that the church age is not included in the prophecies addressed to the Jewish nation.

We believe that Jesus is the Son of God, our Lord, and that He has established a spiritual kingdom, the kingdom of light. Now we await Him as **Lord** and **Husband** of a people chosen for Him. But the Jew who has not believed in Jesus Christ as the Son of God still waits for his **Messiah** and **King**.

However, it is important to point out the position currently held by Israel in the Word of God. Chapter 11 of the Epistle to the Romans is wonderful, because it offers an inspired word which opens our eyes to see Israel's current place before God, and His purpose to be fulfilled soon.

Romans 11:25–29 describes how "blindness in part has happened to Israel until the fullness of the Gentiles has come in. And so all Israel will be saved." The whole passage shows how God stopped dealing with Israel as a nation, turning then to deal with everyone (Jews and Gentiles), thus giving rise to His church.

When God finishes His purpose with the church on earth, He will deal again with Israel to fulfill His promise—"and so all Israel will be saved." This will happen in the millennial kingdom, after completion of the Great Tribulation.

Let us see now what the Scriptures say about the "Prophetic Clock" halting. Figure 10 shows a prophetic clock model.

In Daniel 9:20–27, the prophet speaks about the time that God has chosen to finally fulfill His purpose with the people of Israel (not the church). I think this is one of the greatest relevant prophecies within eschatology, particularly related to the future of Israel. In verses 9:22–23 we see that the angel Gabriel has been commissioned to teach and make Daniel to understand the vision. What is the vision he refers to here when he says, "Therefore consider the matter [understand the command], and understand the vision"?

It seems that what Gabriel will unveil in the next verses is an explanation of the vision Daniel had just received. When we read the previous chapter 8 of Daniel, we find Daniel's vision about a ram and a male goat, which I have described its meaning in detail. The angel Gabriel explains a few things to Daniel, but the prophet remains without understanding. Daniel 8:17 and 19 say,

> ... but he said to me, 'Understand, son of man, that the vision refers to the time of the end.'
> And he said, 'Look, I am making known to you what shall happen in the latter time of the indignation; for at the appointed time the end shall be.'

43

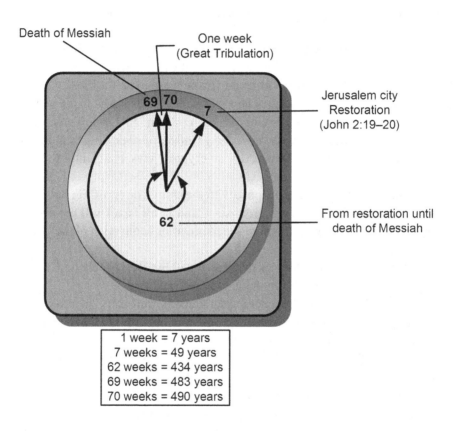

Figure 10: The Prophetic Clock

Then, in verse 8:27 Daniel says, "I was astonished by the vision, but no one understood it."

What do we see in chapter 8's vision? Let us summarize the main points of that vision. As we stated before, the vision shows the ancestry, traits, and actions of the Antichrist. It indicates that from the time the Jewish people begin to offer their sacrifices until the sanctuary is cleansed will be 2,300 days. During that period of time, the sanctuary will be trampled and the continual sacrifice taken away

This chapter 8 also shows that the Antichrist will emerge from one of the kingdoms which sprang from the Greek Empire. In addition, as will be discussed in the next paragraphs, the period of *seventy weeks* is set to start during the lifetime of King Artaxerses (king of Persia), represented here by the ram.

At the beginning of chapter 9, we see that Daniel, as a true man of God, zealous and a lover of the divine truth, prays to the Almighty God. Although he did not fail God and was obedient to His word, he presents himself before God as a sinner, bearing the sin of the people upon himself. This shows how this prophet loved Israel. It is at that time that God again sends the angel Gabriel, to explain the vision to Daniel with more detail. Let us now see those details. Daniel 9:24 says,

> Seventy weeks are determined for your people and for your holy city, to finish the transgression, to make an end of sins, to make reconciliation [expiation] for iniquity, to bring in everlasting righteousness, to seal up vision and prophecy, and to anoint the Most Holy.

This passage is full of details, which we segregate one by one as follows:

• Seventy weeks are determined

God begins the prophecy by establishing a specific time to fulfill it. The Lord wants to make sure we understand the accurate term of its total fulfillment. With the expression *are determined*, God shows His authority and certainty. This is not an invention of men. It is God who has set it up; therefore, its completion is assured. All issues mentioned in this prophecy shall take place throughout the *seventy weeks*—490 years, as we will see later.

- for your people and for your holy city

God speaks to the prophet Daniel and says, "your people [Israel]" and "your holy city [Jerusalem]." Also, verse 10:14 says, "Now I have come to make you understand what will happen to your people in the latter days, for the vision refers to many days yet to come." God is precise and does not play with words. He specifies that this prophecy is for Israel, thus excluding His church. God's plan related to future events for the church is different from His plan for Israel; otherwise, the church ought to be included in this prophecy.

- to finish the transgression, to make an end of sins, to make reconciliation [expiation] for iniquity

There are those who attest that the prophecies of the Old Testament are for the church, because she is the "spiritual Israel." They say that the current Israel has nothing to do with God, because it rejected Christ and is in sin, sentenced as any other pagan nation. The only truth in this assertion is that Israel has indeed rejected Christ, and since then lives in sin, as any other nation.

On the other hand, it is also true that God has not abandoned the people of Israel, although they have sinned. God's promises are firm and true, as we have mentioned:

> For I do not desire, brethren, that you should be ignorant of this mystery, lest you should be wise in your own opinion, that blindness in part has happened to Israel until the fullness of the Gentiles has come in.
> And so all Israel will be saved, as it is written:
>
> "The Deliverer will come out of Zion,
> And He will turn away ungodliness from Jacob;
> For this is My covenant with them,
> When I take away their sins."
>
> Concerning the gospel they are enemies for your sake, but concerning the election they are beloved for the sake of the fathers.
> For the gifts and the calling of God are irrevocable.

Romans 11:25–29

The great day awaited by Israel has come—the day of redemption. The remnant of Israel will be saved. There are so many passages in the Scriptures related to this matter that it is impossible to mention them all here. At the end of the Great Tribulation, the Lord will appear in His glory and will forgive the sin of the remnant of Israel; although we shall see later that many people from other nations will also be blessed.

> 'Behold, I will gather them out of all countries where I have driven them in my anger, in my fury, and in great wrath; I will bring them back to this place, and I will cause them to dwell safely.
> They shall be my people, and I will be their God; then I will give them one heart and one way, that they may fear me forever, for the good of them and their children after them.
> And I will make an everlasting covenant with them, that I will not turn away from doing them good; but I will put my fear in their hearts so that they will not depart from me.
> Yes, I will rejoice over them to do them good, and I will assuredly plant them in this land, with all my heart and with all my soul.'
> For thus says the Lord: 'Just as I have brought all this great calamity on this people, so I will bring on them all the good that I have promised them.
>
> Jeremiah 32:37–42

> For Israel is not forsaken [has not become a widow—RV60], nor Judah, by his God, the Lord of hosts, though their land was filled with sin against the Holy One of Israel.
>
> Jeremiah 51:5

- <u>bring in everlasting righteousness</u>

God's promise is firm, and His righteousness toward Israel will be permanent and forever. This is the promise:

For Zion's sake I will not hold my peace, and for Jerusalem's sake I will not rest, until her righteousness goes forth as brightness, and her salvation as a lamp that burns.

The Gentiles shall see your righteousness, and all kings your glory. You shall be called by a new name, which the mouth of the Lord will name.

You shall also be a crown of glory in the hand of the Lord, and a royal diadem in the hand of your God.

You shall no longer be termed Forsaken, nor shall your land any more be termed Desolate; but you shall be called Hephzibah [my delight is in her], and your land Beulah [bride]; for the Lord delights in you, and your land shall be married.

Isaiah 62:1–4

Also in Isaiah 1:26–27 He says,

I will restore your judges as at the first, and your counselors as at the beginning. Afterward you shall be called the city of righteousness, the faithful city.

Zion shall be redeemed with justice and her penitents with righteousness.

- <u>to seal up vision and prophecy</u>

By this phrase, I understand that God is speaking of something that is firm and final. In other words, this is the plan of God and there is no other one; therefore, at the end of the seventy weeks this prophecy will have its full fulfillment.

- <u>to anoint the Most Holy</u>

Here is the great victory of all time. The long-awaited day is at hand, not only for those who will be saved, but also for the Lord Jesus. This is the day when the Lord Jesus comes to reign as the sovereign King—King of kings and Lord of lords. The people who enter the millennial kingdom will worship the Lord and honor Him as King and Messiah. That will be the time to anoint Jesus as the Most Holy.

> And it shall come to pass that everyone who is left of all the nations which came against Jerusalem shall go up from year to year to worship the King, the Lord of hosts, and to keep the Feast of Tabernacles.
>
> Zechariah 14:16

It should be noted that here we see no interruption in the time established by the Lord for the completion of all these events; they have a continuous fulfillment, one after the other, as it was established previously.

Due to the importance of this next passage, it will be included completely. I firmly believe that this is one of the most important and revealing prophetic passages in the Scriptures, in relation to eschatological matters. Daniel 9:25–27 says,

> Know therefore and understand, that from the going forth of the command to restore and build Jerusalem until Messiah the Prince, there shall be seven weeks and sixty-two weeks; the street shall be built again, and the wall, even in troublesome times.
>
> And after the sixty-two weeks Messiah shall be cut off, but not for Himself; and the people of the prince who is to come shall destroy the city and the sanctuary. The end of it shall be with a flood, and till the end of the war desolations are determined.
>
> Then he shall confirm a covenant with many for one week; but in the middle of the week he shall bring an end to sacrifice and offering. And on the wing of abominations shall be one who makes desolate, even until the consummation, which is determined, is poured out on the desolate.

Let us begin with the meaning of the *seventy weeks*, which are 490 days; however, in the light of the Scriptures 490 days equals 490 years, a day for each year. In Genesis 29:27–28, the Scriptures show this equivalence, "Fulfill her week, and we will give you this one also for the service which you will serve with me still another seven years. Then Jacob did so and fulfilled her week." In Ezekiel 4:4–6, another example is also shown: "… forty days. I have laid on you a day for each year."

From the time the kingdom of Babylon destroyed the city of Jerusalem and the temple until the reign of Media-Persia, there were four orders or decrees related to the restoration of Jerusalem. Let us see these decrees, carried out under the orders of kings, and some other events (Ref. 6):

- King Cyrus (around 538 BC)

  Decree to **rebuild the temple** (house of God) in the first year of King Cyrus (Ezra 1:1–3). The work was directed by Zerubbabel, appointed governor of Judah, and was stopped by the opposition of Judah's enemies (Ezra 4:1–5, 24). They could only begin the work, settling the altar on its place (Ezra 3:3) and beginning to lay down the foundations of the temple (Ezra 3:11–12).

- King Darius (around 519 BC)

  Decree to **rebuild the temple** in the second year of King Darius (Ezra 6:1–12). The work was directed by Zerubbabel (Zech. 4:9) and it included finishing the foundation of the temple (Hag. 2:10, 18). The work was completed in the sixth year of Darius (Ezra 6:15).

- King Artaxerxes (around 458 BC)

  Decree to **restore service in the temple** in the seventh year of King Artaxerxes (Ezra 7:6–28). The mission requested and granted to Ezra did not include rebuilding the temple, because it was already completed. The work was directed by Ezra, priest and scribe, who devoted himself to teach the law and commandments. During his stay in Jerusalem, the religious services, sacrifices, celebrations, and other activities in the temple, were restored.

- King Artaxerxes (around 450–445 BC)

  Decree to **rebuild the city**, including the **walls** and doors, in the twentieth year of King Artaxerxes (Neh. 1:3; 2:1–8). The work was directed by Nehemiah, firstly the king's cupbearer (Neh. 1:11) and later appointed governor of Judah (Neh. 5:14).

When we look at these four decrees or orders, we immediately realize that the only one involving the **restoration and rebuilding of the city** and **walls of Jerusalem** was the last one, granted around 450–445 BC under Artaxerxes, king of Persia. The Book of Nehemiah describes how the Jews had great opposition from their enemies as they finished the work of restoring the walls. According to Daniel's prophecy, the period of the seventy weeks begins with "the going forth of the command to **restore and build Jerusalem**."

The prophecy also says that "the street shall be built again, and the **wall**, even in troublesome times." King Artaxerxes' reign began around 470–465 BC. This period of years is used because when Artaxerxes' father, Emperor Xerxes I, was lying ill, it was understood by some scholars that King Artaxerxes I, third son, was coregent with his father for his last five to ten years.

Nehemiah 2:1 locates the order for rebuilding the city in the twentieth year of this king: "And it came to pass in the month of Nisan, in the twentieth year of king Artaxerxes ..." After establishing these analogies, we conclude that the seventy-week count—490 years—begins in around 450–445 BC.

According to Daniel's prophecy, the time from the command to restore and build Jerusalem until the death of the Messiah is sixty-nine weeks (483 years). The prophecy divides these sixty-nine weeks into two parts—seven weeks (forty-nine years) for the reconstruction of Jerusalem, and sixty-two additional weeks (434 years) up to the death of the Messiah ("And after the sixty-two weeks Messiah shall be cut off"). We know from history that these events were fulfilled: the rebuilding of Jerusalem and its walls, and the death of the Messiah.

Daniel prophesied that "the people of the prince who is to come shall destroy the city and the sanctuary" (Dan. 9:26), and that it would occur after the death of the Messiah. He does not say that a prince will come to destroy, but the people of a prince who is to come (in the future) shall destroy the city and the sanctuary. This "people" is the Roman Empire, which ruled Judea at the time of Jesus. Jesus predicted this event of the destruction of the temple and the city, when He said,

> O Jerusalem, Jerusalem, the one who kills the prophets and stones those who are sent to her! How often I wanted to gather your children together, as a hen gathers her chicks under her wings, but you were not willing!
> See! Your house is left to you desolate.
> Then Jesus went out and departed from the temple, and His disciples came up to show Him the buildings of the temple.

And Jesus said to them, 'Do you not see all these things? Assuredly, I say to you, not one stone shall be left here upon another, that shall not be thrown down.'

Matthew 23:37–38; 24:1–2

The Scriptures in Luke 19:43–44 also cite Jesus saying,

For days will come upon you when your enemies will build an embankment around you, surround you and close you in on every side, and level you, and your children within you, to the ground; and they will not leave in you one stone upon another, because you did not know the time of your visitation.

As mentioned before, this prophecy was completely fulfilled in the year AD 70, when a Roman general named Titus Flavius Vespasian, along with his army, destroyed the city of Jerusalem and the temple. Hundreds of thousands of Jews were killed and other thousands were scattered ("Your house is left to you desolate."), pursuant to the declaration "till the end of the war desolations are determined."

Now, who is "the prince who is to come"? The army that fulfilled the prophecy was the Roman army. The Antichrist, who will rule the world in the Great Tribulation, will use a people with Roman roots to execute his perverse actions against Israel and the whole world. This people is the European Union, as explained previously in detail.

This is why it is said, "the people of the prince who is to come shall destroy the city and the sanctuary." It is as if there were no interruption between the people who started the events in AD 70 and the coming of the Antichrist during the Great Tribulation. Therefore, I surely affirm that the "prince who is to come" is no other than the Antichrist.

The sixty-nine weeks mentioned in Daniel's prophecy have already been entirely fulfilled with the death of the Messiah Jesus Christ, when he was crucified by Roman hands, and with the destruction of Jerusalem and its temple by the Roman army. The next thing to be accomplished, according to the prophecy, is mentioned in verse 27,

Then he shall confirm a covenant with many for one week [seven years]; but in the middle of the week [three and a half years] he shall bring an end to sacrifice and offering. And on the wing of abominations shall be one who makes desolate, even until the consummation, which is determined, is poured out on the desolate.

We see that there is no pause between the destruction of Jerusalem and its temple (v. 26), and what shall come to pass in the last week (v. 27). As per the Jewish history, we see that the *prophetic clock* stopped on Jesus' death and the destruction of Jerusalem and its temple (v. 26), to bring a way for the new covenant of the church (approximately 2,000 years); then the last week of the seventy will be consummated (v. 27)—the seven years of the Great Tribulation. Figure 11: Seventy Weeks, shows a summary of the events already accomplished and those to be fulfilled according to Daniel's prophecy.

Verse 27 mentions that the Antichrist "shall confirm a covenant with many for one week [the last seven years]." What is the covenant that the prophet Daniel is speaking of? After the rapture of the church, the entire world will be in a tremendous state of confusion and desperation, especially those who know a bit about apocalyptic issues. At that time, more than ever before, the world will look for a leader to take them through this global chaos.

That will be the moment the Antichrist will emerge, appearing as a leader with great worldwide influence, including with Jewish and Arab peoples. Initially, this charismatic leader will not show himself as the Antichrist, but as a wise leader who can solve the problems of humanity. The shrewdness, craftiness, influence, and power of this leader will be so great that through agreements he will convince the Muslims/Arabs to cede their actual sacred place of the Temple of the Rock (Dome of the Rock) to the Jews.

The Temple of the Rock is currently erected on the same place where Solomon's temple was built. Therefore, this covenant could include a transfer or barter of the present territory of the Muslim's temple to the Jews, to make a way for the construction of the new Jewish temple (their third temple). I think this will be one of the first transcendental events in which the Antichrist will play a very important role. In this way he will convince Israel, and the entire world, that he is the great leader expected by all nations.

I firmly believe that these agreements between Jews and Muslims/Arabs will be part of the "covenant" mentioned in Daniel 9:27, ratified by the Antichrist—"He shall confirm a covenant with many for one week." This covenant will also include other aspects related to the Jews' law and commandments. Daniel 11:22 mentions a "prince of the covenant" who will be part of the destruction to be carried out by the Antichrist halfway through the period of seven years. "With the force of a flood they shall be swept away from before him and be broken, and also the prince of the covenant."

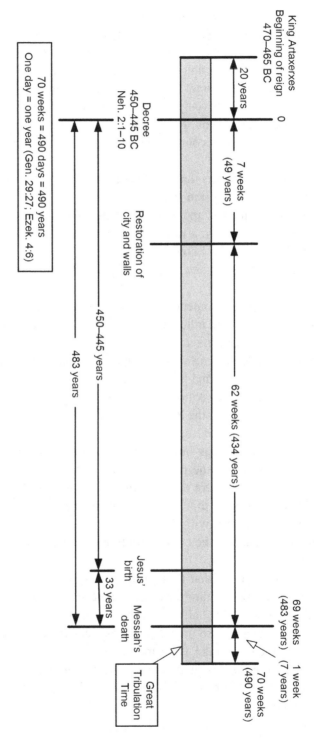

Figure 11: Seventy Weeks

Maybe this prince is the leader ruling in Israel at that time, who will ratify the agreements with the Antichrist. The Antichrist will betray and attack him and his people. At the beginning of the Great Tribulation, the people of Israel will return to the sacrifices, rites, and offerings mentioned in the old law.

In chapter 8 the prophet Daniel inquires, "How long will the vision be, concerning the daily [continuous] sacrifices and the transgression of desolation, the giving of both the sanctuary and the host to be trampled underfoot?" The answer was: "For two thousand three hundred days; then the sanctuary shall be cleansed" (Dan. 8:14).

According to this prophecy, there will be 2,300 days from the beginning of the "daily [continuous] sacrifices," up to the end with the coming of Christ, when "the sanctuary shall be cleansed." If we subtract 2,300 from 2,520 days (equal to seven years of 360 days per year, as the Jewish calendar), we get 220 days, and that divided by thirty days equals seven months and ten days. We see that the Israelites will begin their religious rites of sacrifices at approximately seven months from the beginning of the seven years of the Great Tribulation, after the covenant is ratified with the Antichrist.

Figure 12: Division of Years in the Great Tribulation, shows a correlation of the periods of years referred to in the books of Daniel and Revelation, in relation to the different events to occur in the Great Tribulation.

Matthew 24:20–21 also alludes to the Jewish law observance at the time of the Great Tribulation, when it says,

> And pray that your flight may not be in winter or on the *Sabbath.*
> For then there will be great tribulation, such as has not been since the beginning of the world until this time, no, nor ever shall be.

This warning comes because when keeping the day of rest (Sabbath), the Jews will be inhibited to work or move with freedom. Daniel 7:25, talking about what the Antichrist will do at the halfway point of the seven years, says, "and shall intend to *change times and law* [of the Jews]. Then the saints shall be given into his hand for a time and times and half a time [three and a half years]."

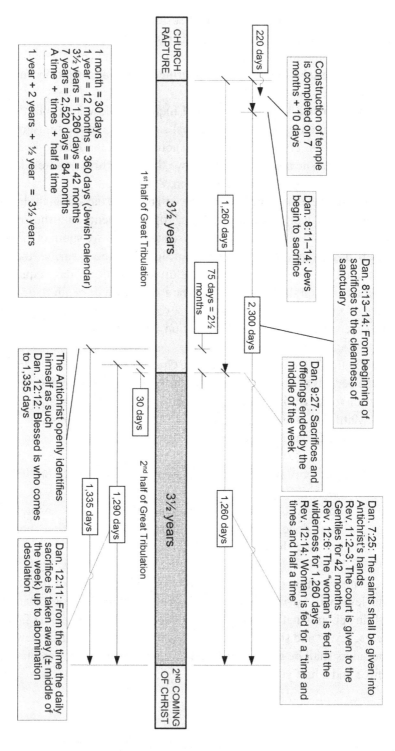

Figure 12: Division of Years in the Great Tribulation

The Third Temple of the Jews

Let us begin this section by considering this question: Why is the Jewish temple so important? Maybe in the sight of many people this temple is like thousands of temples located around the world. For others, this temple is just a religious issue between Jews and Arabs/Muslims.

But the reality is that the importance of this temple has been given by God Himself. This temple can be seen as a testimony of God on the earth, as it happened in the time of its restoration and the walls of Jerusalem.

A few hundred years before Christ, there were some valiant and committed men who dedicated to the reconstruction of the first temple, the city of Jerusalem, and its walls. The Babylonian army had destroyed the temple. Nehemiah was one of these brave men who, led by God, rebuilt the walls of Jerusalem. Nehemiah 6:15–16 says,

> So the wall was finished on the twenty-fifth day of Elul,
> in fifty-two days.
> And it happened, when all our enemies heard of it, and all
> the nations around us saw [feared—RV60] these things,
> that they were very disheartened in their own eyes; for
> they perceived that this work was done by our God.

Therefore, talking about the rebuilding of the walls is talking about the restoration of the testimony of God. The nations close to Jerusalem feared when they saw the walls completely restored. We know that God does not dwell in earthly temples, but this temple in Jerusalem showed the testimony of God, especially for the Hebrew people. The following paragraphs provide more details about the description and importance of the future third temple of the Jews.

I want to clearly set down as definite that the Hebrews will build their *third temple* in Jerusalem. How would it be possible for the Jews to carry out sacrifices and offerings continuously without temple and sanctuary? Which is the sanctuary mentioned in Daniel 8:11–13 and 11:31, to be established in the last "week"?

Which is the holy place mentioned in Matthew 24:15, where the Antichrist will be? Which is God's temple of 2 Thessalonians 2:4, where the wicked Antichrist will sit? Which are God's temple and the altar of Revelation 11:1–2 that the apostle John saw shortly before the completion of the half time of the Great Tribulation? Let us take, for example, this last passage of Revelation:

> Then I was given a reed like a measuring rod. And the angel stood, saying, 'Rise and measure the temple of God, the altar, and those who worship there.
> But leave out the court which is outside the temple, and do not measure it, for it has been given to the Gentiles. And they will tread the holy city underfoot for forty-two months [three and a half years].'

The apostle John saw the temple, the altar, and those who worship in it. The phrase "and those who worship there" suggests that, so far, the Jews still have freedom and access to the temple for their religious services. The apostle John saw very active religious services in the temple. At the end of the first part of the three and a half years, the Antichrist and his army will lunge with all their strength against Israel, and "will tread the holy city underfoot for forty-two months," that is, the remaining three and a half years.

It is well known that God chose only one location for the construction of the Jewish temple—on Mount Moriah in Jerusalem. In this place currently is the Temple of the Rock, also known as Dome of the Rock, a sacred Muslim place, where according to their beliefs, Muhammad, their spiritual leader, ascended to heaven. Mount Moriah was also the place chosen by God for Abraham's son, Isaac, to be offered in sacrifice. Genesis 22:1–2 says,

> Now it came to pass after these things that God tested Abraham, and said to him, 'Abraham!' And he said, 'Here I am.'
> Then He said, 'Take now your son, your only son Isaac, whom you love, and go to the land of Moriah, and offer him there as a burnt offering on one of the mountains of which I shall tell you.'

In 2 Chronicles 3:1, the Scriptures mention the place appointed by God for the construction of the first Jewish temple: "Now Solomon began to build the house of the Lord at Jerusalem on Mount Moriah, where the Lord had appeared to his father David, at the place that David had prepared on the threshing floor of Ornan the Jebusite" (see also 1 Chronicles 21:22–25 and 22:1).

Let us consider now some interesting comments regarding the location of Jerusalem and Solomon's temple. Jerusalem has occupied an important position in history in every age. A custom in the medieval world was to place Jerusalem at the center of the maps of the world. This coincides with the Scriptures, which place Jerusalem as the center of all the nations, and much more, as the center of all the earth

Ezekiel 5:5 says, "Thus says the Lord God: 'This is Jerusalem; I have set her in the midst of the nations and the countries all around her.'" Ezekiel 38:12, talking about Israel, says, "and against a people gathered from the nations, who have acquired livestock and goods, who dwell in the midst of the land."

According to ARV Bible (translated to English)—see *References*, the last phrase of this verse 12 says "who dwell in the navel of the land." Seeing God's perspective, putting Jerusalem at the center or navel of the earth, we can conclude that Jerusalem is the base or foundation of all the earth.

Both in the Scriptures and today's teaching, the foundation is also known as the cornerstone or stone of foundation. The main function of the cornerstone is to serve as a basis to sustain any structure built on it. In Job 38:4–6 we find a tremendous revelation about the creation of the earth:

> Where were you when I laid the foundations of the earth?
> Tell Me, if you have understanding.
> Who determined its measurements? Surely you know! Or
> who stretched the line upon it?
> To what were its foundations fastened? Or who laid its
> cornerstone?

God shows here that He laid a cornerstone as the basis of all the earth, and I definitely believe, considering the other related passages of Scriptures, that here He refers to Jerusalem, specifically Mount Moriah. Isaiah 28:16 says, "Therefore thus says the Lord God: 'Behold, I lay in Zion a stone for a foundation, a tried stone, a precious cornerstone, a sure foundation; whoever believes will not act hastily [will not be put to shame—1 Peter 2:6].'" Zion is used in the Scriptures as parallel to Jerusalem and the Temple Mount.

How great and marvelous is God, the Almighty God! How wonderful and accurate is His word! Praised be the Lord forever!

Let us look now at some characteristics of Mount Moriah in the city of

Jerusalem, where Solomon's temple was built. According to archaeological studies, Mount Moriah is a natural horizontal stone platform, with large rocky mass and solid bedrock. It is an impressive rock.

Genesis 22:4 says, "Then on the third day Abraham lifted his eyes and saw the place afar off." Ask yourself, what was special about the place chosen by God for Abraham to sacrifice his son Isaac, so that he could see and recognize it from afar? Something should distinguish it from all the other hills.

After considering all this information, we can conclude that Mount Moriah is located on the cornerstone, or stone of foundation, of the whole earth. Mount Moriah is the foundation of all the earth; therefore, if God touches this mount, the entire earth will tremble.

This is precisely what will happen at the time of the Great Tribulation, with an earthquake so strong that even the islands will be removed from their places (Rev. 6:12–14). God only needs to touch this cornerstone, and this judgment will be performed (although He just needs to say it, without touching it). This is precisely the place chosen by God to build the third temple of the Jews.

Within God's plan, there is also a connection between the cornerstone that holds the Hebrew temple (and the entire earth), and the Messiah and Savior Jesus Christ. In the Scriptures we find the spiritual meaning of this cornerstone. In 1 Peter 2:6–7 we read:

Therefore it is also contained in the Scripture,

"Behold, I lay in Zion
A chief cornerstone, elect, precious,
And he who believes on Him will by no means be
put to shame."

Therefore, to you who believe, He is precious; but to those who are disobedient,

'the stone which the builders rejected has become the chief cornerstone.'

In spiritual meaning, Jesus is that cornerstone. Similarly, in Ephesians 2:20, speaking to all those who are part of the church of Christ, Paul says, "having been built on the foundation of the apostles and prophets, Jesus

Christ Himself being the chief cornerstone." Jesus is the foundation of our lives; He is the one who holds us, the cornerstone.

It is not a coincidence that God commanded Abraham to sacrifice his son Isaac on the summit of Mount Moriah. Isaac is a type of Jesus and he was "sacrificed" over the cornerstone, Jesus Himself being the cornerstone. Thus, Isaac was "sacrificed in Christ."

In addition, through the sacrifice of Isaac (Christ), Mount Moriah was sanctified and separated unto God for the construction of the temple hundreds of years later (Ezek. 43:12). How great is God who makes everything perfect and forgets nothing!

Let us see what the Scriptures say about Isaac's sacrifice:

> So Abraham took the wood of the burnt offering and laid it on Isaac his son; and he took the fire in his hand, and a knife, and the two of them went together.
> But Isaac spoke to Abraham his father and said, 'My father!' And he said, 'Here I am, my son.' Then he said, 'Look, the fire and the wood, but where is the lamb for a burnt offering?'
> And Abraham said, 'My son, God will provide for Himself the lamb for a burnt offering.' So the two of them went together.
> Then they came to the place of which God had told him. And Abraham built an altar there and placed the wood in order; and he bound Isaac his son and laid him on the altar, upon the wood.
>
> Genesis 22:6–9

This is a wonderful passage! Isaac took the wood for the burnt offering and bore it on his shoulder; then, Abraham laid Isaac on the altar, upon that wood. This is a picture of Jesus Christ, who bore the cross on His shoulder, and then was laid on it and finally crucified. "And He, bearing His cross, went out to a place called the Place of a Skull, which is called in Hebrew, Golgotha" (John 19:17). Isaiah 53:7 says, "… yet He opened not His mouth; He was led as a lamb to the slaughter, and as a sheep before its shearers is silent, so He opened not His mouth."

Abraham said to Isaac, "My son, God will provide for Himself the lamb for a burnt offering." This lamb is Jesus, provided by God Himself, for the redemption of mankind. "And Abraham called the name of the place, The-Lord-Will-Provide; as it is said to this day, 'In the Mount of the

Lord it shall be provided'" (Gen. 22:14). This wonderful event occurred on the Mount of the Lord, Mount Moriah.

After Abraham finished the burnt offering, God spoke to him and uttered a prophecy to be fulfilled through the person of Jesus Christ,

> I will multiply your descendants as the stars of the heaven and as the sand which is on the seashore; and your descendants shall possess the gate of their enemies.
> In your seed [Jesus] all the nations of the earth shall be blessed.
>
> Genesis 22:17–18

This is why God gave such importance to Mount Moriah.

In the vision of the temple given to the prophet Ezekiel, God made reference to Mount Moriah when He said, "This is the law of the temple: The whole area surrounding the mountaintop is most holy. Behold, this is the law of the temple" (Ezek. 43:12).

I have read that some people think that the new Jewish temple could be built beside the Dome of the Rock, with a huge wall dividing the two places. I believe that this will not happen in that way, for certainly our God is not a small god subjected to circumstances or any other thing or person. Our God is God Almighty and very jealous with His plan and purpose.

Mount Moriah, chosen by God for the construction of the temple, will not be shared with another temple where another god is worshiped. God, through the prophet Ezekiel, said that the law of the temple is that the "whole area surrounding the mountaintop is **most holy**."

There must be no doubt, for it is God who established this law: "This is the law of the temple." This place was sanctified and separated for God by Isaac's sacrifice, who was Christ in a figurative sense. Psalm 78:68–69 says, "But chose the tribe of Judah, Mount Zion which He loved. And He built His sanctuary like the heights, like the earth which He has **established forever**." God will not change this place chosen for the construction of the temple; therefore, the Dome of the Rock must be destroyed or removed from the place currently built.

The third Jewish temple will be built near or at the beginning of the period of seven years of the Great Tribulation. From the beginning of the seven years, there will be approximately seven months (220 days) to complete the construction of the temple. The explanation of these 220 days is found in the previous section.

It would seem a very short time, if the design and construction of the

62

temple were to begin from scratch. But the reality is that according to current news, several Jewish groups have already committed to complete the details of the future temple, including its design, the utensils to be used, and all the objects required for the services and religious activities.

Indeed, these groups have been searching out the priesthood requirements, and they are looking for descendants of the sons of Zadox, of the tribe of Levi (Ezek. 44:15; 1 Chron. 6:1–8; 2 Sam. 8:17), to be considered as candidates for priestly services.

I firmly believe that the design of the temple has been completed using the vision of the temple through the prophet Ezekiel. The Book of Ezekiel provides meticulous descriptions that provide the basis of the design of the last temple. God wanted to show this prophet something very important, so He begins this prophecy by saying to him: "Son of man, look with your eyes and hear with your ears, and fix your mind on everything I show you; for you were brought here so that I might show them to you. Declare to the house of Israel everything you see" (Ezek. 40:4).

From chapter 40 to 44, God shows Ezekiel the details and measurements related to the future third temple, the priesthood, and other services. Then, after the vision, the Lord warns Ezekiel again, telling him, "Son of man, mark well, see with your eyes and hear with your ears, all that I say to you concerning all the ordinances of the house of the Lord and all its laws. Mark well who may enter the house and all who go out from the sanctuary" (Ezek. 44:5).

God clearly shows in these words the importance of this vision of the temple, so He alerts the prophet to watch and be mindful from the beginning to the end of the revelation.

It seems that everything in Israel is ready for the construction of the third temple, and the only missing thing is the availability of the site. If so, I think that in seven months the temple might be completed, because they can use prebuilt walls and assemble them on-site.

In this way is also fulfilled what is mentioned in the law about the noise of iron tools that should not be heard as they build the temple. "And the temple, when it was being built, was built with stone finished at the quarry, so that no hammer or chisel or any iron tool was heard in the temple while it was being built" (1 Kings 6:7; see also Exodus 20:25 and Joshua 8:31).

The previously described covenant of the Antichrist with the Jews is mentioned in several other passages in the Book of Daniel, such as Daniel 8:22–23 and 30–32. Now, what will happen at the halfway point of the seven years?

What we see is that these religious services by the people of Israel will not last long, because after the first three and a half years, they will be interrupted by the Antichrist ("in the middle of the week he shall bring an end to sacrifice and offering"). The Antichrist will break the covenant previously confirmed with the Jews, because this covenant was only used to introduce himself to them, and in this way deceive the people.

The time has come when the "great leader" accepted by Israel and other nations will take off his mask and present himself as what he had always wanted to be, the "Messiah" (but according to the Scriptures, the Antichrist). This person, although possessed by demons, will continue being a man who looks for the favor of other Jews through his wiles, so that in this way the Jews abandon the observance of the law.

> ... and return in rage against the holy covenant, and do damage. So he shall return and show regard for those who forsake the holy covenant.
> And forces shall be mustered by him, and they shall defile the sanctuary fortress; then they shall take away the daily sacrifices, and place there the abomination of desolation. Those who do wickedly against the covenant he shall corrupt with flattery ...
>
> Daniel 11:30–32

As we see in these passages, it is clear that the Antichrist will use the temple built by the Jews as his throne, pretending to be God. Revelation 16:10 says, "Then the fifth angel poured out his bowl on the throne of the beast," that is, the Antichrist. This third temple and its sanctuary will be destroyed during the Great Tribulation (Dan. 8:11–13; Rev. 11:1–2).

Dear reader, this will be the darkest hour that humanity will live through, especially the Hebrew people. This moment is when the Antichrist, before destroying the sanctuary, will profane it, sitting in the most holy place and placing images to be worshiped by people.

> ... and the man of sin is revealed, the son of perdition, who opposes and exalts himself above all that is called God or that is worshiped, so that he sits as God in the temple of God, showing himself that he is God.
>
> 2 Thessalonians 2:3–4

Therefore when you see the 'abomination of desolation,' spoken of by Daniel the prophet, standing in the holy place (whoever reads, let him understand), then let those who are in Judea flee to the mountains.

Matthew 24:15–16

Mark 13:14 mentions an additional detail: "So when you see the 'abomination of desolation,' spoken of by Daniel the prophet, *standing where it ought not*." Jesus warned us about the coming of the Antichrist when He said,

> Then if anyone says to you, 'Look, here is the Christ!' or 'There!' do not believe it.
> For false christs and false prophets will rise and show great signs and wonders to deceive, if possible, even the elect.
> See, I have told you beforehand.
> Therefore if they say to you, 'Look, He is in the desert!' do not go out; or 'Look, He is in the inner rooms!' do not believe it.

Matthew 24:23–26

The Scriptures describe these latter days as the "time of Jacob's trouble [distress]" and "great tribulation, such as has not been since the beginning of the world until this time, no, nor ever shall be." Nevertheless, God is great in mercy and keeps His covenant; He does not shatter it as the Antichrist, but is faithful to all. At the end of the seven years, the Desired will come and fulfill His promises, and "which is determined, is poured out on the desolate." The Antichrist shall manifest "and shall prosper till the wrath has been accomplished; for what has been determined shall be done" (Dan. 11:36).

Summarizing, after the sixty-nine weeks, the fulfillment of the prophecy will continue during the last week, with events that have not yet been fulfilled. Therefore, the prophetic clock stopped after sixty-nine weeks were completed, and all that was prophesied for that period of time has happened. In that time when the prophetic clock stopped, God established His church.

After the end of the church period, the prophetic clock will move again to finally complete the last seven years (the last week mentioned by the prophet Daniel). In this last period of seven years, God will deal again with the people of Israel. This will be the true time of the Great Tribulation. But since God still loves Israel (as I also do), He has provided this last chance to them, and the entire world too, to repent and believe in Jesus the Messiah, and be saved.

The End Time

Daniel Chapter 12

This chapter begins by describing, in general terms, the last days on the earth:

> At that time Michael shall stand up, the great prince who stands watch over the sons of your people; and there shall be a time of trouble, such as never was since there was a nation, even to that time. And at that time your people shall be delivered, every one who is found written in the book.

We have already seen the calamity that awaits the earth and its inhabitants. SO IT IS WRITTEN, AND SO IT WILL BE FULFILLED. Everything will be fulfilled. But there is still hope for those who devote their lives to the Lord with all their hearts, and live according to His word. There will not be many, because if in the "green wood" they are now living wantonly, how will it be in the "dry wood" time (Luke 23:31)?

The angel Michael will fight against the devil (the dragon), and will cast him out to the earth together with his angels (Rev. 12:7–9). It is then that the devil, knowing that he has a short time, will lunge with all his fury against the Israelites and all the other believers in the Lord. "Woe to the inhabitants of the earth and the sea! For the devil has come down to you, having great wrath, because he knows that he has a short time" (Rev. 12:12).

This will be the most anguished time on earth, as Satan attempts to deceive all men, to then destroy them. He will use all available resources, including false miracles and signs through the Antichrist and the False Prophet.

God shows Daniel that all these things are not for his time, but will have their fulfillment at the end of days. That is why God says to him, "But you, Daniel, shut up the words, and seal the book until the time of the end;

many shall run to and fro, and knowledge shall increase" (Dan. 12:4). Then the Lord, responding to Daniel's question, repeats, "Go your way, Daniel, for the words are closed up and sealed till the time of the end" (Dan. 12:9).

God closed and sealed Daniel's prophecy, that this word might not be understood until the time when the generation to which it was directed had come. With the coming of the prophets and apostles of the new covenant, God began to reveal what was previously hidden. God brings understanding and heavenly interpretation to the apostles of those closed and sealed prophecies.

One of the books that brings more light on these prophecies is the Book of Revelation. The Lord gives a vision to the apostle John which opens the sealed visions of the Book of Daniel. In Revelation 22:10 the Lord says to John, "Do not seal the words of the prophecy of this book, for the time is at hand." The time to reveal the hidden mysteries of everything that shall happen to Israel and the whole world has come. The prophecy of the Book of Revelation is the revelation of the sealed Book of Daniel.

How great is God! His mercy surpasses our understanding, since He alerts us again and again, in that way to save us from the trial which shall come upon the entire world. "Behold, I am coming quickly! Hold fast what you have, that no one may take your crown" (Rev. 3:11).

What does the prophet Daniel say about the time of fulfillment of this prophecy?

> And one said to the man clothed in linen, who was above the waters of the river, 'How long shall the fulfillment of these wonders be?'
> … that it shall be for a time, times, and half a time; and when the power of the holy people has been completely shattered, all these things shall be finished.
> Although I heard, I did not understand. Then I said, 'My Lord, what shall be the end of these things?'
> And he said, 'Go your way, Daniel, for the words are closed up and sealed till the time of the end.
> … And from the time that the daily sacrifice is taken away, and the abomination of desolation is set up, there shall be one thousand two hundred and ninety days.
> Blessed is he who waits, and comes to the one thousand three hundred and thirty-five days.'
>
> Daniel 12:6–12

This passage shows the duration for the fulfillment of all these events to come: "... shall be for a time, times, and half a time." As shown in figure 12, time, times and half a time means approximately three and a half years (1,260 days). By this we understand that the cruelest part of the Great Tribulation will have duration of about three and a half years, which agrees with verse 12:12 where it says, "Blessed is he who waits, and comes to the one thousand three hundred and thirty-five days."

At the beginning of these 1,335 days, the "great leader," who is raised to deceive the nations, will take off his mask and let his true face as Antichrist be seen. At that time, the Antichrist will begin to oppose the Jews continuing their religious rites in the temple. About two and a half months later (see figure 12), the Antichrist shall trigger the greatest persecution against Israel. This is the time of *Jacob's trouble*.

Only the brave ones who believe in the Lord Jesus can be part of those blessed who will arrive at the end of this distressing and terrible time. "... in the middle of the week he shall bring an end to sacrifice and offering. And on the wing of abominations shall be one who makes desolate, even until the consummation, which is determined, is poured out on the desolate" (Dan. 9:27). This also coincides with the verse in Daniel 12:11 which says, "And from the time that the daily [continuous—RV60] sacrifice is taken away, and the abomination of desolation is set up, there shall be one thousand two hundred and ninety days."

Summarizing, after this opposition begins, it will be approximately forty-five days (a month and a half) until the Antichrist stops the continuous sacrifice; in other words, the activities of the Jews in the temple in Jerusalem will not be allowed any more. This is equivalent to the 1,290 days from the end of the continuous sacrifice until the end of the Great Tribulation, which coincides with the "half of the week" of verse 9:27. From the time that the Antichrist openly identifies himself and begins to oppose the Jews until the coming of the Lord Jesus will be 1,335 days.

The second part of Daniel 12:4 says that at the end of days, "many shall run to and fro, and knowledge shall increase." By this statement I can understand that the end times will be distinguished by a great interest in knowledge and information. Men will go to and fro, searching and searching. That was the sin of the first inhabitants of the earth, Adam and Eve—they ate of the tree of knowledge of good and evil.

The apostle Paul said that "knowledge puffs up;" this is so when man fills his head with only letter and not with the life, purpose, and truth of God. Therefore, as we see in Daniel's prophecy, this last generation will be distinguished by having great knowledge about everything, but will be without understanding of the signs of the times. On this, we were warned by the Lord when He said,

> Now learn this parable from the fig tree: When its branch has already become tender and puts forth leaves, you know that summer is near.
> So you also, when you see all these things, know that it is near—at the doors!
> Assuredly, I say to you, this generation will by no means pass away till all these things take place.
> Heaven and earth will pass away, but My words will by no means pass away.
>
> Matthew 24:32–35

With all conviction, I bear witness that this current generation is the generation of the signs; therefore, as the Lord said, "My words will by no means pass away." "And when the power of the holy people has been completely shattered, all these things shall be finished" (Dan. 12:7).

In chapter 12 of Daniel, God reveals a word that brings great light on our understanding of what will happen to all those faithful men, who in the past, before Christ, died without receiving the promise—as it is said in Hebrews 11:39–40.

God's promises are firm and He will fulfill them in His time. God promised from the time of Abraham that He would give a land to the Israelites as inheritance, which would extend from the Mediterranean Sea shores as far as Babylon, now Iraq. This promise will be fulfilled when Jesus Christ returns in His second coming, after the Great Tribulation. He will bring with Him the faithful men who lived in the old covenant, resurrecting them from the dead to then enter into this Promised Land.

This is mentioned in the second part of Zechariah 14:5, which says, "Thus the Lord my God will come, and all the saints with you [Zechariah]." This is also confirmed in Daniel's prophecy when God, speaking directly to the prophet, says, "But you, go your way till the end; for you shall rest, and will arise to your inheritance at the *end of the days*" (Dan. 12:13). God reveals to Daniel that he will arise from the dead and will receive his inheritance, along with many other faithful who lived before Christ. This is why verses 12:2–3 say,

And many of those who sleep in the dust of the earth shall awake, some to everlasting life, some to shame and everlasting contempt.

Those who are wise shall shine like the brightness of the firmament, and those who turn many to righteousness like the stars forever and ever.

It is clear that these faithful ones and saints of the old covenant will be resurrected to receive the promise, as it also says in Luke 13:28–29,

There will be weeping and gnashing of teeth, when you see Abraham and Isaac and Jacob and all the prophets in the kingdom of God [Millennium], and yourselves thrust out. They will come from the east and the west, from the north and the south, and sit down in the kingdom of God.

God not only gives them the land as inheritance, but those faithful ones who served God as prophets, kings, and other types of leadership will be assigned to reign together with Christ in different positions in the Millennium, according to the capacity of each. We will see later that alongside these saints of the old covenant resurrected in the second coming of Christ, there will also be the resurrected who were killed in the Great Tribulation, and will be rewarded too. These are referred to in Revelation 11:18 and 20:4:

The nations were angry, and Your wrath has come, and the time of the dead, that they should be judged, and that You should reward Your servants the prophets and the saints, and those who fear Your name, small and great, and should destroy those who destroy the earth.

And I saw thrones, and they sat on them, and judgment was committed to them. Then I saw the souls of those who had been beheaded for their witness to Jesus and for the word of God, who had not worshiped the beast or his image, and had not received his mark on their foreheads or on their hands. And they lived and reigned with Christ for a thousand years.

This is our faithful God who does not forget what He proposed to do on His time. There is no other like Him. To Him be glory and honor forever, amen!

CHAPTER 4

Gospel According to Matthew

T he Gospel of Matthew is known by many as the "Gospel of the Kingdom." It is so called because the book dedicates much of its content to the message associated with the kingdom of God. Matthew 24:14 establishes this when it says, "And this **gospel of the kingdom** will be preached in all the world as a witness to all the nations, and then the end will come." This gospel presents Christ as the King.

At His first coming, Christ was identified to the Hebrews as King, although the people of Israel did not receive Him as such: "Tell the daughter of Zion, 'Behold, your King is coming to you, lowly, and sitting on a donkey, a colt, the foal of a donkey'" (Matt. 21:5).

When Jesus was approximately two years old, wise men from the East came to Jerusalem, asking, "Where is He who has been born King of the Jews? For we have seen His star in the East and have come to worship Him" (Matt. 2:2).

In His second coming, Christ will come again to the Jews as King, but this time they will receive Him, and He will reign as King from "the throne of His glory," which will be established in the Millennium. In Luke 1:32–33, the angel Gabriel announces to Mary that the child she will deliver

> will be great, and will be called the Son of the Highest; and the Lord God will give Him the throne of His father David. And He will reign over the house of Jacob forever, and of His kingdom there will be no end.

The future reign of Christ is prophesied from ancient times by many prophets, among them Jeremiah: "But they shall serve the Lord their God, and David [Jesus] their king, whom I will raise up for them" (Jer. 30:9).

There are many other passages in the Scriptures that speak of this topic, but they cannot all be mentioned here; some of these are Matthew 16:28; 19:27–28; 25:31–34, and Revelation 19:16 and 20:4.

In Jesus' lifetime many inhabitants of Israel kept their hope alive for the establishment of the kingdom of God in their midst. An example of this can be seen in Luke 19:11: "Now as they heard these things, He spoke another parable, because He was near Jerusalem and because they thought the kingdom of God would appear immediately."

In other passages, such as John 1:49; 6:15, and Acts 1:6, this fact can be seen clearly. For this reason, when we read the Gospel of Matthew, it is important to recognize the essence and purpose of each part of it. This gospel contains many passages which refer, even in a prophetic way, only to the people of Israel.

Dear reader, let me now insert a parenthesis to encourage you to see and understand two types of messages of Jesus which have different objectives and goals. One is God's message related to promises and prophecies about the people of Israel, and the other one is related to the church, the body of Christ. Israel waits for the Messiah and King; the church waits for her Lord and Husband. Note the intention of Jesus in each message.

Israel has a very important place within the prophecy related to future events. Because the ancient prophets did not see the church, for purposes of prophecy fulfillment, the next step after the destruction of the temple in Jerusalem (AD 70) will be the attack of Russia against Israel and the Great Tribulation. Israel will suffer its punishment, caused by its rejection of Christ. However, thanks to the Lord's mercy, He has not yet dismissed Israel, as mentioned by the apostle Paul in Romans 11:1–2:

> I say then, has God cast away His people? Certainly not!
> For I also am an Israelite, of the seed of Abraham, of the
> tribe of Benjamin.
> God has not cast away His people whom He foreknew.

God continues His purpose concerning the people of Israel, which we will see more clearly through the Gospel of Matthew.

In this book, we will be considering only some chapters of the Gospel of Matthew—chapter 24 in particular—which provides a clear picture of the role of Israel related to the events of the latter days. After considering the previous chapters of this book, together with chapter 24 of Matthew, we can mark out the following outstanding events:

- Israel's rejection of the prophets and Jesus the Messiah
- Destruction of the temple in Jerusalem by the Roman General (and later emperor) Titus in AD 70, which marks the beginning of the judgment of God against Israel
- Signs and trials before the end (Great Tribulation)
- Visible second coming of Christ to earth
- Establishment of the kingdom of Christ in the Millennium

Jesus describes the fulfillment of these events without interruption. This is so, as we have already mentioned, because the accomplishment of this word is not for the church. The church is greatly edified by this word, like any other word that comes from the mouth of God, but the content of this word in particular has nothing to do with the purpose of God for His church.

The Scriptures clearly teach that the Great Tribulation is a judgment for the unbelievers, not for the faithful people. Judgment of God means wrath of God, and it is prepared for those who displease God and live in disobedience to His word.

> For the wrath of God is revealed from heaven against all ungodliness and unrighteousness of men, who suppress the truth in unrighteousness.
> But we know that the judgment of God is according to truth against those who practice such things.
>
> Romans 1:18; 2:2

Matthew 24:34 says that "this generation will by no means pass away till all these things take place." The generation referred to here is the generation of the signs described in the whole chapter 24. *This generation* has its full expression from the beginning of the first century with Israel's rejection of the Messiah, till its final consummation in the Great Tribulation. The same Christ connects the period of His death with the events of the Great Tribulation, bypassing the period of the church.

We see this picture in Jesus statement when they were taking Him to be crucified, and a group of women were mourning and lamenting for Him,

> But Jesus, turning to them, said, 'Daughters of Jerusalem, do not weep for Me, but weep for yourselves and for your children.

> For indeed the days are coming in which they will say,
> "Blessed are the barren, wombs that never bore, and
> breasts which never nursed!"
> Then they will begin to say to the mountains, "Fall on us!"
> and to the hills, "Cover us!"
> For if they do these things in the green wood, what will
> be done in the dry?'
>
> Luke 23:28–31

Jesus speaks here to Israel, the "daughters of Jerusalem," and connects His own time with events to take place in the Great Tribulation. (See also Revelation 6:16–17.)

It is important to note that it was the Roman Empire that ruled politically during Jesus' lifetime. In the same way, the Roman Empire will have a great part and authority in the Great Tribulation, including political and religious authority. Therefore, for the purpose of prophecy fulfillment, the basis of government in the Great Tribulation will be relatively the same as the one established during Jesus' lifetime.

Chapter 24 of the Gospel According to Matthew

Matthew 24:1–3

To rightly understand the message of chapter 24, it is necessary to first consider the message of the previous chapter. In chapter 23, Jesus reproaches the Jews for their life and behavior. It is a strong message that shows the deceit that these people lived in. Jesus calls them (among other things) hypocrites, fools, and blind. The apostle Matthew ends chapter 23 with these words of Jesus:

> O Jerusalem, Jerusalem, the one who kills the prophets
> and stones those who are sent to her! How often I wanted
> to gather your children together, as a hen gathers her
> chicks under her wings, but you were not willing! See!
> Your house is left to you desolate.

Jesus speaks to those Israelites who did not love the truth and who lived a life of appearances, like most of the current inhabitants of the earth. God tried to join them as one ("as a hen gathers her chicks"), but they were stiff-necked and rebellious. Jesus warns them now, saying that Jerusalem, along with her temple, will be made desolate. Jesus declares in Matthew 24:2, "Do you not see all these things? Assuredly, I say to you, not one stone shall be left here upon another, that shall not be thrown down."

This would be the time of the beginning of God's judgment, also prophesied in Daniel 9:26, "And after the sixty-two weeks Messiah shall be cut off, but not for Himself; and the people of the prince who is to come shall destroy the city and the sanctuary. The end of it shall be with a flood, and till the end of the war desolations are determined." As we have mentioned several times, the destruction of Jerusalem and the temple, with its sanctuary, had its entire completion in AD 70.

As we see in chapter 23, Jesus speaks to the Jews, not to the church (although the church is edified through all these messages). Then, the disciples ask Jesus about the signs of the end and His second coming. Jesus responds by declaring what shall come to pass in the Great Tribulation— overlooking the timespan of the church. This is so because Jesus is directing His message to the Jews who do not believe in Him as the Messiah.

There is a great difference between the answers to the question of verse 24:3, "Tell us, when these things will be? And what will be the sign of Your coming, and of the end of the age?" and the question in Acts 1:6, "Lord, will You at this time restore the kingdom to Israel?" Although both questions touch on the same subject, the responses of Jesus were very different.

In Matthew, Jesus responds by describing the events that will happen by the end of *this generation*. He warns them as if all these events were to happen soon, during their own lifetime. In His message, He announces the future trials (Matthew 24) and He promises to establish the kingdom of God on the earth (Matthew 25).

However, in the Book of Acts, Jesus diverts the disciples from the final events, telling them that "It is not for you to know times or seasons which the Father has put in His own authority" (Acts 1:7). Then He encourages them to receive the Holy Spirit in order to be witnesses in all parts of the world.

The message of the future earthly kingdom was not the need of these disciples who were close to becoming the first members of the "body of Christ"—the church of the Lord. Their need was to be filled with the power of the Spirit to express the image of the Lord Jesus in this world. Therefore, the judgments referred to in Matthew 24 are not prophecies to the members of the church, those who are born again and love the truth of God.

The Great Tribulation is a unique event that will affect the entire world. But many of the signs described in the Scriptures will be seen mainly in the land of Israel and its surrounding countries.

The Scriptures call that period of trials in various ways: "the time of Jacob's [Israel] trouble [distress]" (Jer. 30:1–7; Dan. 12:1); a time when God "will make you pass under the rod" (Ezek. 20:33–38); "as silver is melted in the midst of a furnace, so shall you be melted" (Ezek. 22:19–22); and "a day of wrath, a day of trouble and distress, a day of devastation and desolation, a day of darkness and gloominess, a day of clouds and thick darkness" (Zeph. 1:15); "For then there will be great tribulation, such as has not been since the beginning of the world until this time, no, nor ever shall be" (Matt.24:21).

Matthew 24:4–12

From Matthew 24:4 Jesus began to describe the events to be fulfilled by the end of days. It is true that throughout all ages there have been wars, false prophets, and deceivers. But the events mentioned in this chapter 24 are unique, and we have to visualize them in the light of all the Scripture, that is, taking into consideration what other books of the Bible say, such as Revelation, Corinthians, Thessalonians, Daniel, Isaiah, and many others. The events described in chapter 24 have not been fulfilled yet.

Jesus warns the world, especially the Jews, about the tribulations that the inhabitants of the earth will experience before the kingdom of God is established in the Millennium. According to Jesus, life in the Great Tribulation will be full of pain and suffering, if one even survives.

> Then they will deliver you up to tribulation and kill you,
> and you will be hated by all nations for My name's sake.
> And then many will be offended, will betray one another,
> and will hate one another.
> Then many false prophets will rise up and deceive many.
> And because lawlessness will abound, the love of many
> will grow cold.
>
> Matthew 24:9–12

In this period of time, true faithfulness and friendship among friends and family will be scarce. People will hate and betray each other, giving others up to governmental authorities. Wickedness will grow to levels unimaginable, since deceit, hate, and bitterness shall be their "daily bread." "And because lawlessness will abound, the love of many will grow cold."

The true *great tribulation* will extend for a span of time of approximately three and a half years. This period of great distress will begin with wars between nations, diseases, hunger, and earthquakes in different places. And if "all these are the beginning of sorrows" (Matt. 24:8), what shall it be when the Antichrist takes control of the entire world?

There are people who say that they will resist until the end, because they will hide in remote places to not be found. This is a very misguided thought, because technology has increased so much that a person can be traced through satellites, no matter where he is.

It is already known that clothes, shoes, and many other items of clothing sold in large chain stores contain an electronic device (chip) able to identify the user—so it will not be difficult to locate a person through the use of the satellite systems. The Great Tribulation is real; it is not a story for films.

> And there will be signs in the sun, in the moon, and in the stars; and on the earth distress of nations, with perplexity, the sea and the waves roaring; men's hearts failing them from fear and the expectation of those things which are coming on the earth, for the powers of the heavens will be shaken.
>
> Luke 21:25–26

Matthew 24:13–14

"But he who endures to the end shall be saved. And this gospel of the kingdom will be preached in all the world as a witness to all the nations, and then the end will come." The salvation mentioned in this passage is different from the one offered by the Lord Jesus Christ to the members of the church.

Christians are saved by the grace of God through faith in the Lord Jesus (Eph. 2:8). This grace is the source or ground of salvation and faith is the instrument or the door to enter into that salvation. The result of this salvation will be the escape of the Great Tribulation and the transformation of our earthly bodies into incorruptible bodies (1 Cor. 15:50–54) to be with the Lord in heaven.

On the other hand, the "salvation" in Matthew 24 refers to the entrance into the millennial kingdom on this earth. To the conquerors who survive the Great Tribulation, God promises a life of at least a thousand years under the reign of Christ. The Millennium is God's promise to Israel, not to the church.

To reiterate, the "Gospel of the Kingdom" mentioned in this passage, which Jesus also preached to the Jews (Matt. 4:23), is the message associated with the millennial kingdom. This is not the gospel now preached by the church.

The church preaches Christ as Lord and Savior of the soul. This message transforms our whole lives and brings us to the ground of grace, where the Holy Spirit leads our steps in Him. The final result of this salvation is eternal life, enabling us to be true witnesses unto Jesus.

However, the gospel of the kingdom will be preached during the Great Tribulation, bringing a message of hope to those who believe in Jesus and resist until the end, without denying the Lord. These are the ones who will have access to the millennial kingdom.

Chapters 7 and 14 of the Book of Revelation describe 144,000 chosen people (12,000 from each tribe of Israel), for whom part of their tasks will be preaching the gospel of the kingdom before the second coming of Christ. These 144,000, together with other believers of that time, will be the ones who will fulfill the word that "this gospel of the kingdom will be preached in all the world, … and then the end will come."

After the Great Tribulation, since the earth will be completely destroyed, it will need to be restored in order to be occupied by the nations which are saved. Although the whole chapters 60 and 61 of Isaiah tell us about the Millennium, I will only quote verse four of chapter 61, which describes some of the work of restoration to be carried out in the Millennium: "And they shall rebuild the old ruins, they shall raise up the former desolations, and they shall repair the ruined cities, the desolations of many generations."

Because there are many passages in the Scriptures which describe the Millennium and the way of life in it, we cannot include them all here, but will mention some of them:

> For the children of Israel shall abide many days without king or prince, without sacrifice or sacred pillar, without ephod or teraphim.
> Afterward the children of Israel shall return and seek the Lord their God and David [Jesus] their King. They shall fear the Lord and His goodness in the latter days.
> Hosea 3:4–5

And it shall come to pass that everyone who is left of all
the nations which came against Jerusalem shall go up from
year to year to worship the King, the Lord of hosts, and to
keep the Feast of Tabernacles.

Zechariah 14:16

Isaiah 11:6–9 describes the harmony, in which the wild animals will
live in the Millennium,

The wolf also shall dwell with the lamb, the leopard shall
lie down with the young goat, the calf and the young lion
and the fatling together; and a little child shall lead them.
The cow and the bear shall graze; their young ones shall
lie down together; and the lion shall eat straw like the ox.
The nursing child shall play by the cobra's hole, and the
weaned child shall put his hand in the viper's den.
They shall not hurt nor destroy in all My holy mountain,
for the earth shall be full of the knowledge of the Lord as
the waters cover the sea.

Matthew 24:15–22

Let us remember the previously discussed word related to the last week
of Daniel's prophecy. That week represents the seven years of the Great
Tribulation. The prophecy says that at the halfway point of the *week*,
the sacrifice and offering will cease, and the sanctuary will be trampled
underfoot (Dan. 9:27; 8:13–14; 11:31; 12:11).

This clearly shows that the people of Israel will return back to the
old law, observing the solemn feast days and offering sacrifices. For this
reason, Matthew 24:20 says to pray that "your flight may not be in winter
or on the Sabbath."

About the winter it could be the intensely cold preventing them of any
movement. About the Sabbath it would be that if they, trying to comply
with the old law, would be unable to move and flee from the Antichrist's
persecution. This is the time when the Antichrist will seat on the temple
as God. Matthew 24:15–16 says,

Therefore when you see the 'abomination of desolation,'
spoken of by Daniel the prophet, standing in the holy place

(whoever reads, let him understand), then let those who are
in Judea flee to the mountains.

Mark 13:14 presents an additional detail when, speaking about the
abomination of desolation, Jesus says, "standing where it ought not"—in
the temple of the Hebrews in Jerusalem. In 2 Thessalonians 2:3–4, the
Scriptures offer more clearness about this subject when Paul says,

> Let no one deceive you by any means; for that Day will
> not come unless the falling away comes first, and the
> man of sin is revealed, the son of perdition, who opposes
> and exalts himself above all that is called God or that is
> worshiped, so that he sits as God in the temple of God,
> showing himself that he is God.

This is not a fairy tale. The Antichrist will present himself as divine,
as God, and will come to execute all the authority that he can, even though
within the limits God has established.

All these passages clearly show that the abomination of desolation
(the Antichrist, the man of sin, the son of perdition) will occupy the "holy
place," that is, he will sit on a place in the temple of Jerusalem, profaning it.

These passages confirm again that the people of Israel, at some time
in the future, will return to build their temple in the same place where
Solomon's ancient temple was. In this way, the Jews can go back again to
celebrate their religious rites and to declare the sanctuary of the temple as
the "holy place."

The reason that the daily sacrifice ceases at the middle of the week is
that at that time, the Antichrist begins to reign openly with all authority
and wickedness. He will no longer hide his true identity behind the face of
the "great leader" that the nations received and believed. That leader who
misled Israel and all the other nations now begins to reign as if he were
the expected Messiah. In this way he will deceive many, but not all Israel,
because the Jewish people will now realize that he is a false Messiah.

This will be the most difficult time in history for every inhabitant of
the earth, especially the people of Israel, who will suffer the direct impact
of these events. That is why the Lord warns them saying that when they
see the Antichrist taking a place in the temple, pretending to be God, those
who are in Jerusalem should flee out of the city. The greatest persecution
and tribulation of all time has come (Matt. 24:21).

The women who are pregnant or raising children in those days will suffer much by not being able to feed their children, and worse, not being able to flee because of their condition.

This is a tribulation which has never been, nor will ever be on the earth until this time. Luke 21:20 says, "But when you see Jerusalem surrounded by armies, then know that its desolation is near." Also, in Revelation 11:2, God reveals to John what will happen to the city of Jerusalem at the middle of the week: "But leave out the court which is outside the temple, and do not measure it, for it has been given to the Gentiles. And they will tread the holy city underfoot for forty-two months [three and a half years]."

The crucial time for the great city of Jerusalem has come, and the Antichrist will take her; for this reason, God tells the inhabitants of Jerusalem to flee out of the city. But where will the Jews flee? Will they keep out of the hands of the Antichrist? I would like to leave the answers to these questions for when we consider the 12th chapter of Revelation.

Matthew 24:23–26

In those days, there will be many deceivers, pretending to be prophets and even Christ. Many people who do not believe in Jesus and live in accordance with their own rules and will, will be deceived by the Antichrist and by many other false prophets. Jesus warns them that these deceivers will "show great signs and wonders to deceive, if possible, even the elect."

When the population realizes who the Antichrist really is, and begins to experience suffering and tribulation, many will remember their bad works and those that their ancestors did when they killed the true Messiah, Jesus Christ. Then many of them will humble before God and repent.

2 Thessalonians 2:8–12 clearly describes the person of the Antichrist; I will only quote one verse: "The coming of the lawless one is according to the working of Satan, with all power, signs, and lying wonders" (v. 9). The Antichrist comes with misleading and lying signs. He is a false Christ, and when he removes his mask and reveals his true identity, it will be too late for many, because they shall have fallen already into his trap.

Matthew 24:27–31

In this passage, Jesus shows the contrast between the ways the false christs will appear (previous passage) and how the true Christ will appear at His second coming ("and they will see the Son of Man coming on the clouds of heaven with power and great glory").

Jesus also says that He will be seen as lightning—He will appear suddenly. Revelation 1:7 says, "Behold, He is coming with clouds, and every eye will see Him, even they who pierced Him." "They who pierced Him" refers to the Jews, as their ancestors were those who killed Jesus (Acts 2:36–37).

"Every eye will see Him" means that the people who are at that time in Jerusalem and surrounding areas will see Him, because Christ will come down and place his feet on the Mount of Olives in Jerusalem. "Behold, the day of the Lord is coming ..." "And in that day His feet will stand on the Mount of Olives, which faces Jerusalem on the east ..." (Zech. 14:1, 4).

These prophecies refer to the Jews, as it is also confirmed in Mathew 26:64, which says:

> Jesus said to him [high priest], 'It is as you said. Nevertheless, I say to you, hereafter you will see the Son of Man sitting at the right hand of the Power, and coming on the clouds of heaven.'

Jesus spoke to the high priest and the Jews who were with him. The second coming of Jesus will be seen by the inhabitants of Jerusalem and surrounding areas. (Please refer to the section in which Revelation 1:7 is discussed in more detail.) At this time Jesus will come as King to establish His kingdom on the earth.

> I was watching in the night visions, and behold, One like the Son of Man, coming with the clouds of heaven! He came to the Ancient of Days, and they brought Him near before Him.
> Then to Him was given dominion and glory and a kingdom, that all peoples, nations, and languages should serve Him. His dominion is an everlasting dominion, which shall not pass away, and His kingdom the one which shall not be destroyed.
>
> Daniel 7:13–14

In contrast to this visible second coming of Christ to the Mount of Olives, in the rapture of the church, Christ does not descend to the earth, for we "shall be caught up together with them [the resurrected] in the clouds to meet the Lord in the air. And thus we shall always be with the Lord" (1 Thess. 4:17).

In the rapture, Jesus receives the church in the air and then both continue together to heaven. But in His visible second coming, after the defeat of the devil and his armies in Armageddon, Jesus establishes His kingdom of a thousand years on the earth (not in heaven).

> And He will send His angels with a great sound of a trumpet, and they will gather together His elect from the four winds, from one end of heaven to the other.
>
> Matthew 24:31

> When the Son of Man comes in His glory, and all the holy angels with Him, then He will sit on the throne of His glory.
> All the nations will be gathered before Him, and He will separate them one from another, as a shepherd divides his sheep from the goats.
> And He will set the sheep on His right hand, but the goats on the left.
> Then the King will say to those on His right hand, 'Come, you blessed of My Father, inherit the kingdom prepared for you from the foundation of the world.'
>
> Matthew 25:31–34

Hallelujah! This is the great day awaited by those who kept the word and the testimony of Jesus. They shall inherit the kingdom prepared and promised since the time of the patriarch Abraham.

Matthew 24:30 says that when they see Christ coming down from heaven, "all the tribes of the earth will mourn." This passage is discussed in the section on Revelation 1:7; please refer to it.

Another interesting fact that we see in this passage of Matthew is that even nature and the stars of heaven will suffer the impact of the events on the earth. The sun, the moon, and the stars will be shaken, as prophesied also in Joel 2:10, 30–31. Isaiah also prophesied about the "suffering" and "moans" of the earth, when he said,

> The land shall be entirely emptied and utterly plundered, for the Lord has spoken this word.

The earth mourns and fades away, the world languishes
and fades away; the haughty people of the earth languish.
The earth is violently broken, the earth is split open, the
earth is shaken exceedingly.
The earth shall reel to and fro like a drunkard, and shall
totter like a hut; its transgression shall be heavy upon it,
and it will fall, and not rise again.

Isaiah 24:3–4, 19–20

We will see later how nature has been currently experiencing the
effects of the sin of man, and how it is also awaiting the redemption that
will be manifested at the great day of the coming of the Lord Jesus (Rom.
8:19–23).

Although we will consider more details in the Book of Revelation, I
would like to mention, in general terms, something about Matthew 24:28,
"For wherever the carcass is, there the eagles will be gathered together."

I understand that this passage refers to what will happen in the so-
called Battle of Armageddon, with the second coming of Christ. A large
army commanded by the Antichrist will meet at Armageddon, or the
Valley of Jezreel, located in Israel, to try to finally destroy the people of
Israel. Is at that time that the King of kings and Lord of lords will appear
with the clouds, along with the heavenly angels (Matt. 24:27, 30; Rev.
19:11–21). "Then the Lord will go forth and fight against those nations, as
He fights in the day of battle" (Zech. 14:3).

The angels will be responsible for destroying the army of the enemy.
That battle will produce so many dead that it will be a "banquet" for the
birds of prey, sent for that specific purpose and time (Rev. 19:21; Luke 17:37;
Ezek. 39:17–22). Therefore, the passage of Matthew says that "wherever the
carcass is, there the eagles will be gathered together." Zechariah 14:12–13
says,

And this shall be the plague with which the Lord will
strike all the people who fought against Jerusalem: Their
flesh shall dissolve while they stand on their feet, their
eyes shall dissolve in their sockets, and their tongues shall
dissolve in their mouths.
It shall come to pass in that day that a great panic from the
Lord will be among them. Everyone will seize the hand
of his neighbor, and raise his hand against his neighbor's
hand.

The Lord, together with His angels, will overcome, and none of His enemies will escape.

Matthew 24:32–36

Jesus used plants and trees to bring specific messages, in particular to the Jews. We can see in the Scriptures the use of several plants; three excel among them: the vine, the olive, and the fig tree. In most cases, they are used to identify people. For example, the vine is representative of Jesus: "I am the true vine, and My Father is the vinedresser" (John 15:1). We also see that God relates the vine to His church: "I am the vine, you are the branches" (John 15:5).

On the other hand, the olive tree, from which oil is extracted, is clearly representative of the Holy Spirit. The fig tree has also its meaning—it represents Israel. We see in Jeremiah 24:1–10 how the figs are representative of the people of Israel. In the referenced passage of Matthew, Jesus uses the fig tree,

> Now learn this parable from the fig tree: When its branch
> has already become tender and puts forth leaves, you know
> that summer is near.
> So you also, when you see all these things, know that it is
> near—at the doors!

The fig tree has the peculiarity that when summer approaches in Israel, between August and September, it begins to sprout tender leaves. So the sprout of new leaves in the fig tree marks the opening of summer—a clear and precise signal. Similarly, Jesus has given a series of events and specific signs that will occur prior to His second coming, which will announce that the time of His coming is close.

On the other hand, there are no signs for the rapture. It may occur at any time, without previous notice or accomplishment of any specific event. In the latter part of this book, more detail about the important subject of the rapture is included.

"But of that day and hour no one knows, not even the angels of heaven, but My Father only." Although anyone may read and see the signs that Christ's second coming is drawing near, the Lord is categorical when He says that the date and the specific time of His coming shall remain secret. Why then do many people attempt to calculate the day of His second coming? Since Jesus has expressly said that only His Father knows it, we cannot speculate.

We must be satisfied with what God reveals, and not go beyond trying to use our imagination. "The secret things belong to the Lord our God, but those things which are revealed belong to us and to our children forever, that we may do all the words of this law" (Deut. 29:29). Jesus was also very clear with His disciples when He said, "It is not for you to know times or seasons which the Father has put in His own authority" (Acts 1:7).

Matthew 24:34 says that "this generation will by no means pass away till all these things take place." Matthew 23:36 also says: "Assuredly, I say to you, all these things will come upon this generation." What does *this generation* refer to? Jesus Christ Himself answers this question when He says, **this** generation, that is, the same generation or time in which He was living.

The first chapter of the Gospel of Matthew describes the genealogy of Jesus Christ on behalf of Joseph, Mary's husband. Verse 17 says, "So all the generations from Abraham to David are fourteen generations, from David until the captivity in Babylon are fourteen generations, and from the captivity in Babylon until the Christ are fourteen generations." The generations ended in Christ. Jesus marked the last generation, and the phrase *this generation* refers to the timespan of His own generation.

As mentioned before, with the death of Christ the prophetic clock stopped in the sixty-ninth week. There is only one week (seven years) lacking to fulfill the entire prophet Daniel's prophecy. When Jesus speaks of "this generation," He refers to the time in which He lived, **plus** the seven years for the Great Tribulation.

For purposes of fulfillment of Israel's prophecy, the seven years of the Great Tribulation are part of *this generation*, without any separation. (For more details on this subject of the union between Jesus' time and the Great Tribulation, see chapter 2 *What the Old Prophet Did Not See*.) Therefore, *this generation* refers to the generation or timespan in which the signs described in Matthew will be fulfilled, which includes the period of the Great Tribulation.

Matthew 24:37–51

But as the days of Noah were, so also will the coming of the Son of Man be.

For as in the days before the flood, they were eating and drinking, marrying and giving in marriage, until the day that Noah entered the ark, and did not know until the flood came and took them all away, so also will the coming of the Son of Man be.

Matthew 24:37–39

It is amazing that with all the signs that will take place throughout all the world, the coming of the Lord will surprise the majority of the inhabitants of the earth. They will neither believe the advertisements, nor the word of God. Man is rebellious and does not hear or believe in God, although the Lord works with mercy and justice. It was the same when God warned, through Noah, of the trials to come, but the people scoffed at the message of the prophet; therefore, all of them perished.

Verses 40 and 41 say, "Then two men will be in the field: one will be taken and the other left. Two women will be grinding at the mill: one will be taken and the other left." (See also Luke 17:34–37.) Who are the *taken* and who are the *left* in this passage? Many people think that Jesus is speaking here about the rapture, saying that the "taken" are the Christians in the rapture. But this is not so, because this chapter 24 of Matthew does not talk about the church.

We must understand that Jesus, in His second coming, will come to establish a kingdom amongst the people who are living on this earth at the time of the Great Tribulation. The people will be already on the earth—they do not need to be moved to another place. In addition to these chosen people, there will be another people on the earth, those who neither serve nor believe in God. These latter, the unbelievers, will not be part of the millennial kingdom to be established on the earth.

Understanding this, we can then say that the "taken," in this passage, are the sinners and transgressors, the disobedient and rebels, who did not believe the truth, but had pleasure in unrighteousness (2 Thess. 2:12). God separates these unbelievers from the people who will inherit the kingdom, that is, the "left." Therefore, the *taken* are the sinners who will go away into everlasting punishment and the *left* are the righteous who will inherit the millennial kingdom.

Matthew 25:31–46 shows how the Lord, at the time of His second coming, will separate the inhabitants of the earth in two groups: "sheep" (righteous, believers) and "goats" (sinners, unbelievers). King Jesus will give the *sheep* access to the millennial kingdom; in other words, these are the *left* on the earth, who will enter into the new kingdom.

87

"Then the King will say to those on His right hand, 'Come, you blessed of My Father, inherit the kingdom prepared for you from the foundation of the world" (Matt. 25:34).

The *goats* are the *taken*:

> Then He will also say to those on the left hand, 'Depart from Me, you cursed, into the everlasting fire prepared for the devil and his angels.
> And these will go away into everlasting punishment.
>
> Matthew 25:41, 46

Matthew 24:39–40 indicates that "the flood came and *took them all away*, so also will the coming of the Son of Man be. Then two men will be in the field: one *will be taken* ..." We cannot separate the message of these verses from the previous passage. The message is the same. In the judgment of the flood, Noah and his family were "left" on earth. The sinners were "taken" or destroyed (see also Luke 17:26–27).

The salvation of Noah from the judgment of the flood is a representation of what will happen in the Great Tribulation. Noah and his family represent those people, who, although they will pass through the judgment of the Great Tribulation, they will be victorious; they will be left to enter the Millennium.

In order to visualize this subject even better, let us consider other passages provided in the Scriptures. Let us see the parable of the wheat and tares in Matthew 13:24–30, and its explanation by Jesus in verses 13:36–43.

According to the Lord's explanation, the sower is the Son of Man, Jesus; the field is the world; the good seeds are the children of the kingdom (those who will enter the millennial kingdom); the tares are the sons of the wicked; the enemy who sowed the tares is the devil; the harvest is the end of the age (the end of the Great Tribulation), and the reapers are the angels.

In this parable, Jesus identifies the *kingdom of heaven* with the kingdom of the Millennium, which He will establish at His second coming. He gives us to understand that at the end of the Great Tribulation, He will send the angels, saying, "Let both grow together until the harvest, and at the time of harvest I will say to the reapers, *'First gather together the tares* and bind them in bundles to burn them, but gather the wheat into my barn'" (Matt. 13:30). The first "taken" are the tares, that is, the wicked—then the wheat, those who remain, "the left."

Therefore as the tares are gathered and burned in the fire, so it will be at the end of this age.

The Son of Man will send out His angels, and they *will gather* out of His kingdom all things that offend, and those who practice lawlessness, and will cast them into the furnace of fire. There will be wailing and gnashing of teeth.

Then the righteous will shine forth as the sun in the kingdom of their Father [the Millennium]. He who has ears to hear, let him hear!

Matthew 13:40–43

In the parable of the fish collection of Matthew 13:47–50, the Lord also illustrates how it will be at His second coming. The scripture says that the angels "*will separate* the wicked from among the just, and cast them into the furnace of fire." Just as in the previous examples, here He shows that the wicked will first be taken and the good will be left.

Dear reader, stop now for a moment and meditate in the Lord. Are you prepared to escape the judgment which shall come upon all the earth? If you are not prepared for it, now is the time to look unto God and pour out your heart before Him. Ask God to put His love and fear in your heart, so you can love and serve Him with all your heart, with all your soul, with all your mind, and with all your strength. The Lord loves mankind very much.

We see at the end of this wonderful chapter 24 that the Lord exhorts us to watch and be prepared, "for the Son of Man is coming at an hour you do not expect." So, "Blessed is that servant whom his master, when he comes, will find so doing."

The Lord is wonderful and great indeed in truth and righteousness. His power extends throughout all the earth. To Him be the glory and praise forever. Certainly He is our Shepherd and watches over every one of us. Let us lift our hands and give Him glory, because everything is already prepared. Hallelujah, amen!

CHAPTER 5

Book of Revelation

The Book of Revelation contains a prophetic word that will be fulfilled in the last days. Many individuals and organizations have ventured to say that most of what is written in this book has been already accomplished. They have tried to force several events of history into a sense of prophetic-apocalyptic fulfillment.

For example, the First and Second World Wars, in particular what happened with the dictator Adolf Hitler in Germany, have been seen by some groups of people as the fulfillment of the prophecies of Revelation, implying that Hitler was the Antichrist.

On the other hand, some have said that the Antichrist is not a person, but a system or institution, thus invalidating the purpose of God to judge even the devil and his followers. Others say that the word of the Book of Revelation is being fulfilled at this time, because every word found in it is symbolic and fits with events that are currently happening in the world. Finally, others simply say that God is love and that He will not allow such a great tribulation to occur in this world.

These are just a few versions of the many diverse opinions related to this topic. We could write a book on the various views currently taught to people. But that is not the purpose of this book. Inside my heart beats a pure desire to share with others the riches that God has given me. That is why I will focus on sharing, with all sincerity, on those areas of Scripture which are clear in my understanding, not trying to add to or remove anything from that prophetic word that will be fulfilled soon.

The Lord showed the prophet Daniel what would happen in the final days, although Daniel did not understand its meaning. Daniel 10:14 says, "Now I have come to make you understand what will happen to your people in the latter days, for the vision refers to many days yet to come."

Then God says to Daniel that the word received by him would not be revealed in all its meaning at that time, because it was not yet the time for its accomplishment. That is why the Lord tells Daniel, "But you, Daniel, shut up the words, and seal the book until the time of the end" (Dan. 12:4). Daniel 12:8–9 also says,

> Although I heard, I did not understand. Then I said, 'My Lord, what shall be the end of these things?'
> And he said, 'Go your way, Daniel, for the words are closed up and sealed till the time of the end.'

Through these biblical quotations, we can realize that God sealed the prophecy and kept it secret because the time of its fulfillment had not yet come. We may then infer that when the time was at hand, God would open the prophecy and give understanding. And this was what happened with the revelation of God to the apostle John. The Book of Revelation opens what was sealed in the Book of Daniel. God tells the apostle John, "Do not seal the words of the prophecy of this book, for the time is at hand" (Rev. 22:10).

Dear reader, Christ is at hand. The time came, and now is, for all prophecy given through the prophets to have its faithful fulfillment. I encourage you to read this book with an open heart, looking unto Jesus, the author and finisher of our faith. May the Lord enlighten us to understand this word related to the last days on this planet Earth.

The Prophetic Book

Revelation 1:1–8

The Book of Revelation starts by establishing categorically the source of the revelation in this prophetic book. This is done that there might be no doubt about its divine inspiration, and that no person would take its content lightly. The author and sole source of this prophetic Book of Revelation is the Lord Jesus Christ.

Therefore, every word found in this wonderful and divine jewel will have its entire fulfillment in the time prescribed by God, our Father. As Matthew 24:35 says, "Heaven and earth will pass away, but My words will by no means pass away."

This last book shows the tremendous authority that the Word of God has. John was chosen to write exactly what the Lord Jesus spoke to him. John did not have the choice to include any thoughts of his own in this prophecy. Jesus said to him:

> 'I am the Alpha and the Omega, the First and the Last,' and, 'What you see, write in a book and send it to the seven churches which are in Asia ...'
> Write the things which you have seen, and the things which are, and the things which will take place after this.
>
> Revelation 1:11, 19

Therefore, John wrote exactly what he *saw* and *heard* through the direct revelation from the Lord. This means that this prophetic book contains a powerful word of revelation which comes directly from God. Even in the messages to the seven churches of Asia (chapters 2 and 3) a phrase referring to Jesus as the author of those messages is included at the beginning of each. Some examples are the following:

> These things says He who holds the seven stars ...
> These things says the First and the Last ...
> These things says the Son of God ...

So, it is of great importance that we, as members of the church, know and understand the prophetic message of this Book of Revelation, because it was conceived from the own vocabulary and style of the Lord Jesus. Verse 19:10 says: "For the testimony of Jesus is the spirit of prophecy." This means that through this prophetic book we can see and touch Jesus' own character and personality.

We are blessed with this book: "Blessed is he who reads and those who hear the words of this prophecy, and keep those things which are written in it; for the time is near" (v. 1:3). To read, hear, and obey the word of this prophetic book will make us blessed, because these words come directly from the mouth of Jesus. God is so zealous about the content of this book that at the end of it, He says:

> For I testify to everyone who hears the words of the prophecy of this book: If anyone adds to these things, God will add to him the plagues that are written in this book; and if anyone takes away from the words of the book of

this prophecy, God shall take away his part from the Book of Life, from the holy city, and from the things which are written in this book.

Revelation 22:18–19

John was the last of the twelve apostles to die. Speaking of John, Jesus said, "If I will that he [John] remain till I come ... Then this saying went out among the brethren that this disciple would not die" (John 21:22–23).

Jesus did not tell Peter that John would not die, but that he would be present (*remain*) until the second coming of Christ. This saying implied that John would remain on Earth, not in the flesh, but through the Book of Revelation, which contains the last prophecy to be fulfilled prior to the return of Jesus Christ to the Earth.

John would therefore be present on Earth through the last witness of Jesus and the word of God, proclaimed by this wonderful Book of Revelation. God chose the apostle John for this great responsibility because he was a faithful believer "who bore witness to the word of God, and to the testimony of Jesus Christ, to all things that he saw" (v. 1:2).

It is interesting to see that of the four gospels, only the Gospel According to John does not mention anything about apocalyptic events—and this was the apostle chosen to bring the greatest of all revelations related to that topic. John was very loved by the Lord Jesus, to the extent that he leaned on the chest of the Master.

Now there was leaning on Jesus' bosom one of His disciples, whom Jesus loved.
Then, leaning back on Jesus' breast ...

John 13:23, 25

This deep relationship with the Lord enabled John to be the holy and faithful instrument that was chosen by God to reveal His last word in written form to the mankind, especially to the church.

According to what the Apostle saw and heard, Jesus is described in the first chapter of Revelation using several phrases about who He is and what He did for mankind, namely: *who is, who was, and who is to come; the faithful witness, the firstborn from the dead; the ruler over the kings of the earth; the alpha and the omega, the beginning and the end; the Almighty; the first and the last.*

Then John depicts Jesus in a glorious way, with splendor and great power: "like the sun shining in its strength." This is Jesus, our Savior, the

One who overcame, and now holds the keys of death. Who is like Jesus? There is no comparison.

This referenced passage also speaks about "the seven Spirits who are before His throne" (vv. 1:4; 4:5; 5:6). The prophet Isaiah gives us a little more light about these seven Spirits: "The Spirit of the Lord shall rest upon Him, the Spirit of wisdom and understanding, the Spirit of counsel and might, the Spirit of knowledge and of the fear of the Lord" (Isa. 11:2). All these attributes tell us of the greatness and majesty of our Lord Jesus.

From the beginning to the end of the Book of Revelation, we do not read that God commanded to seal the book, or that those who read this prophecy will not understand it. It is clear that God wants this word to be received and understood. The book begins by saying that this revelation is "to show His servants things which must shortly take place" (v. 1:1).

What does *must shortly take place* mean? It has been two thousand years, and we have not seen the entire fulfillment of this book. To answer this question, we must remember what was said previously about the completion of the seventy weeks of Daniel's prophecy. Only the events to take place within the seven years described in Revelation are missing from the entire fulfillment of Daniel's prophecy. Therefore, seven years is "soon"; but I repeat, this is from the point of view of the fulfillment of Daniel's prophecy.

On the other hand, because we cannot look in only one direction, we must understand that this warning for the swift completion of apocalyptic events is also an edifying message for the church. We, who love and serve Jesus, wait for Him to appear very soon—to call us to be with Him forever—before the beginning of the Great Tribulation. This is our glorious hope.

"Blessed is he who reads and those who hear the words of this prophecy, and keep those things which are written in it; for the time is near" (vv. 1:3; see also vv. 22:6–7). There are three important points in this beatitude: those who read, those who hear, and those who keep (obey) this word. God, in His goodness, reveals what has to happen soon, not as mere apocalyptic information, but for our obedience. Likewise, Romans 16:25–26 says,

> Now to Him who is able to establish you according to my gospel and the preaching of Jesus Christ, *according to the revelation of the mystery* kept secret since the world began but now made manifest, and by the prophetic Scriptures *made known to all nations*, according to the commandment of the everlasting God, *for obedience to the faith.*

This is the main reason for God to openly reveal what will happen at the end of time. The time has come for these prophecies related to the final judgment to be fulfilled. So everyone who believes in Him must walk as He walked: in holiness and faithfulness to Him and to His word. Verse 22:10 says, "And he said to me, 'Do not seal the words of the prophecy of this book, for the time is at hand.'" Therefore, the Book of Revelation is the revelation of the sealed book of the prophet Daniel, now opened for us.

Dear reader, you can be blessed when you have contact with the Book of Revelation. Hear what God tells your heart, believe in Him with a sincere heart and keep His word, and you will see the door of your salvation open.

The apostle John wrote the revealed word in a book and sent it, by God's instruction, to the believers of the seven churches which were in Asia at that time (v. 1:11). The Book of Revelation was written at the end of the first century.

Due to the great persecutions that arose and the entry of false and misleading elements into the churches, it seems that only seven churches remained in Asia. This is why the Lord Jesus commands John to write in a book the things which he sees and the things which will take place, and send them to the seven churches in Asia. This was an admonition to wake up and live committed to God and His word.

This passage of the first chapter also mentions that Christ "has made us kings and priests to His God and Father" (v. 1:6). A king is one who reigns or governs, and has authority. A priest is one who intercedes, advises spiritually, and is in continuous service for the people before God. Therefore, the church will be working with Christ in a way of authority and priesthood. This is a promise to be fulfilled in the new earth which the Lord will create, where the church will dwell together with Jesus.

Here I would like to stop momentarily to comment a little more on this promise of God to the church. The Book of Revelation speaks of three kingdoms: the Antichrist's kingdom which will last seven years (until the second coming of Christ), the kingdom of a thousand years (commonly called the Millennium), and the kingdom in the new earth and the new heaven for eternity (which I call the Father's kingdom).

We must understand that the promise for Israel is the Millennium and the promise for the church is the Father's kingdom. The Antichrist's kingdom, which is of short duration, is a kingdom of judgment of all nations, including the final verdict on the "evil trinity."

The Millennium is the kingdom of Christ, where Israel will be *head of nations,* and those who have the capacity, as God chooses, will reign together with Jesus. "And I saw thrones, and they sat on them, [those who received authority to judge—RV60] and judgment was committed to them" (v. 20:4). My understanding is that prophets such as Abraham, Daniel, and others will be the chosen ones to reign with Jesus in the Millennium.

Luke speaks of the presence of these prophets in the Millennium, "There will be weeping and gnashing of teeth, when you see Abraham and Isaac and Jacob and all the prophets in the kingdom of God, and yourselves thrust out" (Luke 13:28). Here *the kingdom of God* refers to the Millennium.

God promised, "Blessed and holy is he who has part in the first resurrection. Over such the second death has no power, but they shall be priests of God and of Christ, and shall reign with Him a thousand years" (v. 20:6). All the prophets and other faithful men and women will be part of this first resurrection which will occur at the second coming of Christ. This subject has already been discussed. This is the kingdom of Jesus, and He will reign, as prophesied by the angel Gabriel in his message to Mary:

> He will be great, and will be called the Son of the Highest;
> and the Lord God will give Him the throne of His father
> David.
> And He will reign over the house of Jacob forever, and of
> His kingdom there will be no end.
>
> Luke 1:32–33

Daniel 7:21–22 says,

> I was watching; and the same horn was making war
> against the saints, and prevailing against them, until the
> Ancient of Days came, and a judgment was made in favor
> of the saints of the Most High, and the time came for the
> saints to possess the kingdom.

This is the kingdom promised to the people of Israel (*the house of Jacob*). The church will not be present in this kingdom, because the time to descend from heaven as the bride of Christ has not come yet. In our discussion of Revelation 21, we will expand more on this important issue.

Continuing with chapter one, we see that Jesus announces His coming, a visible coming where "every eye will see Him, even they who pierced Him. And all the tribes of the earth will mourn because of Him" (v. 1:7).

Let us look closely at this passage. This event will happen at the end of the Great Tribulation. Who will truly see Him at His advent, and who will mourn because of Him? I have heard and read that the second coming of Jesus will be seen by television through satellite, and in this way the prophecy that *"every eye will see Him"* will be fulfilled.

I wonder is it likely that the world population will be sitting with their families and friends, watching television, at a time when almost everything is destroyed and there will be no electricity in many parts of the world, due to catastrophic events. Will families have this time of peace and quiet to sit and watch TV?

How is it possible that all of the world's population will see the specific moment of Christ's arrival, for the Scriptures describe this event as occurring "as lightning" (Matt. 24:27)—very fast? Could many reporters be available and ready in Jerusalem to film this great event, when the Scriptures say that no one knows the time of His coming?

It is also known that there will be chaos in Jerusalem at that time, because the city will be under siege and controlled by the Antichrist. I believe that the answer to these questions is that it will not be possible for the whole world's population to see the coming of the Lord Jesus.

Who, then, will be those who see Him? The same Scriptures have the answer to this question: "they who pierced Him," the people of Israel. The ancestors of the current inhabitants of Israel were those who pierced Christ—who killed Him. The Scriptures are wonderful; they themselves explain the mysteries of God. In the Gospel According to John, we find a passage stating these truths, which will be accomplished at the second coming of the Lord.

> But when they came to Jesus and saw that He was already dead, they did not break His legs.
> But one of the soldiers *pierced* His side with a spear, and immediately blood and water came out.
> And he who has seen has testified, and his testimony is true; and he knows that he is telling the truth, so that you may believe.
> For these things were done that the Scripture should be fulfilled, 'Not one of His bones shall be broken.'
> And again another Scripture says, '*They shall look on Him whom they pierced.*'
>
> John 19:33–37; see also Zechariah
> 12:10 and Acts 2:36–37

THE REVELATION OF THE SEALED BOOK

This is not a matter of logic; it is a biblical fact that the judgment manifested in the Great Tribulation is primarily for the people of Israel, for having rejected and killed Jesus (although we know that non-Jews who do not serve the Lord will meet the same fate). When Jesus was arrested, He was brought before the Sanhedrin, where He answered questions of the high priest:

> But Jesus kept silent. And the high priest answered and said to Him, 'I put You under oath by the living God: Tell us if You are the Christ, the Son of God!'
> Jesus said to him, 'It is as you said. Nevertheless, I say to you, hereafter you will see the Son of Man sitting at the right hand of the Power, and coming on the clouds of heaven.'
>
> Mathew 26:63–64

Here Jesus prophesies to the highest religious representative and all the Jews, that *they* will see Him "coming on the clouds of heaven" (at His second coming). When Jesus came for the first time, "He came to His own, and His own did not receive Him" (John 1:11).

Now Jesus comes again to His own for the second time, and on this occasion, yes, many will receive Him! Although the majority of the world's population will opt to not serve the Lord, there will be a remnant that will believe and wait for Him anxiously, because by then they will have experienced the suffering of the furnace of fire of the Great Tribulation.

Those who *pierced* Jesus will be those who will see Him now coming with great power and glory. This scripture refers to the Jews, as stated in the previous paragraph. Therefore, by *every eye will see Him* we must understand that the people who are in Jerusalem and surrounding areas at that time are the ones who will see Him. This will occur when He descends and places His feet on the Mount of Olives in Jerusalem (this will happen after His victory over the army of the Antichrist, as we will see later).

> Then the Lord will go forth and fight against those nations, as He fights in the day of battle.
> And in that day His feet will stand on the Mount of Olives, which faces Jerusalem on the east. And the Mount of Olives shall be split in two, from east to west, making a

very large valley; half of the mountain shall move toward
the north and half of it toward the south.

Zechariah 14:3–4

This valley will be the new creation of the Lord, to be used as part
of the area from which He will reign over the nations. In Acts 1:11, the
angels tell the disciples: "This same Jesus, who was taken up from you
into heaven, will so come in like manner as you saw Him go into heaven."
Acts 1:12 gives us to understand that Jesus was taken up from the Mount of
Olives, the place where some disciples were with Him. So, He will descend
to the same place from which He ascended to heaven, so the inhabitants of
Jerusalem and surrounding areas will see Him.

There are phrases in the Scriptures which literally mean the entire
earth or the world population; on the other hand, in other passages, the
same phrases often are used to represent limited areas or the inhabitants
of only some nations. There is not a general rule to be applied in all cases;
therefore, to understand these passages with more certainty, we must see
them on a case-by-case basis, in accordance with the entire context of each
passage.

Another phrase with the same interpretation is "all the tribes of the
earth will mourn because of Him." If we see this phrase literally, we
have to say that all the inhabitants of the earth shall see Christ at His
second coming. I do not believe this will happen in that way (although the
whole world will mourn when they hear about His advent). As an example,
Jeremiah 47:2 says,

> Thus says the Lord: 'Behold, waters rise out of the north,
> and shall be an overflowing flood; they shall overflow the
> *land and all that is in it* [*the earth and its fullness*—RV60],
> the city and those who dwell within; then the men shall
> cry, and *all the inhabitants of the land* shall wail.'

Then, verse 47:4 says that it refers only to "all the Philistines ... from
Tyre and Sidon." In Hebrew, the word used for *land* (אֶרֶץ) is also used
for *earth*.

The passage of Revelation, "all the tribes of the earth will mourn
because of Him," is a reference to two other passages in the Scriptures:

> Then the sign of the Son of Man will appear in heaven,
> and then all the tribes of the earth will mourn, and they

will see the Son of Man coming on the clouds of heaven
with power and great glory.

Matthew 24:30

And I will pour on the house of David and on the inhabitants
of Jerusalem the Spirit of grace and supplication; then they
will look on Me whom they pierced. Yes, they will mourn
for Him as one mourns for his only son, and grieve for
Him as one grieves for a firstborn.

In that day there shall be a great mourning in Jerusalem,
like the mourning at Hadad Rimmon in the plain of
Megiddo.

And the land shall mourn, every family by itself: the
family of the house of David by itself, and their wives by
themselves; the family of the house of Nathan by itself ...

Zechariah 12:10–14

When we look at these references, we see that the *mourning* refers
to the great sorrow that the Israelites will feel for rejecting Christ at His
first coming. It is a cry of pain for their sin of not having believed in the
Messiah, who now shows Himself to them for the second time. But this
time, many (*a remnant*) will receive and believe in Him.

The *tribes of the earth* of Revelation; the *tribes of the earth* of Matthew;
the *house of David* and the *inhabitants of Jerusalem* of Zechariah, are all
the same, that is, the Israelites who are in Judea at the time of the second
coming of the Lord.

These are those who "pierced" Jesus, who "will mourn for Him as
one mourns for his only son." This lament is not the same as the lament
of the inhabitants of the other nations, which will occur when they hear
of the coming of the Lord Jesus. The lament of the believing Jews will be
unto repentance, but the lament of the nations will be for judgment and
condemnation.

After this, Jesus will separate the bad (goats) from the good (sheep).
The bad, those who do not serve the Lord, will be thrown into hell, and
the servants of God will inherit the earth in the millennial kingdom.
Hallelujah, Jesus will reign on the righteous, as the King of kings and Lord
of lords! To God be the glory forever—honor and magnificence! His Name
is great and majestic! "Blessed is He who comes in the name of the Lord!"

The Vision of the Son of Man and the Things Which Are

Revelation 1:9–20

After the destruction of Jerusalem and the temple in AD 70, the Roman rulers lashed out with even more force against the Hebrews. In the years after AD 80, there were great persecutions against the Christians. The apostle John was no exception, because he was possibly exiled at the same time to the island called Patmos, "for the word of God and for the testimony of Jesus Christ."

This is why John, a humble and faithful servant of the Lord, is writing to the churches saying, "I, John, both your brother and companion in the tribulation and kingdom and patience of Jesus Christ" (v. 1:9). Without overlooking the sufferings of the apostle John, it was in Patmos that the Lord was pleased to reveal, through this servant, the riches of His wisdom and purpose for mankind in the latter days on the earth.

John describes how he saw Jesus in his revelation on Patmos. He describes Him as someone splendid, glorious, and majestic. The vestment and face of Jesus show purity, glory, majesty, and power.

The Lord commands John, saying, "What you see, write in a book and send it to the seven churches which are in Asia" (v. 1:11). John obeyed faithfully, writing everything that was shown to him, and sent it to the churches in Asia.

This message of God (although it describes the judgments of God for all nations) opens our understanding to see that it is a revelation for the church of the Lord, to be understood clearly by her. Although the church will escape the hour of trial which shall come upon the whole world, to her has been granted the revelation and understanding of this last prophecy, as expressed clearly in the first verse, "to show *His servants* things which must shortly take place."

We all know that the apostle John was with Jesus; he walked, ate, and even slept with Him. When Jesus died and was resurrected, the Apostle was also beside Him. John knew Jesus, because he had a very close relationship with Him.

It is interesting to see now, that facing this same Jesus, John says, "And when I saw Him, I fell at His feet as dead" (v. 1:17). Although this is the same Jesus who John knew, this time his Lord has shown Himself with so much glory and magnificence that John could not even stand on his feet. This is the Christ who overcame death, and now lives forever. Hallelujah!

The Lord then lays His right hand on John, strengthens him, and says, "Write the things which you have seen, and the things which are, and the things which will take place after this" (v. 1:19). The "things which are" refer to current things about the spiritual status of the seven churches and the life and atmosphere of that time, governed by the Roman Empire. The Lord exhorts most of these churches to repent of their sins and errors before the prophesied judgment starts.

Chapters two and three of Revelation describe the condition of the churches in Asia at that time, by the end of the first century, when the Book of Revelation was written.

The "things which will take place after this" are the events to happen in the near future, after the *things which are*—in other words, things which were not happening during John's lifetime. As we have emphasized, the prophetic eye sees everything as continuous until the end of days, overlooking the time of the church. In this way, the period of the Roman Empire, after the death of Christ, is joined with the *things which will take place after this*, as if they were under that same political power (Luke 23:27–31).

The judgments in the Great Tribulation are part of the *things which will take place after this*, which will be experienced by all who reject the Lord Jesus, not living according to His word and purpose.

The first three chapters of Revelation cover, in essence, the *things which are*, or in other words, the things which occurred or were taking place during the apostle John's time. All revelation written in the first three chapters was received by John here on the earth, when Jesus visited him in the island of Patmos.

Then, chapter 4 begins by saying, "Come up here, and I will show you things which must take place after this." Therefore, after chapter 4 John describes what is prepared to take place after the period of the church, after she is taken up into heaven. (More details about this are provided in the comments on chapter 4 of Revelation.)

After chapter 4, there is no more direct mention of the church living on the earth—until the end of the Book of Revelation, when she is shown as the "holy city, New Jerusalem, coming down out of heaven from God, prepared as a bride adorned for her husband" (v. 21:2). All revelation received by John from chapter 4 onward was entirely shown in heaven.

Here, in the first chapter, the seven churches are now represented by seven golden candlesticks, which are around the presence of the Lord Jesus (vv. 1:11–13, 20). In the same way, the apostle Paul describes the church located in heavenly places with Christ Jesus. Ephesians 2:6–7 says,

> And raised us up together, and made us sit together in the
> heavenly places in Christ Jesus, that in the ages to come
> He might show the exceeding riches of His grace in His
> kindness toward us in Christ Jesus.

These *heavenly places* are in spiritual sense, because the church has not yet overcome finally; she continues on earth.

There are also seven stars at the right hand of the Lord, which represent the angels of the seven churches. It is somewhat difficult to understand the meaning of these angels. I do not see clearly that they are the heavenly creatures commonly known as angels, because the apostle John writes and sends the Book of Revelation to them. What would angels do with this book?

Nor do I see that each angel means the so-called "pastor" of each church, because according to biblical teaching, more than one pastor (same as elder or bishop) should function at the same time in every individual church. The concept of a "single pastor" has no basis in the Scriptures. (This is a topic which could be explored at length elsewhere.)

However, each church could have an angel, or messenger, who ministers in favor of her, similar to those who watched over and worked in defense of an entire city (see Daniel 10:13, 20).

> For He shall give His angels charge over you, to keep you
> in all your ways.
>
> Psalm 91:11

> The angel of the Lord encamps all around those who fear
> Him, and delivers them.
>
> Psalm 34:7

The Seven Churches

Revelation 2 and 3

In these two chapters, the Lord proclaims a message to the seven churches remaining in Asia, as a warning, so that they can be kept from the trial which shall come upon the whole world. God locates the final "conquerors" from the churches in heaven: "To him who overcomes I will grant to sit with Me on My throne, as I also overcame and sat down with My Father on His throne" (v. 3:21). Therefore, these saved ones will be delivered from the Great Tribulation described in the next chapters of Revelation.

While the events of the Great Tribulation occur, these conquerors will be enjoying the presence of God in His glory.

> Because you have kept My command to persevere, I also
> will keep you from the hour of trial which shall come upon
> the whole world, to test those who dwell on the earth.
> Behold, I am coming quickly! Hold fast what you have,
> that no one may take your crown.
> He who overcomes, I will make him a pillar in the temple
> of My God, and he shall go out no more. ...
>
> Revelation 3:10–12

Another reference to this truth is found in Luke 21:36, where Jesus, preaching to the Jews, says: "Watch therefore, and pray always that you may be counted worthy to escape all these things that will come to pass, and to stand before the Son of Man."

The messages to each church show that not all who gathered together were pleasing God. Although the churches, represented by the candlesticks, were located around Jesus, they could be removed from that place, due to the presence of sin in them. "Remember therefore from where you have fallen; repent and do the first works, or else I will come to you quickly and remove your lampstand from its place—unless you repent" (v. 2:5). This shows that many members of these churches had not overcome finally.

The churches mentioned in these two chapters were those established by the Lord Jesus in different cities of Asia. There was one church per city, as the Scriptures teach, particularly in the Book of Acts and the epistles of Paul.

Another point of view to consider is that these seven churches, in addition to what we have already mentioned, may also represent seven periods in the history of the church—from the beginning of the Christian era until the day of the Christians' disappearance in the rapture.

Each message should then represent the spiritual condition of the believers in each of the seven periods during the approximately two thousand years since the first church in the city of Jerusalem. If this is so, we would be living in the period of the message to the church in Laodicea (vv. 3:14–22).

Certainly, the message presented to this last church fits very well with the time in which we live today. The majority of people live with the idea that they are serving God and that they are saved. I am not in a position to judge people, for judgment only belongs to God and the Lord Jesus, but I believe they themselves express what they are in Christ. The Lord Jesus said, "by their fruits you will know them" (Matt. 7:20).

It is not for us to convince a friend, neighbor, or family member that we are Christians. The fruits Jesus spoke of are the fruits of the Spirit the expression and conduct of one who has been born again, has known God, and walks in Christ continually. These are the conquerors in the faith of God. In His message to the church in Laodicea, Jesus describes those Christian as *lukewarm;* they are neither cold nor hot. The Lord tells them "I will vomit you out of My mouth."

In other words, He will dismiss or separate them from Himself, because they displease Him. They have a hypocritical testimony. Before many others, they are seen and act as Christians, but they are not. They have the appearance of sheep, but God knows them and says to them: "and do not know that you are wretched, miserable, poor, blind, and naked" (v. 3:17). "As many as I love, I rebuke and chasten. Therefore be zealous and repent" (v. 3:19).

I could write a lot about the content of chapters 2 and 3, but my immediate priority in this writing is with the message of the next chapters of this great Book of Revelation. I only wish to conclude these two chapters by saying that the message of the entire Book of Revelation is for all believers; that is why at the end of each message to each church, the Lord says, "He who has an ear, let him hear what the Spirit says to the churches." I emphasize the plurality of the phrase *the churches,* for this is all believers.

This prophetic book contains a powerful word of revelation which comes directly from God. Each message to the seven churches begins with a phrase indicating that Jesus is the author of those messages; therefore, hear what the Lord says to you.

The Vision of God's Throne

Revelation 4:1–11

> After these things I looked, and behold, a door standing
> open in heaven. And the first voice which I heard was like
> a trumpet speaking with me, saying, 'Come up here, and
> I will show you things which must take place after this.'
> Immediately I was in the Spirit ...
>
> Revelation 4:1–2

As described in the first three chapters, the Book of Revelation records an experience of the apostle John on the island of Patmos. Jesus visited this island and revealed Himself to John. From chapter 4 onward, all revelation was no longer given on earth (Patmos), but shown in heaven. John was taken to heaven, where he saw and received the revelation, and then he wrote it.

On the other hand, the prophet Daniel received the revelation through visions of God on the earth, in the territory where he resided, or nearby. Daniel did not see the things in heaven, but on the earth. This is interesting, because although both revelations show things to come in the latter days, each provides different elements and different points of view, thus enriching one another.

Daniel sees the actions of the enemies of God as crude, savage, and without mercy. He sees the cruelty and diabolical deceit in every movement of the Antichrist. Although John sees the sufferings and tribulations, he does not see the details experienced by the individuals who dwell on the earth. Here is the wisdom of God, as He unites these two revelations to show us the reality of everything that will happen soon.

According to the first verses of chapter 4, the Lord gives these new events a chronological nature. That is, after the things described in the previous three chapters have taken place, then the things revealed in chapter 4 onward will be fulfilled.

It is important to note that not all the events described in Revelation are chronological when we see them in reference to the whole book. What I do see is that the book was structured into chronological periods; in other words, John presents a group of events that will happen chronologically, but then describes another group of events that will happen chronologically in relation to themselves, but not in relation to the first group. The first group can be accomplished in parallel with the events of the second group.

That is why the Book of Revelation is chronological, but by stages or periods of events, not from the point of view of the entire book. An example of this will be shown later in chapter 6 of Revelation, which describes the events as the six seals are opened.

The Twenty-Four Elders

> Immediately I was in the Spirit; and behold, a throne set in heaven, and One sat on the throne.
> And He who sat there was like a jasper and a sardius stone in appearance; and there was a rainbow around the throne, in appearance like an emerald.
> Around the throne were twenty-four thrones, and on the thrones I saw twenty-four elders sitting, clothed in white robes; and they had crowns of gold on their heads.
> Revelation 4:2–4

> The twenty-four elders fall down before Him who sits on the throne and worship Him who lives forever and ever, and cast their crowns before the throne, saying:

> "You are worthy, O Lord,
> To receive glory and honor and power;
> For You created all things,
> And by Your will they exist and were created."
> Revelation 4:10–11

The apostle John sees a throne and one sitting on it, and twenty-four elders sitting on thrones around it. There is no doubt that the throne in the center is the throne of God. The twenty-four elders are also sitting on thrones and have crowns of gold on their heads, suggesting that they have the authority of kings.

In verse 5:10, the twenty-four elders say: "And have made us kings and priests to our God; and we shall reign on the earth." This mirrors what John said in verse 1:6 (including himself in the statement): "… and has made *us* kings and priests to His God and Father."

These twenty-four elders are dressed in white clothes, which represent holiness. They are sitting in front of God's throne, at rest, in a privileged place. Verses 5:8–10 say,

> Now when He had taken the scroll, the four living creatures and the twenty-four elders fell down before the Lamb, each having a harp, and golden bowls full of incense, which are the prayers of the saints.
> And they sang a new song, saying:
>
> > "You are worthy to take the scroll,
> > And to open its seals;
> > For You were slain,
> > And have redeemed us to God by Your blood
> > Out of every tribe and tongue and people and nation,
> > And have made us kings and priests to our God;
> > And we shall reign on the earth."

Let us see in detail what these passages show about the twenty-four elders:

- They are called to be kings and priests of God.
- They are sitting on thrones with crowns of gold on their heads.
- They are dressed in white clothes.
- They have harps and golden bowls full of incense, which are the prayers of the saints.
- They were redeemed by the blood of Christ.
- They come from every part of the earth (every lineage, tongue, people, and nation).
- It is clearly established that up to this point, Christ has not yet opened the seals (chapter 6) of the scroll presented here. In other words, the events of the Great Tribulation have not started yet.
- The Lamb is Christ, and the elders recognize that Christ is the only one worthy to open the seals, because He was slain (sacrificed).

Considering these points, I can affirm that the twenty-four elders are people, not other creatures, who come from every part of the earth, not from heaven. I do not see in the Scriptures that angels or other heavenly creatures are redeemed by the blood of Christ; this has been a fact and blessing only awarded to people on the earth.

In addition, I have never seen the angels of God, or any other creature, seated on thrones with golden crowns on their heads. We also see that the events of chapter 4 are happening before Christ begins to open the seals described in chapter 6. There should be no doubt that these twenty-four elders are persons who have not gone through the Great Tribulation on the earth, because they are already sitting on thrones beside Christ prior to the start of the apocalyptic events.

The phrase of verse 4:8, "and is to come," suggests that hitherto the Lord had not yet come to earth in His visible second coming, which shall come to pass at the end of the Great Tribulation. The white vestments are representative of holiness and purity (absence of sin), and identify the conquerors (v. 3:5).

When I see all the above, I can say that there are many similarities between these elders and the church of the Lord, as described in the Scriptures. For example, the promise to be kings and priests was also given to the church (Rev. 1:6; 1 Peter 2:5, 9). The church of the Lord will not go through the Great Tribulation. While the catastrophic events never seen before are happening on the earth, the twenty-four elders are sitting at rest, before the presence of God.

Also, I firmly believe that the church is the only one who could sing the new song of Revelation 5:9–10, which mentions the redemption through the blood of Christ in His sacrifice. Therefore, I firmly believe that these twenty-four elders represent the victorious church, which shall be brought into the presence of God in the rapture (vv. 3:10–12). "To him who overcomes I will grant to sit with Me on My throne, as I also overcame and sat down with My Father on His throne" (v. 3:21).

The rapture will take place in the span of time between the end of chapter 3 and beginning of chapter 4 of Revelation. As stated above, chapters 2 and 3 may describe the condition of the church from the first until the current century.

Then, chapter 4 shows the twenty-four elders, representing the church of all times—in other words, the faithful members of Christ from the day of Pentecost until the day of the rapture—sitting victorious in the presence of God. These are those to whom the Lord says: "Because you have kept My command to persevere, I also will keep you from the hour of trial which shall come upon the whole world, to test those who dwell on the earth" (vs. 3:10).

As we saw above, the churches mentioned in the first three chapters, represented by the candlesticks, were told they could lose their privileged place with the Lord because of the presence of sin in them. This shows that these churches still not had triumphed finally. On the other hand, the church represented by the twenty-four elders in chapter 4 is a church of total and final victory. It is located in front of the throne of God and will never lose this place. This is the church caught up to heaven in the rapture.

As you will find later in Revelation 20:11–15, *The Final Judgment*, Daniel 7:9–10 brings more light to see the meaning of these twenty-four elders. The passage says:

> I watched till thrones were put in place, and the Ancient of Days was seated; His garment was white as snow, and the hair of His head was like pure wool. His throne was a fiery flame, its wheels a burning fire; a fiery stream issued and came forth from before Him. A thousand thousands ministered to Him; ten thousand times ten thousand stood before Him. The court was seated, and the books were opened.

The "thrones" (plural) seen by Daniel before the Ancient of Days (the Judge, the Father) in verse 7:9 refer to the "thousand thousands [who] ministered to Him" of verse 7:10. Therefore, these thrones seen by the prophet Daniel are the twenty-four thrones, with the twenty-four elders seated on them, seen by the apostle John; that is, Daniel was watching the church (*thousand thousands*) serving God in the final judgment.

Now, what could be the significance of the number twenty-four? Ephesians 2:11–22 tells us how God reconciled both Jews and Gentiles in "one body," "making peace." Also, Romans 11:11–24 describes God's desire that Israel be part of His eternal purpose for mankind in the church. I refer to the last two verses of this passage in Romans,

> And they also, if they do not continue in unbelief, will be grafted in, for God is able to graft them in again.
> For if you were cut out of the olive tree which is wild by nature, and were grafted contrary to nature into a cultivated olive tree, how much more will these, who are natural branches, be grafted into their own olive tree?

When the Lord describes the New Jerusalem, which refers to the church, which descends from heaven, He mentions twelve doors which will carry the names of the twelve tribes of the sons of Israel (v. 21:12), and twelve foundations which shall bear the names of the twelve apostles of the Lord Jesus (v. 21:14). Therefore, it could be that the twenty-four elders represent the church of the Lord in all His fullness, including believers of all nationalities, Jews and non-Jews.

> And He put all things under His feet, and gave Him to be head over all things to the church, which is His body, the fullness of Him who fills all in all.
>
> Ephesians 1:22–23

The Gentile believers are represented by the names of the twelve apostles and the Jewish believers by the names of the twelve tribes of Israel, all now united together in *one new man,* and reconciled in *one body,* the church.

> For He Himself is our peace, who has made both [Gentiles and Jews] one, and has broken down the middle wall of separation, having abolished in His flesh the enmity, that is, the law of commandments contained in ordinances, so as to create in Himself one new man from the two, thus making peace, and that He might reconcile them both to God in one body through the cross, thereby putting to death the enmity.
>
> Ephesians 2:14–16

It is important to understand that chapters 4 and 5 of Revelation describe events occurring in heaven ("and behold, a door standing open in heaven"—v. 4:1), prior to the beginning of the seven years of the Great Tribulation. The apocalyptic events prophesied by ancient prophets, and then by some of the apostles, will start when the first seal of the scroll is opened, described in Revelation chapter 6.

The Four Living Creatures

In this passage (vv. 4:6–9), we see four living creatures, each having six wings, and full of eyes around and within. The first was like a lion, the

111

second like a calf, the third had the face of a man, and the fourth was like a flying eagle.

We see a close relationship between these four creatures and the twenty-four elders. Both the creatures and the elders are always in front of the throne of God, and do not cease worshiping Him.

The prophet Ezekiel also saw in a vision some creatures very similar to these. Ezekiel 1:4–12 describes these creatures, just like the ones in Revelation, as having the appearance of a lion, ox, man, and eagle.

It is not easy to understand the presence and meaning of these four living creatures. But if we look at every creature in more detail, we will see a great intrinsic message in each.

The four gospels show the life and work of Jesus; thereby, through them we can see who Christ is. These gospels present the Lord Jesus from four different points of view. This is possibly the answer to many people who ask why there are four similar gospels. Here the answer: there are four facets of Christ's person and work that we can see through the four gospels. We can also see these four facets of the life of Jesus through the four creatures which are around the throne of God.

Following is a comparison of the message of each gospel, which corresponds to the image of each creature:

- The creature like a lion is compared with the Gospel of Matthew. The lion is considered "the king of the beasts." In Matthew, we see Christ as King, one who prepares the people for a future kingdom. For this reason, the Gospel of Matthew is called the Gospel of the Kingdom (Matt. 4:23; 9:35; 24:14).

   As we saw at the beginning of this book, the Gospel of Matthew shows the events to take place at the time when Christ returns to the earth to establish His millennial kingdom. Jesus is the King; Jesus is the Lion. "But one of the elders said to me, 'Do not weep. Behold, the *Lion of the tribe of Judah*, the Root of David [King], has prevailed to open the scroll and to loose its seven seals'" (v. 5:5).

- The second creature with a likeness of a calf is compared with the Gospel of Mark. The calf or ox (according to Ezekiel) is considered an animal of work, such as a servant, one who is always serving others. In addition, the calf was used as a sin offering, carried outside the camp to be burnt on wood with fire. The Gospel of Mark shows Jesus as a servant, one called and separated to work and to give His life as a sacrifice for others.

- The third creature is like a man and is compared to the Gospel of

Luke, which gives emphasis to Christ as a man. Luke presents the Lord as one who came down, leaving His glory and coming in the likeness of man among the inhabitants of the earth. That is why the phrase "the Son of Man" abounds in the Gospel of Luke.

- Finally, we have the living creature like an eagle, compared with the Gospel of John. The eagle is a bird of heights, with extremely acute vision enabling it to see across long distances. The Gospel of John, although it contains a simple message, is very deep. It presents Christ as God. John touches the heights, the spiritual and the divine. John 1:1, 14, and 14:9 say:

> In the beginning was the Word, and the Word was with God, and the Word was God.
> And the Word became flesh and dwelt among us, and we beheld His glory, the glory as of the only begotten of the Father, full of grace and truth.
> Jesus said to him, 'Have I been with you so long, and yet you have not known Me, Philip? He who has seen Me has seen the Father; so how can you say, "Show us the Father"?'

The eagle can represent God Himself or the divine.

> As an eagle stirs up its nest … So the LORD alone led him …
>
> Deuteronomy 32:11–13

> You have seen what I did to the Egyptians, and how I bore you on eagles' wings and brought you to Myself.
>
> Exodus 19:4

> For thus says the High and Lofty One who inhabits eternity, whose name is Holy: 'I dwell in the high and holy place …'
>
> Isaiah 57:15

The four creatures are bearing witness of Jesus and His work in a continuous way, until He completes His work of redemption in all those who will be saved from the earth. These living creatures are always around the throne of God in heaven. We never see them out of heaven. In the section *The Final Judgment* (Rev. 20:11–15), we will see a very important role of these creatures.

When God establishes His throne with Christ and the church in the new earth, the four living creatures will be gone. This is so, because Christ no longer needs that "something else" or creature to represent Him in the new earth. From now on, everything will be in its real state, without symbols—and it will be an eternal kingdom. The four facets of Christ presented in the four gospels, and shown through the four creatures, will then be an integral part of the person of Christ.

Ephesians 1:10 speaks about the eternal purpose of God in Christ, which is "that in the dispensation of the fullness of the times He might gather together in one all things in Christ, both which are in heaven and which are on earth—in Him." Jesus Christ is the Lord and He fills everything.

When we imagine these four creatures, they may seem monstrous beings, without any beauty or attractiveness. But for God they are special, and perform a very important role, being in the most privileged place around the throne of God.

> Oh, the depth of the riches both of the wisdom and knowledge of God! How unsearchable are His judgments and His ways past finding out!
>
> "For who has known the mind of the Lord?
> Or who has become His counselor?"
> Romans 11:33–34

In the state we are now, we cannot understand all the wonders of God, because now we know only in part; but when that which is perfect comes, then that which is in part will be done away, and we shall know just as we were known. Each of us must learn to judge things as God judges them, and to see them through the divine eye, because what to man may be worthless, for God can be a great treasure.

Jesus, the Only One Worthy to Open the Scroll

Revelation 5:1–14

This is one of the most wonderful passages in the Scriptures; it is my favorite. The chapter begins when the apostle John, fixing his eyes upon the throne, says,

> And I saw in the right hand of Him who sat on the throne
> a scroll written inside and on the back, sealed with seven
> seals.
> Then I saw a strong angel proclaiming with a loud voice,
> 'Who is worthy to open the scroll and to loose its seals?'
> And no one in heaven or on the earth or under the earth
> was able to open the scroll, or to look at it.
> So I wept much, because no one was found worthy to open
> and read the scroll, or to look at it.
>
> Revelation 5:1–4

Here a book or scroll sealed with seven seals and held by the right hand of God the Father is presented. A book was also presented to the prophet Daniel, which also seemed to contain secret things:

> But I will tell you what is noted in the scripture [book]
> of truth.
> Daniel, shut up the words, and seal the book until the time
> of the end.
>
> Daniel 10:21; 12:4

These words to Daniel were shut up and sealed to be clearly disclosed when the time for their completion had come. Is the book that John saw the same as the one Daniel had in his hands? I think we cannot affirm it with all certainty, but we can see that both contain a word to be fulfilled at the end of days. The prophet Daniel was ordered to close and seal the book; the apostle John was commanded not to seal the book (Rev. 22:10). The book is now opened; therefore, we can know and understand what is written in both Daniel and John's books.

When I read chapter 5, I am truly shaken and excited to see the greatness of Christ, our Lord, and God, our Father. The apostle John

115

weeps disconsolately because in all heaven and on the earth, no one was found worthy to take the book out of the hand of God and loose its seals. But glory to God, hallelujah! One appeared who has the honor, and who paid the highest price—His own life—in order to be worthy to proceed to take the scroll from the hand of the Supreme God, loose its seals, and read it.

> But one of the elders said to me, 'Do not weep. Behold, the Lion of the tribe of Judah, the Root of David, has prevailed to open the scroll and to loose its seven seals.'
>
> Revelation 5:5

When Jesus took the book in His hands, the heavenly hosts could not restrain themselves and be still and quiet; all kinds of sounds and praises were heard. The heavens shook.

> Now when He had taken the scroll, the four living creatures and the twenty-four elders fell down before the Lamb, each having a harp, and golden bowls full of incense, which are the prayers of the saints.
> And they sang a new song, saying:
>
> > "You are worthy to take the scroll,
> > And to open its seals;
> > For You were slain,
> > And have redeemed us to God by Your blood
> > Out of every tribe and tongue and people and nation,
> > And have made us kings and priests to our God;
> > And we shall reign on the earth."
>
> Then I looked, and I heard the voice of many angels around the throne, the living creatures, and the elders; and the number of them was ten thousand times ten thousand, and thousands of thousands, saying with a loud voice:
>
> > "Worthy is the Lamb who was slain
> > To receive power and riches and wisdom,
> > And strength and honor and glory and blessing!"
>
> Revelation 5:8–12

Praise is to God! What joy is seen and heard in heaven to find who is worthy to complete the work for all ages! I ask myself, what did the apostle John feel when he heard millions of voices, those of all who dwell in heaven, praising and glorifying God, all at the same time? I think that his entire body trembled, and even the core of his being shook inside him. What a great honor for that humble apostle to be there, witnessing that wonderful and powerful spectacle!

Glory to God for each of the seven seals which Jesus will open! He takes to Himself that which always belonged to Him; but by the presence and work of the devil, the creation could not recognize Him as such. The Lamb who was slain is worthy to receive the power, the riches, the wisdom, the strength, the honor, the glory, and the blessing (v. 5:12). Glory to God for Jesus Christ!

Today we can serve God and recognize all of His attributes (one for each seal to open). Will there be any direct link between the events to happen as the seven seals are open, the information contained in the book, and these seven elements which exalt Jesus as the powerful conqueror? Answer this question for yourself as we go on reading this book.

Something interesting that I would like to highlight is that it was one of the elders, representing the church, who recognized that Jesus, the Lamb, was the only one worthy to open the seals of the scroll. This is a great privilege given to the church—to identify and recognize the work that Christ accomplished here on the earth.

The victorious church is chosen by God for this future great event, because she is the only one who has been experiencing true redemption and sanctification while she is on this lost world. She is now seated on thrones around the Father, bearing the true testimony of what the Lord Jesus is and has done for mankind. To God be the glory forever for this great honor given to the members of the church.

When the Scriptures present Christ as a slain Lamb, it is a direct reference to the price paid with His sacrifice and death for mankind, by which He redeemed us for God and His kingdom. Jesus is worthy to open the book because only He suffered as nobody else has done. All of mankind's sins and diseases were placed on His shoulders. By this, every member of the church can identify the Lamb, as described in this passage.

In heaven, the members of the victorious church will have the spiritual capacity to recognize that Jesus, the Lamb, is the only one worthy to open the seals of the scroll. Do you now have that testimony of holiness and fear of God, enough to show forth the image of Christ in this world, and then to identify and lift up Christ, proclaiming what the elder says in verse 5:5,

"Behold, the Lion of the tribe of Judah, the Root of David, has prevailed to open the scroll and to loose its seven seals"?

Although we must be able to do this every moment of our lives, there is something the Lord commands us to do in the church, which offers us the opportunity to witness that Jesus is the Lamb and worthy to be our Lord, and to take the book and open its seals. In 1 Corinthians 11:23–26, the apostle Paul declares what Jesus commanded us to do:

> ... that the Lord Jesus on the same night in which He was betrayed took bread; and when He had given thanks, He broke it and said, 'Take, eat; this is My body which is broken for you; do this in remembrance of Me.'
> In the same manner He also took the cup after supper, saying, 'This cup is the new covenant in My blood. This do, as often as you drink it, in remembrance of Me.'
> For as often as you eat this bread and drink this cup, you proclaim the Lord's death till He comes.

So, by eating the bread and taking the cup, we remember Jesus as the Lamb offered in sacrifice for us. By doing this, we declare Him worthy to be the Lamb and the Redeemer. Therefore, similar to Revelation 5, now through our testimony we must proclaim and identify Him as the Lamb, the Worthy.

On the other hand, Jesus was chosen by the heavenly Father to execute all judgment on the earth.

> For the Father judges no one, but has committed all judgment to the Son, that all should honor the Son just as they honor the Father. He who does not honor the Son does not honor the Father who sent Him.
>
> John 5:22–23

As we will see later, as each seal is opened, many catastrophic events will take place on the earth, causing great tribulation to its inhabitants. Everything seems to indicate that the scroll in the Father's hands contains all information related to the judgments of God upon the nations, to be carried out as commanded by the Lord Jesus. Based on all the reasons mentioned above, we can then say that the Lamb, Christ, is the only one worthy and able to open the seals of the book.

The events that will happen at the opening of the first seal indicate the start of the countdown of the seven years of the Great Tribulation. It is remarkable to see that the twenty-four elders continue in their same positions, sitting around the throne of God, as the Lamb begins to open the seals. These elders, representing the church, are in a secure place, kept from the trial which shall come upon all nations.

I would like to highlight here what the position of the twenty-four elders truly means. Through all the trials to come, we will see the twenty-four elders always seated on their thrones, in that place of privilege around the throne of God. This shows that the church will not be part of what will be happening at the same time on the earth. There are several passages in Revelation which confirm this statement.

In chapter 7, John sees a multitude of believers who die on earth during the Great Tribulation, and immediately they are seen saved in a special place in heaven. Verse 7:11 says, "All the angels stood around the throne and the elders and the four living creatures, and fell on their faces before the throne and worshiped God." We see here that the church, represented by the twenty-four elders, has not moved from her place around the throne, while the earth is in its greatest crisis of tribulation. It is one of the elders who identifies this multitude that comes from the earth:

> Then one of the elders answered, saying to me, 'Who are these arrayed in white robes, and where did they come from?'
> And I said to him, 'Sir, you know.' So he said to me, 'These are the ones who come out of the great tribulation, and washed their robes and made them white in the blood of the Lamb.'
>
> Revelation 7:13–14

We also see the elders worshiping God at the time of the judgments announced by the seventh trumpet: "And the twenty-four elders who sat before God on their thrones fell on their faces and worshiped God …" (vv. 11:16–18).

In addition, after the turbulence on the earth due to the soon coming of the Lord Jesus, we once again see the twenty-four elders, this time becoming part of the victory of our Lord Jesus: "And the twenty-four elders and the four living creatures fell down and worshiped God who sat on the throne, saying, 'Amen! Alleluia!'" (v. 19:4). Therefore, it is certain that the church will not go through the Great Tribulation.

Chapter 5 of Revelation concludes by presenting the twenty-four elders, four living creatures, and millions of angels praising God, because the time to open the seals and finish with sin in the world has come.

The First Six Seals

Revelation 6:1–17

Before beginning with the opening of the seals, I would like to establish the way in which the next apocalyptic events in this writing will be presented, from chapter 6 until the end of the Book of Revelation. When we see this prophetic book from a macro viewpoint—not by separate sections, but the entire book at the same time—we can notice that God, in His great wisdom, did not present the events as happening in strict chronological order.

It might seem that the book would be easier to understand if written in strict chronological order. But I do not think this was what God designed for us. I see that the way God presents these prophetic events has a hidden purpose. That is, God desires that we can touch and search His mind, pouring out our lives to Him to know His word and true purpose. The Lord seeks true worshipers, who worship Him in spirit and truth, rather than those who merely comply with a series of religious rituals or rules.

I see that Revelation was written in groups of events that are chronological within themselves, but not in relation to the entire book. The events prophesied to occur from the second seal until the seventh seal, those to take place with the sound of the seven trumpets, those to happen with the pouring out of the seven bowls of God's anger, and those to occur during the time of the two witnesses, will be accomplished simultaneously during the last three and a half years.

In order to bring the greatest clarity possible to the previous statement, let us consider the example of chapter 6, in relation to other passages from Revelation.

- Group 1

    Chapter 6 of Revelation mentions the events and judgments to be fulfilled during the seven years of the Great Tribulation. This passage describes the judgments following each opening of the seals, but in general form, without details.

Verses 6:14–17 describe the preamble to the second coming of Christ. Here the sky recedes as a scroll when it is rolled up, and the throne of God is revealed. Many inhabitants of the earth mourn greatly, and others, knowing the consequences of denying God, declare, "For the great day of His wrath has come, and who is able to stand?" (v. 6:17).

- Group 2

In the passages that speak about the seven trumpets (vv. 8:6—9:21; 11:15–19), the judgments are described in more details. Almost all of them are related to rare atmospheric disturbances and phenomena. Verses 11:15–19 describe what shall happen at the sound of the seventh trumpet. This passage shows the open sky: "Then the temple of God was opened in heaven, and the ark of His covenant was seen in His temple. And there were lightnings, noises, thunderings, an earthquake, and great hail" (v. 11:19).

This is a picture of the return of Christ at His second coming. Loud voices in heaven are heard and the twenty-four elders announce that the end-time has come and the kingdoms of this world have become the kingdoms of Christ.

- Group 3

In verses 14:14–20, after the completion of the sound of the seven trumpets, we see the arrival of Christ to reap "the harvest of the earth."

Then I looked, and behold, a white cloud, and on the cloud sat One like the Son of Man, having on His head a golden crown, and in His hand a sharp sickle.
And another angel came out of the temple, crying with a loud voice to Him who sat on the cloud, 'Thrust in Your sickle and reap, for the time has come for You to reap, for the harvest of the earth is ripe.'
So He who sat on the cloud thrust in His sickle on the earth, and the earth was reaped. ...

This passage describes the great killing which will occur in the battle in Edom, including the strip of 1,600 furlongs, at the end of the Great Tribulation.

- Group 4

Chapter 16 of Revelation describes the catastrophic events to take place on the earth during the pouring out of the seven bowls. Verses 19:11–21 describe the rejoicing in heaven, because now is the time for Christ to take the kingdom. This passage seems to be the continuation of the scenes showed with the seventh angel pouring out the last bowl (vv. 16:17–21).

"Now I saw heaven opened, and behold, a white horse. And He who sat on him was called Faithful and True, and in righteousness He judges and makes war" (v. 19:11). Here we see the second coming of Christ with power and great glory, and the encounter between the Lord, with His heavenly armies, and the Antichrist (the beast), with the kings of the nations and their armies, during the last battle in Armageddon.

Having this account, an important and interesting question should arise in our minds: Will the sky roll up four times to give way to four comings of Christ to the earth? There is only one return of Christ, not four. Therefore, these are not descriptions of four different events which show the coming of the Lord at different points within the time of the Great Tribulation.

As we see, the last events of these four groups relate to the only one return of Christ. All the events within each specific group will occur chronologically, but the four groups themselves are not chronological in relation to the entire Book of Revelation. Therefore, when we look at the four groups at the same time, it is not difficult to note that these are the same events, but described in different ways.

Summarizing, the judgments in the Great Tribulation are described in the Book of Revelation through different points of view, but they relate to each other. The judgments shown through the seven seals, the seven trumpets, and the seven bowls are similar, some are the same, and some are even the same as the signs through the two witnesses (v. 11:6). All these events will happen during the same period of time: the last three and a half years of the Great Tribulation. This will be discussed later in more details.

The Lamb, the only one worthy in heaven and under the heaven, begins to open the seals. With each opening of the seals, a series of events will occur which will affect all the inhabitants of the earth, but more directly, the people of Israel and its surrounding areas.

The first four seals are characterized by the emergence of four horses of different colors, with their four horsemen. According to the events that we will see, related to each horse in particular, we can understand that the four horsemen are the same. Each rider represents the Antichrist, who will be a man with great intellectual abilities and worldwide leadership.

The horses, with their different colors, represent different strategies or incidents which will occur during specific periods of time. These strategies will be designed and developed by the Antichrist, a demon-possessed man, who will use his power with all sagacity against all mankind, especially against the Jewish people. The prophet Daniel describes the Antichrist, with his different strategies, in this way:

> And in the latter time of their kingdom, when the transgressors have reached their fullness, a king shall arise, having fierce features, who understands sinister schemes.
>
> His power shall be mighty, but not by his own power; he shall destroy fearfully, and shall prosper and thrive; he shall destroy the mighty, and also the holy people.
>
> Through his cunning he shall cause deceit to prosper under his rule; and he shall exalt himself in his heart. He shall destroy many in their prosperity. He shall even rise against the Prince of princes; but he shall be broken without human means.
>
> Daniel 8:23–25

The Antichrist will use all kinds of resources, including very smart and influential people in society, to control the leaders of every nation, and thus persecute those who do not support his evil plans.

From the second seal onwards, we will see the different judgments with their corresponding calamities, to be experienced by the inhabitants of the earth. It was already prophesied by the former prophets that these judgments would come.

> For thus says the Lord God: 'How much more it shall be when I send My four severe judgments on Jerusalem—the

sword and famine and wild beasts and pestilence—to cut
off man and beast from it?'

Ezekiel 14:21

These are precisely the four kinds of judgment that will be manifested
from the opening of the second seal until the fourth one. It is very important
to note that the first seal will cover the first three and a half years and the
remaining seals will cover the next three and a half years of the Great
Tribulation.

First Seal

Revelation 6:1–2

At the opening of the first seal, "behold, a white horse. He who sat on it
had a bow; and a crown was given to him, and he went out conquering
and to conquer."

The white color of the horse means peace. The Antichrist will emerge
publicly at the beginning of the seven years, but he will do so as a charismatic
and convincing leader, promoting peace among nations, especially between
Israel and its Arab neighbors. This happens at a time of great uncertainty
and confusion around the world, because of the fulfillment of two huge and
unexpected events: firstly, the faithful Christians have left the earth in the
rapture of Christ, and second, Russia attacks Israel (for more detail, see
chapter 6 *Russia Will Attack Israel Soon*).

Then this evil Antichrist appears, promoting peace and quietness
through all the earth. When the relations between Jews and Arabs/Muslims
are in their greatest difficulty, there appears one who can solve all these
international and even global problems—a peacemaker, a man capable of
developing agreements between both peoples.

Using many wiles and his great eloquence, the Antichrist will be
accepted by all nations, to then become the axis of the entire world.
"Through his cunning he shall cause deceit to prosper under his rule;
and he shall exalt himself in his heart. He shall destroy many in their
prosperity" (Dan. 8:25).

As mentioned in sections of the Book of Daniel (chapter 3 of this book),
there will be some people who will not fully agree with the Antichrist and

will challenge him, but they will not prevail. "But news from the east and the north shall trouble him [the Antichrist]; therefore he shall go out with great fury to destroy and annihilate many" (Dan. 11:44).

The first period of the Great Tribulation will characterize as a period of apparent peace and security, where the people of Israel will again celebrate their rites and religious holidays, as they did in the old covenant. This period of peace will last approximately three and a half years, and "when they say, 'Peace and safety!' then sudden destruction comes upon them, as labor pains upon a pregnant woman. And they shall not escape" (1 Thess. 5:3). These events are presented in the great passage of Daniel 9:27,

> Then he shall confirm a covenant with many for one week; but in the middle of the week he shall bring an end to sacrifice and offering. And on the wing of abominations shall be one who makes desolate, even until the consummation, which is determined, is poured out on the desolate.

The agreement mentioned in this passage will be in effect during the first three and a half years, when Israel shall enjoy peace and freedom, until the true purpose of the Antichrist is revealed.

Many will be deceived. Daniel 11:21–23 says that a vile prince shall arise and seize the kingdom by flatteries, and he will rise and become conqueror. In this first seal, the rider comes with a crown, which means that he comes to reign; he comes conquering and to conquer. Nobody on the earth can stop him. It is therefore in the time of the first seal that the Antichrist lays down strong and deep roots, seizing the entire world.

The bow without arrows in the hand of the horseman means that the Antichrist comes to prepare for war in a secret way, to be manifested in the middle of the seven years (with the opening of the second seal). So, the first white horse speaks about a vile man bringing peace to the world, but with war in "his hands" (plans). This is an old strategy used by many other dictators throughout history, such as Hitler, Stalin, and others.

Second Seal

Revelation 6:3–4

At the opening of the second seal, behold, "Another horse, fiery red, went out. And it was granted to the one who sat on it to take peace from the earth, and that people should kill one another; and there was given to him a great sword." The red color speaks of blood's shedding. To this rider, the Antichrist, was given the power to take peace from the earth. That "good leader" who had sought peace and security among nations now removes his mask and shows his true face and identity—the wrecker and hater of humanity.

Daniel 11:21–24 says that this new leader will remove peace and make great spoils,

> And in his place shall arise a vile person, to whom they will not give the honor of royalty; but he shall come in peaceably, and seize the kingdom by intrigue.
> With the force of a flood they shall be swept away from before him and be broken, and also the prince of the covenant.
> And after the league is made with him he shall act deceitfully, for he shall come up and become strong with a small number of people.
> He shall enter peaceably, even into the richest places of the province; and he shall do what his fathers have not done, nor his forefathers: he shall disperse among them the plunder, spoil, and riches; and he shall devise his plans against the strongholds, but only for a time.

The time of fulfillment of this second seal will begin at the second half of the seven years of the Great Tribulation; it is when the Antichrist will break the agreement ratified with Israel, to continue then with his evil plan of destruction. As mentioned in the previous section, it is in the opening of the second seal that Daniel 9:27's prophecy is fulfilled.

> Then he shall confirm a covenant with many for one week; but in the *middle of the week* he shall bring an end to sacrifice and offering. And on the wing of abominations shall be

one who makes desolate, even until the consummation,
which is determined, is poured out on the desolate.

Daniel 8:23–24, speaking about the Antichrist, says, "… a king shall
arise, having fierce features, who understands sinister schemes. His power
shall be mighty, but not by his own power …" Satan will be like a father to
the Antichrist, and will grant him his authority. "Now the beast [Antichrist]
which I saw was like a leopard, his feet were like the feet of a bear, and his
mouth like the mouth of a lion. The dragon [Satan] gave him his power, his
throne, and great authority" (v. 13:2).

The Antichrist will come with great shrewdness and deception
("having fierce features, who understands sinister schemes"), and will
receive power from his master, Satan. The devil and his ministers of evil
will be the faithful political advisers of the Antichrist. I have no doubt
that many renowned people among the nations, experts in different fields
(economics, politics, technology, military, etc.) will give unconditional
support to the evil plans of the Antichrist.

We must remember that throughout history, certain leaders have
emerged with same characteristics of the Antichrist. One example we
have mentioned before was the Syrian King Antiochus Epiphanes (168
BC), who executed many plans similar to those of the Antichrist. However,
he had only local or regional authority, and could not dominate the whole
world (though it was his desire). The Antichrist will have authority over
the entire world.

The great sword which was given to the rider means that a great war
will take place in that period of time—the World War III—which will be
commanded by the Antichrist. The red color speaks of shedding of much
blood, which points out the many thousands who will die in that war.

This second seal introduces all the inhabitants of the earth to what
will truly be the Great Tribulation. It will be a time of trouble and anguish
which has never been, nor will ever again be on earth. After these terrible
events begin, there will be no more rest in any part of the earth. Fear and
desperation will take over the entire world's population.

The mere fact of knowing that the "son" of the devil is ruling the
nations will be enough to terrify anyone who realizes it. Remember what
the Lord Jesus said: "The thief [devil] does not come except to steal, and
to kill, and to destroy." This has been the purpose and working of the devil
for all times, and now he has the opportunity to put it into full action.

Third Seal

Revelation 6:5–6

> When He opened the third seal, I heard the third living creature say, 'Come and see.' So I looked, and behold, a black horse, and he who sat on it had a pair of scales in his hand.
> And I heard a voice in the midst of the four living creatures saying, 'A quart of wheat for a denarius, and three quarts of barley for a denarius; and do not harm the oil and the wine.'

The black color of the horse represents hunger. Lamentations 4:8–9 and 5:10 describe what the bodies of those who die by hunger are like:

> Now their appearance is blacker than soot; they go unrecognized in the streets; their skin clings to their bones, it has become as dry as wood.
> Those slain by the sword are better off than those who die of hunger; for these pine away, stricken for lack of the fruits of the field. Our skin is hot [blackened—RV60] as an oven, because of the fever of famine.

Hunger causes much suffering, and a slow and very painful death. The Great War, mentioned above with the opening of the second seal, will be the main cause of this critical food shortage which will be experienced over the face of the earth.

The destruction of vegetation (all green things) by supernatural events is another important factor that will create this great food shortage. As we will see, parts of the judgments to come are related to the destruction of nature by fires, hailstones, pollution, and other rare phenomena.

The scales in the hand of the rider mean that the food remaining on the earth will be sold by measure. The prophet Ezekiel prophesied in verses 4:16–17 about the shortage of food that is coming:

> Moreover He said to me, 'Son of man, surely I will cut off the supply of bread in Jerusalem; they shall eat bread by weight and with anxiety, and shall drink water by measure

and with dread, that they may lack bread and water, and
be dismayed with one another, and waste away because
of their iniquity.'

History reminds us that in times of hunger and war, human beings act
in a savage way. For example, in chapter 6 of 2 Kings, we find the story of
what happened to the inhabitants of Samaria. Due to the hunger produced
by a Syrian army's siege, the people cooked and ate even their own small
children. They reached the highest limit of the atrocities a human being
can commit. This was the result of their desperation and the lack of God.

In times of war and hunger, selfishness and inhumanity take over the
majority of people and cause these abhorrent actions. If this is already a
fact of history, what will they not do in the Great Tribulation, which will
be much worse and more extensive than any other trial that has occurred
on the earth?

> And I will cause them to eat the flesh of their sons and the
> flesh of their daughters, and everyone shall eat the flesh of
> his friend in the siege and in the desperation with which
> their enemies and those who seek their lives shall drive
> them to despair.
>
> Jeremiah 19:9

Knowing of the hunger and the need to come, Jesus lamented,

> But woe to those who are pregnant and to those who are
> nursing babies in those days!
> For then there will be great tribulation, such as has not
> been since the beginning of the world until this time, no,
> nor ever shall be.
>
> Matthew 24:19, 21

The children and the elderly will be the most vulnerable ones.

According to the Scriptures, a denarius was the wage of a worker for
one day of work (Matt. 20:2). Therefore, at the time of the third seal, wages
for a day of work will buy, at most, two pounds (a quart) of wheat or six
pounds (three quarts) of barley. A man will work the whole day to have
the chance to buy that amount of food. This prophecy gives understanding
about how great the shortage will be over the entire earth.

Now, remember that although you may have money to buy, the purchase and sale of food or anything else will be restricted to those who have a mark (number 666), which identifies them as the servants and subjects of the Antichrist.

> He causes all, both small and great, rich and poor, free and slave, to receive a mark on their right hand or on their foreheads, and that no one may buy or sell except one who has the mark or the name of the beast, or the number of his name.
>
> ... for it is the number of a man: his number is 666.
>
> Revelation 13:16–18

The Antichrist will have full authority from the middle of the *week* of the Great Tribulation, so he will take control of all types of business throughout the entire world. This imposition of the mark will weigh down the situation so much that hunger will increase even more on the earth, for even the people who have money cannot buy.

It is important to note that due to the wars, hunger, and shortages, many companies, factories, and businesses will cease their operations. Unemployment will be at its highest level around the entire world. No one will want to buy things that are not really necessary.

Shortages and hunger will also bring other consequences. If the wage for one day of work will only buy a limited amount of food (I stress: only two pounds of wheat for a denarius), then there will be no money to pay other accounts and services (utilities, rent, etc.) and to support a family. The inhabitants of the earth will be in great trouble.

Children and the elderly, especially, will suffer much in this shortage. Many diseases associated with a lack of adequate food will also be experienced. These events will cause many to abandon their faith in God and surrender to the system controlled by the Antichrist, because they will not be able to endure these trials.

At the end of this passage says, "... do not harm the oil and the wine." According to research of people with knowledge of health and nutrition, olive oil and grape wine contain several ingredients which help in prevention and treatment of certain diseases or conditions. Some of these ingredients are polyphenols, oleic acid, catechins or flavonoids, and others.

These ingredients have been identified with the following uses: stop bleeding, infection, and scarring of wounds and ulcers; laxative in cases of constipation; antioxidant; skin diseases; anti-inflammatory; regulate blood pressure; prevent coronary diseases; diuretic; and stimulate the immune system, among others (Ref. 7).

Chapter 10 of the Gospel of Luke tells the story of the "Good Samaritan." Verse 34 says that the Samaritan "bandaged his wounds, pouring on oil and wine." Perhaps this is why the oil and wine shall not be harmed: to help the injured persons from wars and other events, since medicines will be scarce at that time, and few will be privileged to have access to them. This talks about God's mercy, that although the people are under His judgments, God always thinks in them.

Fourth Seal

Revelation 6:7–8

> When He opened the fourth seal, I heard the voice of the fourth living creature saying, 'Come and see.'
> So I looked, and behold, a pale [yellow] horse. And the name of him who sat on it was Death, and Hades followed with him. And power was given to them over a fourth of the earth, to kill with sword, with hunger, with death, and by the beasts of the earth.

In this period of time there will be deaths of all kinds, such as by the sword (war), hunger, mortality (pestilence, diseases, etc.) and by the beasts of the earth. The former prophets also spoke of these trials to come.

> 'And I will appoint over them four forms of destruction,' says the Lord: 'the sword to slay, the dogs to drag, the birds of the heavens and the beasts of the earth to devour and destroy.'
> Jeremiah 15:3

> So I will send against you famine and wild beasts, and they will bereave you. Pestilence and blood shall pass through you, and I will bring the sword against you. I, the Lord, have spoken.
> Ezekiel 5:17

This will be a time of much suffering, pain, and death. This is why the name of the rider is "Death," for his tactic will be to kill and kill. This fourth seal covers the last time of the seven years of the Great Tribulation.

The phrase "and Hades followed with him" clearly shows the intention of this rider, the Antichrist. It is evident that the main objective of the devil, in this period of time, is to kill and destroy. In this way he can suppress any opportunity of salvation for the inhabitants of the earth, and drive them defeated into hell. There is no doubt that the devil comes with all his anger against all that he can, because he knows he has only a short time.

> Therefore rejoice, O heavens, and you who dwell in them!
> Woe to the inhabitants of the earth and the sea! For the
> devil has come down to you, having great wrath, because
> he knows that he has a short time.
>
> Revelation 12:12

Hades is a Greek word designating the dwelling place of dead, which in the past was equivalent to Sheol in Hebrew. It was believed that Hades was in the depths of the earth. In the New Testament, Hades was used to denote the final destination of bad people, while Abraham's bosom was the place for the faithful ones. Sheol, apparently, was both together. If Hades follows the Antichrist, this means that he will leave a lot of unbelievers dead on his way.

In this period of the fourth seal, one-quarter of the world's population will die; that is, if there were approximately 4,000 million inhabitants at that time, about 1,000 million would die—a great massacre. The fulfillment of all these events suggests that there will be a great persecution against both Jews and Gentile (non-Jew) believers in God—those who have refused to submit to the dominion of the Antichrist and have chosen to serve the Lord, no matter what they have to suffer, even unto death.

Fifth Seal

Revelation 6:9–11

> When He opened the fifth seal, I saw under the altar the souls of those who had been slain for the word of God and for the testimony which they held.
> And they cried with a loud voice, saying, 'How long, O Lord, holy and true, until You judge and avenge our blood on those who dwell on the earth?'
> Then a white robe was given to each of them; and it was said to them that they should rest a little while longer, until both the number of their fellow servants and their brethren, who would be killed as they were, was completed.

The altar mentioned here may be the altar of incense located in front of the throne of God, which represents the prayers of the saints (vv. 8:3–4). It is clearly noted that these souls are those who believe in God after the church is caught up into heaven, those who die during the events to occur in the period of the three previous seals. They die giving testimony of the Lord and His word; therefore, their souls are now put away until the time that the Lord resurrects them at His second coming, at the end of the Great Tribulation.

White robes are given to them and they are told to rest until the number of those who would be killed as they were is completed. Therefore, this passage sets us in a period not far from the end of the Great Tribulation, when there will be great persecution and death throughout the world. This judgment will fall even on those who have refused the Lord and have given to the service of the Antichrist, so these unbelievers will pass through the *furnace of fire* of judgment, and will not escape.

It is important to note that many of these events will be carried out by the Antichrist, but many others will come directly from heaven, sent by God, as we shall see later. Therefore, suffering and death will come to both believers and non-believers.

The souls that John sees are not resurrected bodies, but living souls ("I saw under the altar the souls of those who had been slain"). They are in a state of rest. With certainty, we can say that these souls are not part of the church. They are beneath the altar, not in thrones before God as the twenty-four elders.

In addition, as we have stated previously, the church will not be present in the Great Tribulation, and we have seen that these souls come from the Great Tribulation. A little more explanation about this multitude of souls will be provided later in verses 7:9–17.

Sixth Seal

Revelation 6:12–17

As the sixth seal was open, John saw a great commotion in the earth and in heaven.

> I looked when He opened the sixth seal, and behold, there was a great earthquake; and the sun became black as sackcloth of hair, and the moon became like blood.
> And the stars of heaven fell to the earth, as a fig tree drops its late figs when it is shaken by a mighty wind.
> Then the sky receded as a scroll when it is rolled up, and every mountain and island was moved out of its place.
>
> Revelation 6:12–14

Here we see how nature will also suffer and be affected as a result of the judgment on mankind. Many heavenly bodies will fall to earth, causing great catastrophe. The sun and the moon will darken, and the stars shall fall upon the earth. The earth shall be shaken in such a way that even the mountains will vanish and the islands will be removed from their places. Many parts of the earth will disappear, others will move from their places, and others will be joined with other lands (see vv. 16:18–21).

Matthew speaks also of this disaster to fall upon nature, the same as Isaiah also foretold these unusual events:

> Immediately after the tribulation of those days the sun will be darkened, and the moon will not give its light; the stars will fall from heaven, and the powers of the heavens will be shaken.
>
> Matthew 24:29

The earth is violently broken, the earth is split open, the
earth is shaken exceedingly. The earth shall reel to and fro
like a drunkard, and shall totter like a hut; its transgression
shall be heavy upon it, and it will fall, and not rise again.

Isaiah 24:19–20; see also 34:1–4

The earth will be different from what it was before the Great Tribulation.
And, who will bear all this calamity which shall come upon the earth (Joel
2:10–11, 30–31)? In Isaiah 13:9–13 we find that,

Behold, the day of the Lord comes, cruel, with both wrath
and fierce anger, to lay the land desolate; and He will
destroy its sinners from it.
For the stars of heaven and their constellations will not
give their light; the sun will be darkened in its going forth,
and the moon will not cause its light to shine.
'I will punish the world for its evil, and the wicked for their
iniquity; I will halt the arrogance of the proud, and will
lay low the haughtiness of the terrible.
… Therefore I will shake the heavens, and the earth will
move out of her place, in the wrath of the Lord of hosts
and in the day of His fierce anger.'

God reveals also in Job 9:6, through this beloved servant, that the
earth shall be shaken, "He shakes the earth out of its place, and its pillars
tremble." If the whole earth moves from its place, this means that it will
come out of its orbit. This will produce dramatic changes in the entire
earth. The waters which are currently confined to the rivers, lakes, seas,
and oceans will come out from their boundaries. The temperature of the
whole earth will change, and possibly will be hotter (vv. 7:16; 16:8–9). Both
day and night will have a different time of duration.

All of this speaks about the many disastrous changes to take place on
the earth. The scientists living at that time will be astonished by all these
unexplained events.

The time has come for the wrath of the Lamb, and who will be able to
stand? The sky will roll up as a scroll (v. 6:14), and the one who is seated
on the throne will be seen. Verses 6:14–17 describe the great day of God's
wrath, when the Son of Man, Jesus, comes down to the earth in His second
coming (vv. 1:7; Matt. 24:30). On that day, men will ask the mountains,

which at that time are falling, to fall on them to hide them from the face of Him who sits on the throne (Isa. 2:10; 19–21; Matt. 24:30; Luke 23:30).

The believers remaining on earth will rejoice on that day, but not so the other inhabitants of the earth, who shall now experience the anguish and terror of the presence of the living God. These shall not stand before the magnificent presence of the King of kings and Lord of lords. To Him be the glory and praise forever, amen.

Final Note to Chapter 6

As we have seen, this chapter summarizes, in general terms, the entire period that will elapse after the defeat of Russia in its attack to Israel, until the end of the Great Tribulation. For this reason, we must understand that the events to be described hereafter will not occur chronologically after chapter 6, but will be part of the previously described events—now presented by the apostle John from other points of view and with other details.

The Great Tribulation has many elements similar to the events occurred when the people of Israel were captive in Egypt. Israel lived under the oppression and tribulation of the Egyptians for approximately 400 years (Acts 7:6), until they cried out to God and He heard them (Acts 7:34).

God sent a "deliverer," Moses, who liberated the people with a powerful hand and many signs. Then the people were taken to Mount Sinai to worship and serve God, and receive God's law. From this place, they went to the land of Canaan, which God gave them as possession.

In the Great Tribulation it will happen, in principle, very much like this story of Israel. The believing people of Israel, along with believers of other nations, shall cry out to God at the time of their greatest anguish, and God will hear them. The Lord will make them free with a powerful hand in His second coming, and will lead them to the true Promised Land, where they will dwell for a thousand years. This was the promise to Israel, and God, faithful and powerful, will fulfill it.

The 144,000 Sealed

Revelation 7:1–8

> After these things I saw four angels standing at the four
> corners of the earth, holding the four winds of the earth,
> that the wind should not blow on the earth, on the sea, or
> on any tree.
> Then I saw another angel ascending from the east, having
> the seal of the living God. And he cried with a loud voice
> to the four angels to whom it was granted to harm the
> earth and the sea, saying, 'Do not harm the earth, the sea,
> or the trees till we have sealed the servants of our God on
> their foreheads.'
>
> Revelation 7:1–3

John sees four angels who stop the wind which moves from the four
corners of the earth. This action of the angels will cause the earth to warm
up greatly, causing great havoc on the earth, the sea, and the trees. This
intense heat is confirmed with the assertion of verse 7:16 related to those
who come out of the Great Tribulation, "They shall neither hunger anymore
nor thirst anymore; the sun shall not strike them, nor any heat."

This change in nature will cause great calamity and even death,
especially in children and the elderly, from the intense heat they will suffer.
Even the vegetation will be burned. But the four angels are commanded
not to do any damage till the 144,000 chosen servants of God are sealed
on their foreheads.

Who are these 144,000 men? What is their mission? What attributes
they have? Let us see what the Scriptures say about these 144,000 chosen
by God:

1. They are called servants of God (v. 7:3)

    These believers will be chosen and sealed on their foreheads
    with the seal of God (vv. 7:3; 9:4; 14:1) at the beginning of the
    period of greatest tribulation on the earth (the middle of the seven
    years). As servants of God, they will have the mission to proclaim
    the Gospel of the Kingdom, the word of salvation—the message

which brings the hope of entering the kingdom of the Millennium, where Christ will reign for a thousand years.

"And this gospel of the kingdom will be preached in all the world as a witness to all the nations, and then the end will come" (Matt. 24:14). This word of hope will be preached in the entire world, but especially in Israel and its surrounding areas. This salvation, which shall be manifested in the millennial kingdom, is different from the salvation experienced by the church from Pentecost until today.

The salvation that God provides currently makes us partakers of the "body of Christ," the church, the chosen to be the bride of Christ. There is no greater privilege than this, to be part of the body of Christ. Those who are saved during the Great Tribulation time will not be part of the church; they will be saved to have access to the Millennium.

2. They are of Jewish citizenship (vv. 7:4–8)

The 144,000 servants are men chosen from among all the tribes of the sons of Israel. They are Hebrews, 12,000 from each tribe (vs. 7:4). This passage does not provide for a symbolic interpretation, or for the possibility that these men are chosen from other nationalities.

When the Lord wants to indicate that people are from everywhere, the Scriptures make it clear, as in verse 7:9, "After these things I looked, and behold, a great multitude which no one could number, of all nations, tribes, peoples, and tongues." With reference to the 144,000, the Scriptures are specific in mentioning each tribe of Israel by name.

Dear reader, there are many theories about these chosen ones. There are some who say that both the number 144,000 and the names of the tribes are symbolic. But no group or person has biblical evidence to explain these theories. Their basis is a game of words without foundation in God. The Scriptures are clear—the 144,000 are chosen from the twelve tribes of Israel.

Now, why are these chosen ones Jews and not from other nationalities? The answer is simple: Israel was the people chosen by God, and to them is the promise of inheriting the Promised Land (although this blessing shall also extend to the servants of

God from other nations). Therefore, the Jews are the most suitable to preach the Gospel of the Kingdom.

On the other hand, it is certain that there will also be many other people, not of these selected 144,000, who will preach and encourage others to believe in God and endure the tribulations.

Within the tribes mentioned in this passage, there is one, Manasseh, which was not of the sons of Jacob. Manasseh was Joseph's son. He replaced the tribe of Dan, which does not appear in the list mentioned in this passage.

There are several passages that shed light on the reasons why God did not include the tribe of Dan among the 144,000 elect. In Genesis 49:1, we find that the patriarch Jacob (Israel), at the end of his life, called all his children to declare to them "what shall befall you in the *last days*." The words of Jacob contain prophetic messages for all his children.

Concerning his son Dan, Jacob says, "Dan shall be a serpent by the way, a viper by the path, that bites the horse's heels so that its rider shall fall backward" (Gen. 49:17). In this prophecy, Dan is called a *serpent* and *viper* that makes a rider fall. These are not worthy names for an honored people. (The malevolent future of Dan was described in the section *The Antichrist: His Ancestry,* chapter 3 of this book.)

Another passage mentions that the tribe who serves other gods, or was idolatrous, "The Lord would separate him from all the tribes of Israel for adversity, according to all the curses of the covenant that are written in this Book of the Law" (Deut. 29:21; see also vv. 29:18–20).

Judges 18 and 1 Kings 12:28–31 describe the great idolatry which was in the tribe of Dan. Moreover, we see that this tribe did not have a true eagerness to inherit the land which was appointed to them in Canaan. In addition, if part of the Antichrist's ancestry belongs to the tribe of Dan (as mentioned previously), I think that Dan will not be honored by God placing him on this list of privileged saints, who will be responsible for the spread of the word of God for salvation.

3. They will sing a new song and play harps (vv. 14:1–3; 15:2–4)

The 144,000 elect will play harps and sing the song of Moses and the song of the Lamb. The song of Moses was sung after

God liberated the people of Israel from the oppression in Egypt, after the crossing of the Red Sea (Ex. 15:1). In this song, Moses proclaims the victory of God over the Egyptians and exalts the name of God.

The events now presented in these specific passages (vv. 14:1–3; 15:2–4) will take place at the end of the Great Tribulation. For this reason, the 144,000 servants of the Lord sing two songs: the song of Moses, which proclaims the end of the devil's oppression on the people of Israel and other nations in the Great Tribulation; and the song of the Lamb, to proclaim liberation and salvation by the Lord Jesus.

As we see, there is a great similarity between the events of the Israelites' exodus from Egypt and the events that will take place at the end of the Great Tribulation.

4. They were redeemed from among those who lived on the earth (vv. 14:3–4)

The 144,000 chosen were redeemed from among men of the earth as firstfruits to God. They will have a specific time to complete the mission to which God calls them. In that period of time (last three and a half years), God will keep them from the evil that the devil will want to do against them. "They were commanded not to harm the grass of the earth, or any green thing, or any tree, but only those men who do not have the seal of God on their foreheads" (v. 9:4).

By this passage we can clearly see that these servants cannot be harmed by the Antichrist's followers. The seal of God on them will protect them from being punished by their enemies.

These servants, sealed by God, will be one of the major obstacles to the work of the Antichrist in the world. But when they finish their mission, which shall come to pass at the end of the Great Tribulation, they will be killed by the Antichrist's army. Verse 13:7 says, "It was granted to him to make war with the saints and to overcome them. And authority was given him over every tribe, tongue, and nation."

For this reason, the apostle John sees the 144,000 in a place with Jesus (v. 14:1) at the end of the Great Tribulation. They have experienced the physical death and have been taken up to meet with the Lord. This is why it says that they "were redeemed from the earth."

There is a passage in the Book of Daniel which may refer to these 144,000 chosen.

> And those of the people who understand [wise men of the people—RV60] shall instruct many; yet for many days they shall fall by sword and flame, by captivity and plundering.
> Now when they fall, they shall be aided with a little help; but many shall join with them by intrigue.
> And some of those of understanding shall fall, to refine them, purify them, and make them white, until the time of the end; because it is still for the appointed time.
>
> Daniel 11:33–35

These "wise men of the people," who at the end of their journey will "instruct many," that is, evangelize, "shall fall [die], to refine them, purify them, and make them white," and be finally brought to heaven.

5. <u>They have a blameless testimony (vv. 14:4–5)</u>

> These are the ones who were not defiled with women, for they are virgins. These are the ones who follow the Lamb wherever He goes. These were redeemed from among men, being firstfruits to God and to the Lamb.
> And in their mouth was found no deceit, for they are without fault before the throne of God.

The 144,000 chosen are men who will live without any defilement and with a pleasing testimony before God. They believe God and are surrendered to obey His word, to the point that, for their service to God, they will be virgins.

God, in His great wisdom and knowledge, has separated these 144,000 Israelite men, and keeps them for the hour in which they will be presented as the elect servants of the Lord, prepared for the great preaching of the Gospel of the Kingdom. Only God knows the names of these elect.

The Multitude Clothed with White Robes

Revelation 7:9–17

> After these things I looked, and behold, a great multitude
> which no one could number, of all nations, tribes, peoples,
> and tongues, standing before the throne and before the
> Lamb, clothed with white robes, with palm branches in
> their hands, and crying out with a loud voice, saying,
> 'Salvation belongs to our God who sits on the throne, and
> to the Lamb!'
> All the angels stood around the throne and the elders and
> the four living creatures ...
> Then one of the elders answered, saying to me, 'Who are
> these arrayed in white robes, and where did they come
> from?'
> And I said to him, 'Sir, you know.' So he said to me,
> 'These are the ones who come out of the great tribulation,
> and washed their robes and made them white in the blood
> of the Lamb.
> Therefore they are before the throne of God, and serve
> Him day and night in His temple. And He who sits on the
> throne will dwell among them.'
>
> Revelation 7:9–15

The crowd described in this passage refers to the believers who have
died during the Great Tribulation (v. 7:14). They are not only Jewish, for
they come from "all nations, tribes, peoples, and tongues." They have
washed their clothes and whitened them in the blood of the Lamb. This
means that they believed in Jesus as the Messiah, because it is only through
Christ that redemption and salvation of the soul can be obtained. Jesus
Christ is the only Savior and Messiah. This is why this crowd of people is
described as the redeemed by the blood of the Lamb.

There should be no doubt that this multitude consists of the sum of the
believers described in verses 6:9-11, which at that time were at rest under
the altar, plus the believers who were lacking to complete the final number
of that multitude, according to verse 6:11. When the number of servants
killed for their testimony of Jesus is completed, they will go from beneath

the altar into the presence of God, with great rejoicing, serving the Lord day and night (v. 7:15).

They are not heard anymore crying out, "How long, O Lord, holy and true, until You judge and avenge our blood on those who dwell on the earth?" (v. 6:10), but now they worship and serve the Lord.

These servants have palm branches in their hands, which is a sign of worship to their King. Matthew 21:1–9 describes the time when Jesus entered Jerusalem, and how the people were happy, worshipping and exalting Him as King, with branches of trees in their hands. This way of worship was typical for Jewish holidays, including the Feast of the Tabernacles (Lev. 23:40).

The crowd described in this passage will be resurrected at the end of the Great Tribulation, with the second coming of our Lord Jesus Christ. A more detailed description of all those who enter the millennial kingdom is included in the comments on verses 20:4–6.

Here I would like to emphasize again that the people who will enter the Millennium are not part of the church. Let us remember that the church will be the bride of the Lamb, and will have a very special place with Jesus, which we will describe in more details later. Hebrews 11:39–40, as mentioned before, says, "God having provided something better for us ..."

In other words, the church will not only be a people of God, but something better, the bride of the Son of God. On the other hand, the multitude described above will be shepherded as a people: "for the Lamb who is in the midst of the throne will shepherd them" (v. 7:17).

Seventh Seal

Revelation 8:1–5

Just as the seventh seal is opened, which is the last, after a silence of half an hour in heaven, seven angels with seven trumpets come up. All those who are in heaven (four creatures, twenty-four elders, angels, and those who came out of the Great Tribulation) know that this is the last seal to open. All of them keep silent and all activity in heaven stops.

During his stay in heaven, the apostle John has heard many noises, lightning, voices, praises, and harps—but now comes a great silence. To him, this silence was very strange, making him feel that the half-hour was very long. Let us remember that this is the last seal of seven of that great book which was in the hand of God. It seems as if this would finish a stage to then kick off another one; and by the silence in heaven, we understand that something great and awful is approaching.

The appearance of the seven angels with seven trumpets indicates that something important to take place will be announced. Just before the seven angels start playing their trumpets, another angel takes a golden censer of incense, fills it with fire from the altar, and throws it to the earth. This incense represents the prayers of the saints who dwelled on the earth at the time of the Great Tribulation, who cried out to God day and night.

The cry of these saints was great; that is why to the angel "was given much incense, that he should offer [add] it with the prayers of all the saints" (v. 8:3). This shows that the believers in that time experienced great suffering and tribulations, in such a way that they cried out to God with much anguish. Their prayers were expressions of a mixture of suffering and prayer.

"Then the angel took the censer, filled it with fire from the altar, and threw it to the earth. And there were noises, thunderings, lightnings, and an earthquake" (v. 8:5). The incense with fire poured out on the earth by the angels represents the judgments of God "poured" over the whole world.

These "poured judgments" are the answer of God to the prayers of the saints, when they cried out with a loud voice, saying: "How long, O Lord, holy and true, until You judge and avenge our blood on those who dwell on the earth?" (v. 6:10).

The day has come for the repayment of injustices committed by the despisers of the truth against the servants of the Lord. The Lord Himself, with His angels, will fulfill the final judgment over the nations and over the Antichrist.

The First Four Trumpets

Revelation 8:6–13

These first four angels of this passage are the same four angels referred to in verses 7:1–3, to whom the mission to harm the earth and the sea was given. Just as the first four angels play their trumpets, a series of catastrophic events take place.

Many of these events are similar to those carried out by the hand of Moses when the people of Israel were in Egypt. If these trials happened in the past, why doubt that they will come again at the end of days? It is useful to remember this comment, because in chapter 11 of Revelation we will expand a little more on the similarity of these events.

It is also important to point out again that many of the events which come after the playing of the trumpets refer to the same events and time described by the seven seals—now seen from another point of view. The judgments that come with the playing of the first four trumpets are related to elements of nature (earth, sea and heaven); they are the expression of the weeping and moaning of God's creation.

> For the earnest expectation of the creation eagerly waits for the revealing of the sons of God.
> For the creation was subjected to futility, not willingly, but because of Him who subjected it in hope; because the creation itself also will be delivered from the bondage of corruption into the glorious liberty of the children of God. For we know that the whole creation groans and labors with birth pangs together until now.
>
> Romans 8:19–22

Following are the catastrophic events found in this passage, including some references to similar events which occurred with the exodus of Israel from Egypt.

First Trumpet

> The first angel sounded: And hail and fire followed, mingled with blood, and they were thrown to the earth. And a third of the trees were burned up, and all green grass was burned up.
>
> Revelation 8:7; see also Exodus 9:22–25

These events will produce a great famine, because the food, both vegetable and animal, will become even scarcer than it already was. The cattle will die for lack of green grass. The effects of these judgments are similar to those already mentioned with the opening of the third seal, when a great famine will spread through all the earth.

Second Trumpet

> Then the second angel sounded: And something like a great mountain burning with fire was thrown into the sea, and a third of the sea became blood.
> And a third of the living creatures in the sea died, and a third of the ships were destroyed.
>   Revelation 8:8–9; see also Exodus 7:19–21

The sea mentioned here may be the Mediterranean Sea, which is to the west of Israel. Just as what occurred in Egypt, when the waters became blood and the plague was so extreme that water rotted and nobody could use it, so it will also be in this end-time period.

Third Trumpet

> Then the third angel sounded: And a great star fell from heaven, burning like a torch, and it fell on a third of the rivers and on the springs of water.
> The name of the star is Wormwood. A third of the waters became wormwood, and many men died from the water, because it was made bitter.
>   Revelation 8:10–11

Possibly this star will break into pieces upon entering the atmosphere of the earth, and in this way spread through rivers and other bodies of water. Many men will die because the waters will become bitter. This means that it will be very difficult to get drinking water at this time. The star mentioned here could be a meteorite which will crash to the earth.

Fourth Trumpet

> Then the fourth angel sounded: And a third of the sun was struck, a third of the moon, and a third of the stars, so that

a third of them were darkened. A third of the day did not shine, and likewise the night.

> Revelation 8:12; see also Exodus
> 10:21–23 and Joel 2:30–31

This scenario will produce longer nights, and maybe certain catastrophic changes in nature and in the earth's atmosphere. Matthew 24:29 gives a similar message: "Immediately after the tribulation of those days the sun will be darkened, and the moon will not give its light; the stars will fall from heaven, and the powers of the heavens will be shaken."

If all these things happen at the same time (celestial bodies moving from their places), cataclysms will take place through the entire world, such as major flooding, earthquakes, and tsunamis. Seeing all these things, people will be terrified.

> And there will be signs in the sun, in the moon, and in the stars; and on the earth distress of nations, with perplexity, the sea and the waves roaring; men's hearts failing them from fear and the expectation of those things which are coming on the earth, for the powers of the heavens will be shaken.
>
> Luke 21:25–26

These calamities will not occur consecutively (because there will be a time between them). Although many of these events could occur mainly in Israel and its surrounding regions, the entire world will be greatly affected, and will suffer and be troubled.

Dear reader, do these events not produce a great terror and commotion in your live? But these judgments do not stop here, for another angel rises, flying through the midst of heaven, saying with a loud voice: "Woe, woe, woe to the inhabitants of the earth, because of the remaining blasts of the trumpet of the three angels who are about to sound!" (v. 8:13). It seems that the next trials to happen will be worse than the previous ones.

Fifth Trumpet

Revelation 9:1–21

When the fifth angel sounds his trumpet, which is identified as the *first woe*, a star falls from heaven. The star is given a key to open the bottomless pit, from which smoke arises and darkens the sun and the atmosphere. Then out of the smoke, locusts come upon the earth to torment men for five months.

These locusts do not look like the locusts commonly known at that time, similar to grasshoppers. The locusts at the time of Moses in Egypt consumed all green grass and trees (Exodus 10). The locusts which John sees now,

> to them was given power, as the scorpions of the earth have power.
> They were commanded not to harm the grass of the earth, or any green thing, or any tree, but only those men who do not have the seal of God on their foreheads.
> And they were not given authority to kill them, but to torment them for five months. Their torment was like the torment of a scorpion when it strikes a man.
> > Revelation 9:3–5

These locusts seem strange, like nothing the apostle had ever seen. The description suggests that John may have seen weapons and modern military equipment—things prepared for war.

> They had breastplates like breastplates of iron, and the sound of their wings was like the sound of chariots with many horses running into battle.
> They had tails like scorpions, and there were stings in their tails. Their power was to hurt men five months.
> > Revelation 9:9–10

What we see described here seems like military tanks moving into battle. The locusts are commanded to torment and hurt people who do not have the seal of God on their foreheads (so this exempts the 144,000 elect) for five months.

It seems that this suffering shall be experienced by both believers and unbelievers (including those who have the mark of the devil—666). The five months of this torment shows that the end is not yet, but is close. The king of these locusts is the angel of the abyss, whose name in Hebrew is Abaddon (Apollyon in Greek), which means destroyer (v. 9:11).

"In those days men will seek death and will not find it; they will desire to die, and death will flee from them" (v. 9:6). This means that these events of the fifth trumpet will take place late in the Great Tribulation. Men will be so tired of suffering that all they want is death, but God will not allow it—at least in this specific last period of time.

These things will occur when considerable time has elapsed since the first trumpet, because when the first trumpet sounded, "a third of the trees were burned up, and all green grass was burned up" (v. 8:7). Since verse 9:4 says "not to harm the grass of the earth, or any green thing, or any tree," enough time has passed so that vegetation has recovered.

Sixth Trumpet

When the sixth angel sounds his trumpet, which is identified as the *second woe*, it is said to him:

> 'Release the four angels who are bound at the great river Euphrates.'
> So the four angels, who had been prepared for the hour and day and month and year, were released to kill a third of mankind.
> Now the number of the army of the horsemen was two hundred million; I heard the number of them.
>
> Revelation 9:14–16

This river Euphrates is located in what today is Iraq, the ancient Babylon. Because these angels are tied, we can infer that they are not good angels. The mission of these angels is specific, and with a transcendental meaning; that is why they were "prepared for the hour and day and month and year." These angels will help to gather a large army from all parts of the world.

The army consists of 200 million people riding on horses, with breastplates of fiery red (fire), hyacinth blue, and sulfur yellow. The power of the horses is in their mouths and in their tails. From the horse's mouths come fire, smoke, and brimstone, which will cause the death of one-third of mankind.

What John sees here is very similar to what he described at the fifth trumpet blast. It seems that the trial shown with the sixth trumpet is an extension of what was already happening with the sound of the previous trumpet. The prophecy in Joel 2:1–11 also describes the type of army to come against Jerusalem, with tremendous similarity to what was revealed to the apostle John. Joel 2:2–5 says:

> A day of darkness and gloominess, a day of clouds and thick darkness, like the morning clouds spread over the mountains. A people come, great and strong, nor will there ever be any such after them, even for many successive generations.
> A fire devours before them, and behind them a flame burns; the land is like the Garden of Eden before them, and behind them a desolate wilderness; surely nothing shall escape them.
> Their appearance is like the appearance of horses; and like swift steeds, so they run.
> With a noise like chariots over mountaintops they leap, like the noise of a flaming fire that devours the stubble, like a strong people set in battle array.

Verses 16:12–16 provide few additional details on this same subject:

> Then the sixth angel poured out his bowl on the great river Euphrates, and its water was dried up, so that the way of the kings from the east might be prepared.
> And I saw three unclean spirits like frogs coming out of the mouth of the dragon, out of the mouth of the beast, and out of the mouth of the false prophet.
> For they are spirits of demons, performing signs, which go out to the kings of the earth and of the whole world, to gather them to the battle of that great day of God Almighty.
> Behold, I am coming as a thief. Blessed is he who watches, and keeps his garments, lest he walk naked and they see his shame.

And they gathered them together to the place called in
Hebrew, Armageddon.

I could say that the four previous angels will be helped by the three
demons mentioned in this last passage, who will go out to the nations to
comply with the great charge of bringing together the largest army ever
seen in the history of the earth—200 million soldiers.

God revealed this same episode to several prophets; I will just quote
a couple of them:

> Behold, the day of the Lord is coming, and your spoil will
> be divided in your midst.
> For I will gather all the nations to battle against Jerusalem;
> the city shall be taken, the houses rifled, and the women
> ravished. Half of the city shall go into captivity, but the
> remnant of the people shall not be cut off from the city.
> Then the Lord will go forth and fight against those nations,
> as He fights in the day of battle.
>
> Zechariah 14:1–3

> I will also gather all nations, and bring them down
> to the Valley of Jehoshaphat [Valley of Megiddo or
> Armageddon]; and I will enter into judgment with them
> there on account of My people, My heritage Israel, whom
> they have scattered among the nations; they have also
> divided up My land.
> Assemble and come, all you nations, and gather together
> all around. Cause Your mighty ones to go down there, O
> Lord.
> Let the nations be wakened, and come up to the Valley of
> Jehoshaphat; for there I will sit to judge all the surrounding
> nations.
> Put in the sickle, for the harvest is ripe. Come, go down;
> for the winepress is full, the vats overflow—for their
> wickedness is great.
> Multitudes, multitudes in the valley of decision [Valley of
> Megiddo or Armageddon]! For the day of the Lord is near
> in the valley of decision.

The sun and moon will grow dark, and the stars will
diminish their brightness.

Joel 3:2, 11–15

The horses seen here by John might be tanks and other military
equipment, which are part of the military equipment of latest technology
to be used by the large army of the Antichrist. In verses 16:12–14 we read
that the river Euphrates will be dried up so that the kings of the east,
with their armies, can pass through and be gathered into the valley called
Armageddon (also known as the valley of Megiddo or valley of decision),
which is located south of Nazareth of Galilee, in Israel (v. 16:16).

It is interesting to see that two nations of the world's largest population
are located to the east of the river Euphrates; these are India and China.
The world's estimated population by the middle of 2012 was 7,017 million
people. Of these, there were 1,343 million (more than 19%) in China and
1,205 million (more than 17%) in India (Ref. 8). This totals approximately
36 percent of the world's population in these two nations together.

There is no doubt that the greater part of the 200 million army, which
will be prepared for this moment, will come from India and China. The
armies of the European nations (the ten horns of the beast) will also be part
of this great army that will fight against the Lord, as it is stated as follows:

The ten horns which you saw are ten kings who have
received no kingdom as yet, but they receive authority for
one hour as kings with the beast.
These are of one mind, and they will give their power and
authority to the beast.
These will make war with the Lamb ...

Revelation 17:12–14

It is well known that China is developing militarily as never before
in her entire history. Her military capacity has greatly improved with
the introduction of the latest technology, to the extent that they are
manufacturing (through agreements with other nations) their own fighter
planes and other military equipment. This news was published in the article
China's Arms Race from "Time" magazine (Ref. 9).

We find at the end of this passage of Revelation that the men who were
not killed by these plagues (fire, smoke, and brimstone) did not leave off
worshipping the images, nor did they repent of their works, fornications,
and other sins. Thus are the majority of men and women at this time too;

although they see signs in heavens and hear of the salvation in Christ, yet they do not repent and do not change their lives to the holy way of the Lord.

Dear reader, I stop here a moment to encourage you to be sensitive to God and His word. He is the life and without Him we are lost. The Lord is good and merciful, and always warns us of things to come. The Lord warns us of the days to come:

> Behold, I am coming as a thief. Blessed is he who watches, and keeps his garments, lest he walk naked and they see his shame.
>
> Revelation 16:15

> For the day of the Lord is great and very terrible; who can endure it?
>
> Joel 2:11

The Angel with the Little Book

Revelation 10:1–11

> I saw still another mighty angel coming down from heaven, clothed with a cloud. And a rainbow was on his head, his face was like the sun, and his feet like pillars of fire.
> He had a little book open in his hand. And he set his right foot on the sea and his left foot on the land, and cried with a loud voice, as when a lion roars. When he cried out, seven thunders uttered their voices.
> Now when the seven thunders uttered their voices, I was about to write; but I heard a voice from heaven saying to me, 'Seal up the things which the seven thunders uttered, and do not write them.'
>
> Revelation 10:1–4

I do not want to venture to say what is written in the book mentioned in this passage and what the words heard by John were. What I know is that both messages were very important, and they were related to something of the last days of the Great Tribulation, and the arrival of Christ on the earth.

In verses 10:6–7, the angel says that "… there should be delay no longer, but in the days of the sounding of the seventh angel, when he is about to sound, the mystery of God would be finished." This mystery is the second coming of Christ to the earth.

Then we read that John eats the small book that the angel had in his hand, and it was sweet in his mouth but bitter in his stomach. This means that what is written in the book is something horrifying to happen in the last stretch of this generation.

Then the angel commands John, saying, "You must prophesy again about many peoples, nations, tongues, and kings," that is, this word must be spread all over the world. There is a passage in the Gospel of John which I think directly relates to this command to the apostle.

> Jesus said to him [Peter], 'If I will that he [John] remain till I come, what is that to you? You follow Me.'
> Then this saying went out among the brethren that this disciple [John] would not die. Yet Jesus did not say to him that he would not die, but, 'If I will that he remain till I come, what is that to you?'
> This is the disciple who testifies of these things, and wrote these things; and we know that his testimony is true.
>
> John 21:22–24

This last prophecy in the Gospel of John is fulfilled by the Book of Revelation. The apostle John remains in this last message for mankind, until the return of Jesus.

Dear reader, the end is close, and it is necessary that you hear the last words of hope, so you may separate your life for service to God and love Him with all your heart, soul, mind, and strength. We cannot lose more time—we must move with urgency.

The Lord comes for His church, and those who are prepared, holy, and obedient to His word will be caught up in the clouds, to be kept from the hour of trial which shall come upon the whole world. Now is the opportunity—the door is still open—but not for long. Today is the day of salvation.

The Two Witnesses

Revelation 11:1–14

The catastrophic events of the Great Tribulation will begin in the middle of the prophesied seven years. The events prophesied to occur from the second seal until the seventh seal, those to take place with the sound of the seven trumpets, those to happen with the pouring out of the seven bowls of God's anger, and those to occur during the time of the two witnesses, will be accomplished simultaneously during the last three and a half years.

The Antichrist will have full dominion over the earth during that period of time, especially in the city of Jerusalem.

> Then I was given a reed like a measuring rod. And the angel stood, saying, 'Rise and measure the temple of God, the altar, and those who worship there.
> But leave out the court which is outside the temple, and do not measure it, for it has been given to the Gentiles. And they will tread the holy city underfoot for forty-two months [three and a half years].'
>
> Revelation 11:1–2

Although this passage has been discussed, let me consider some additional comments on this section. The apostle John was ordered to "measure the temple of God, the altar, and those who worship there." This is the third temple of the Jews, described earlier in this book. Through this command to John, God is emphasizing the temple's measurements, as revealed to the prophet Ezekiel in chapters 40 to 44 of his book. God provided Ezekiel a detailed design of the temple with all its measurements.

The phrase "and those who worship there" suggests that until that time (during the first three and a half years) the Jews had freedom and access to the temple for their religious services—by which we can understand that the Antichrist is not known yet as Antichrist, although this is certainly about to be revealed.

Now, it is easy to understand the measuring of the temple and the altar, but what does it mean to measure those who worship in it? I believe that the Lord is giving special importance to the number of people who are worshiping in the temple—so the command means to count them. It seems that these servants are faithful and dedicated Jews, zealous for God, and part of the remnant which will be protected and nourished for the last three and a half years, as it says in verses 12:6 and 14:

> Then the woman fled into the wilderness, where she has a place prepared by God, that they should feed her there one thousand two hundred and sixty days.
> But the woman was given two wings of a great eagle, that she might fly into the wilderness to her place, where she is nourished for a time and times and half a time, from the presence of the serpent.

I will expand on these last two passages later.

When the first half of the seven years is completed, the Antichrist and his army will lash out with all their strength against Israel and "will tread the holy city underfoot for forty-two months." Luke 21:24 says that "Jerusalem will be trampled by Gentiles until the times of the Gentiles are fulfilled."

John then sees two witnesses "clothed in sackcloth," who appear in Jerusalem at the middle of the seven years, who will prophesy for the last 1,260 days—forty-two months (v. 11:3).

These witnesses will have the mission of performing great signs and preaching the Gospel of the Kingdom, in addition to the 144,000 servants. These are the *two elect,* through whom many Israelites will believe in the Lord and turn from their own ways to the way of God. No one can harm them; and God gives them power to hurt with plagues and fire during the last three and a half years.

I would say that the most catastrophic events to take place in the Great Tribulation will be achieved by the command of these two witnesses. There is a direct connection and harmony between the petitions of the two witnesses and the judgments coming from heaven. Verse 11:10 says that "these two prophets tormented those who dwell on the earth." Therefore, the signs that these two witnesses carry out will have a global impact.

Let us see now who these two witnesses and prophets could be. The Scriptures mention three servants of God who disappeared from the earth: Enoch, Moses, and Elijah. Enoch lived before the flood took place in the time of Noah. Enoch, the seventh from Adam, is a clear representation of the church, because he was taken away to heaven before the flood (judgment) would come. "And Enoch walked with God; and he was not, for God took him" (Gen. 5:24).

Because Enoch's testimony pleased God so much, he was kept from that trial and taken alive to heaven. "By faith Enoch was taken away so that he did not see death, and was not found, because God had taken him; for before he was taken he had this testimony, that he pleased God" (Heb. 11:5).

Similarly, the church, which has a testimony pleasing to God, will be taken to heaven before the judgment of the Great Tribulation begins. The Great Tribulation will be a global judgment like the flood. For this reason Enoch will not be one of the witnesses who will appear in the Great Tribulation, because he represents the victorious church that will be in the rapture.

Now, what can we say of Moses and Elijah? We know that God took Elijah alive to heaven: "Then it happened, as they continued on and talked, that suddenly a chariot of fire appeared with horses of fire, and separated the two of them; and Elijah went up by a whirlwind into heaven" (2 Kings 2:11).

Regarding Moses we know that, although the Scriptures say that Moses died, nobody saw him in his death. Deuteronomy 34:5–6 says:

> So Moses the servant of the Lord died there in the land of
> Moab, according to the word of the Lord.
> And He buried him in a valley in the land of Moab,
> opposite Beth Peor; but no one knows his grave to this day.

Nobody saw Moses dying, nor was his body found, because it was God who buried him. I wonder how God buries. Moreover, the people of Israel found out the death of Moses "according to the word [saying—RV60] of the Lord."

Let us consider three points of view concerning Moses' disappearance: first, Moses died as any person dies; second, Moses died and God raised him from the dead, and took him up to heaven; and third, Moses did not die and God took him away alive to heaven, as He took away Elijah. Let us see now what the Scriptures show about this.

In Luke 9:30–31, the prophets Moses and Elijah appear before Jesus as witnesses, in shining garments,

> And behold, two men talked with Him, who were Moses
> and Elijah, who appeared in glory and spoke of His
> decease which He was about to accomplish at Jerusalem.

When this wonderful scene took place, the apostle Peter and some other apostles recognized the two men who appeared as Moses and Elijah. This appearance shows that these two prophets were not dead. The Scriptures clearly establish that the dead cannot appear again unless God resurrects them in the way Jesus did with Lazarus (John 11:38–44).

These two prophets knew the things that would happen to Jesus, because they talked about His decease or departure from this world. A witness is someone who has seen or heard something, to then be able to bear witness of that. Moses and Elijah are witnesses of what was going to happen to Jesus in His last days on earth and His death on the cross.

Moreover, Moses represented the law and Elijah the prophets, so in their appearance on this mountain, they were bearing witness and endorsement of the law and prophets to the Lord Jesus and His work of salvation. The following passages show that these two prophets have the characteristics to be true witnesses unto the Lord Jesus Christ.

> The righteousness of God apart from the law is revealed, being witnessed by the Law and the Prophets.
> Romans 3:21

> Then He said to them, 'These are the words which I spoke to you while I was still with you, that all things must be fulfilled which were written in the Law of Moses and the Prophets and the Psalms concerning Me.'
> Luke 24:44

> Philip found Nathanael and said to him, 'We have found Him of whom Moses in the law, and also the prophets, wrote—Jesus of Nazareth, the son of Joseph.'
> John 1:45

In the Book of Revelation, the apostle John calls the two witnesses "the two olive trees and the two lampstands standing before the God of the earth" (v. 11:4). In Zechariah 4:3 and 13–14 we find that

> Two olive trees are by it, one at the right of the bowl and the other at its left.
> Then he answered me and said, 'Do you not know what these are?' And I said, 'No, my lord.'
> So he said, 'These are the two anointed ones, who stand beside the Lord of the whole earth.'

It seems that John and Zechariah saw the same two persons before the throne, whom God called *my two witnesses* (v. 11:3). Revelation 11:5–6 say,

> And if anyone wants to harm them, fire proceeds from their mouth and devours their enemies. And if anyone wants to harm them, he must be killed in this manner. These have power to shut heaven, so that no rain falls in the days of their prophecy; and they have power over waters to turn them to blood, and to strike the earth with all plagues, as often as they desire.

Moses and Elijah were used by God in ancient times to perform these same or similar signs: sending fire from heaven (Ex. 9:23–24; 2 Kings 1:9–15), turning water into blood (Ex. 7:20–21), sending different kinds of plagues (Exodus 7—10), and stopping the rain (1 Kings 17:1; James 5:17). Deuteronomy 34:10–12 says,

> But since then there has not arisen in Israel a prophet like Moses, whom the Lord knew face to face, in all the signs and wonders which the Lord sent him to do in the land of Egypt, before Pharaoh, before all his servants, and in all his land, and by all that mighty power and all the great terror which Moses performed in the sight of all Israel.

Related to the return of Elijah to Israel, there is a prophecy in Malachi 4:5–6 which says:

> Behold, I will send you Elijah the prophet before the coming of the great and dreadful day of the Lord.
> And he will turn the hearts of the fathers to the children, and the hearts of the children to their fathers, lest I come and strike the earth with a curse.

From the time of this prophecy, there was an expectation in the hearts of the Jews for the return of the prophet Elijah. It is important to note that many prophecies have dual fulfillment. This is one of them, since it was fulfilled in the person of John the Baptist (John 1:21, 25; Mark 9:11–13; Matt. 11:13–14), and it will be accomplished again, but this time with the coming of Elijah himself in person, at the halftime of the Great Tribulation.

We can see that the whole chapter 4 of Malachi speaks about the advent of the Lord. As examples, I will cite parts of verses one and five:

> For behold, the day is coming, burning like an oven …
> Behold, I will send you Elijah the prophet before the coming of the great and dreadful day of the Lord.

It is stated in this passage that the prophet Elijah will be sent before the great day of the Lord, that is, the second coming of Christ.

John the Baptist came to prepare the way to introduce Christ to the people of Israel (Isa. 40:3; Matt. 3:3). This same prophet, "John the Baptist," will prepare the way again, this time in the Great Tribulation and in the "person of the prophet Elijah"—introducing Christ for His second coming, to the people of Israel and the whole world.

The two witnesses will appear in the Great Tribulation so that through their preaching, prophecies, and signs, the people will repent and glorify God, and be saved from the final judgment (v. 11:13). There is a prophecy in Luke 1:16–17 (which refers to the one in Malachi) which seemed to be met in the person of John the Baptist, but when it is considered in more detail, we realize that it will also be fulfilled by the two witnesses in Revelation.

> And he will turn many of the children of Israel to the Lord their God.
> He will also go before Him in the spirit and power of Elijah, 'to turn the hearts of the fathers to the children,' and the disobedient to the wisdom of the just, to make ready a people prepared for the Lord.

This passage clearly shows the mission the two witnesses will have, specifically the prophet Elijah. We can say that the message of John the Baptist was a powerful word, because he introduced Jesus to the people of Israel; so we see the *spirit and power of Elijah,* that is, Elijah's courage.

However, we do not see any demonstration of signs and miracles, or supernatural works through his person, as Elijah did in his time. So these manifestations of the power of God are then left to be shown through the Elijah who will come as a witness at the time of the Great Tribulation. Then the prophecy which says that he shall come *in the spirit and power of Elijah* will have thorough fulfillment.

On the other hand, speaking figuratively, we could say that Elijah and Moses represent two groups of saved ones in the Great Tribulation. Elijah went up alive in a chariot of fire to a place in heaven. Similarly, there will be a faithful people of God who resist the trials of the Great Tribulation and go alive into the Millennium, the Promised Land.

Moses "died" and then it seems that he was "resurrected" and taken away to heaven. Similarly, there will be a believing people who will die during the Great Tribulation and be resurrected at the end, at the second coming of Christ, to then be introduced to the Millennium, too.

In addition, the "death" of Moses represented the end of the law and the old covenant, consummated when the Lord Jesus establishes the new covenant.

On the other hand, the taking away of Elijah alive to heaven points to the continuing function of prophetic ministry in the new covenant, although in a different execution. Luke 16:16 says, "The law and the prophets were until John. Since that time the kingdom of God has been preached, and everyone is pressing into it." In other words, the beginning of the new covenant marked the end of the old covenant, which includes the former law and the prophets.

Having seen this account, I can clearly say that Moses and Elijah are the two olive trees, the two witnesses, who will prophesy and do great works during the last halftime of the Great Tribulation.

There is no doubt that many of the trials and signs executed in that time will be accomplished by God through these two servants; that is why the end of verse 11:10 says, "because these two prophets tormented those who dwell on the earth." These torments are the ones mentioned in verses 11:5–6: fire, drought, water turned into blood, and plagues of all kinds. For this reason the two prophets will be hated by the Antichrist and all the godless people of the earth.

After finishing the mission God gave them to do, Moses and Elijah will be killed by the beast's army. Their bodies will be exhibited publicly in Jerusalem for three and a half days, because the people will not allow them to be buried (vv. 11:7–9).

"And those who dwell on the earth will rejoice over them, make merry, and send gifts to one another, because these two prophets tormented those who dwell on the earth" (v. 11:10). All perverse people will rejoice and celebrate the deaths of God's two witnesses.

But then an unexpected event occurs: "after the three-and-a-half days the breath of life from God entered them, and they stood on their feet, and great fear fell on those who saw them" (v. 11:11). Great terror grips those who see them getting up from the street. Then these two prophets are called by God and taken away to heaven, something which the inhabitants of Jerusalem shall hear and see.

"In the same hour there was a great earthquake, and a tenth of the city fell. In the earthquake seven thousand people were killed and the rest were afraid and gave glory to the God of heaven" (v.11:13). With the departure of Moses and Elijah, "The second woe is past. Behold, the third woe is coming quickly" (v. 11:14).

Seventh Trumpet

Revelation 11:15–19

"Then the seventh angel sounded: And there were loud voices in heaven, saying, 'The kingdoms of this world have become the kingdoms of our Lord and of His Christ, and He shall reign forever and ever!'" (v. 11:15). This is the preparation and proclamation of the return of Christ to the earth, and the culmination of the Great Tribulation.

We see here the twenty-four elders worshiping God, because the time has come for the Lord Jesus to take the kingdoms of this world and reign over the people of Israel and all the other nations of the world. A great and deep rejoicing is seen in the twenty-four elders. These elders represent the church, and for the seven years in which the inhabitants of the earth experienced the judgments of God, her members have been worshiping God from their thrones in heaven. Now, the time of glory and final victory of Christ has come.

On this great day, the works of the devil and his evil agents, and the unrighteousness and rebellion of the inhabitants of the earth, will be done away with. The most wonderful spectacle our eyes could behold will appear at that time: heaven will be opened as a scroll and the temple of God will be shown. The earth will be shaken with lightning, noises, thunders, an earthquake, and great hail. The inhabitants of the earth and all the armies of the Antichrist will be bewildered as they hear and see these last events.

The time has come for the return of the Lamb to the earth with great power and glory. Those who did not believe that these things would happen; they now regret it with great anguish, and fear. The *third woe* is completed.

The Woman Persecuted by the Dragon

Revelation 12:1–17

> Now a great sign appeared in heaven: a woman clothed
> with the sun, with the moon under her feet, and on her
> head a garland of twelve stars.
> Then being with child, she cried out in labor and in pain
> to give birth.
> And another sign appeared in heaven: behold, a great,
> fiery red dragon having seven heads and ten horns, and
> seven diadems on his heads.
> His tail drew a third of the stars of heaven and threw them
> to the earth. And the dragon stood before the woman who
> was ready to give birth, to devour her Child as soon as it
> was born.
> She bore a male Child who was to rule all nations with a
> rod of iron. And her Child was caught up to God and His
> throne.
> Then the woman fled into the wilderness, where she has
> a place prepared by God, that they should feed her there
> one thousand two hundred and sixty days.
>
> Revelation 12:1–6

Much has been said of the meaning of this woman. Some have even said
that she represents Mary, Jesus' mother. But if we look at the Scriptures,
they themselves reveal the key to the meaning of this woman. Genesis
37:9–10 tells the story of Joseph, one of Jacob's sons, having a dream
in which the sun, the moon, and eleven stars bow down to him. Jacob
interprets the dream: the sun represents himself, Jacob (Israel), the moon is
his wife Rachel, Joseph's mother, and the eleven stars are the other eleven
sons of Jacob.

Therefore, the woman *clothed with the sun* represents the nation of
Israel (or better, a remnant of the nation of Israel, which will be explained
later). The son born of this woman is Jesus Christ, who was "caught up to
God and His throne" (fulfilled when Jesus ascended to heaven after His
resurrection from the dead). It also says that this child "was to rule all
nations with a rod of iron." Revelation 19:15, speaking about the coming
of the Lord at the end of the Great Tribulation says,

> Now out of His mouth goes a sharp sword, that with it He
> should strike the nations. And He Himself will rule them
> with a rod of iron. He Himself treads the winepress of the
> fierceness and wrath of Almighty God.

Therefore, Jesus will come with great authority and courage upon the
wicked among the nations (see also Matthew 25:31–46).

The dragon (Satan, serpent of old—v. 12:9) stood in front of the woman
to devour her child as soon as he was born. From the beginning of creation,
the devil has tried to kill the One who will defeat him. After the first man
was tempted by the devil and sinned, God pronounced a judgment against
the author of all temptation. Genesis 3:15 says, "And I will put enmity
between you and the woman, and between your seed and her seed; He [the
seed] shall bruise your head, and you shall bruise His heel."

The word of God states that Satan and his seed will be at enmity with
the woman and her seed forever. Who is the woman mentioned in this
passage of Genesis? Is she Eve? Shall Eve be at enmity with Satan forever?
What is the purpose of this if Eve has died already?

Definitely God is not talking about Eve, but about a future nation,
Israel, the "mother" of Jesus Christ the seed. "Now to Abraham and his
Seed were the promises made. He does not say, 'And to seeds,' as of many,
but as of one, 'And to your Seed,' who is Christ" (Gal. 3:16).

On the other hand, the seed of Satan is the Antichrist. In the same way
that Judas Iscariot was possessed by demons, so also the Antichrist will be,
and in that way he will be under the control of the source of evil, that is, Satan.

> Jesus answered, 'It is he to whom I shall give a piece
> of bread when I have dipped it.' And having dipped the
> bread, He gave it to Judas Iscariot, the son of Simon.
> Now after the piece of bread, Satan entered him. Then
> Jesus said to him, 'What you do, do quickly.'
> John 13:26–27

The Antichrist will be Satan's son. From the time of God's statement
in Genesis, the devil has been seeking that seed, Jesus Christ, who was
prophesied to destroy him. This was confirmed when the devil found out
that the Messiah and King of the Jews was born, and sought an opportunity
to kill Him through King Herod (Matt. 2:13–18).

But God kept Jesus from the hand of the devil. At the end, Jesus is the
one who will defeat Satan and the Antichrist forever, and by this the word

spoken by God in Genesis will be fulfilled, "He [the seed, Jesus] shall bruise your head [Satan, the serpent of old]." The following verses also talk about that great victory:

> Sit at My right hand, till I make Your enemies Your footstool.
>
> Hebrews 1:13

> And the God of peace will crush Satan under your feet shortly.
>
> Romans 16:20

A notable character is introduced in this passage of Revelation, who shall have great authority and worldwide dominion at the time of the Great Tribulation. This "creature" is the dragon, the old serpent (Gen. 3:1), also called the devil and Satan (v. 12:9). Just as in the kingdom of light there is the Trinity of good (Father–God, Son–Jesus Christ, and the Comforter or Helper–Holy Spirit), in the kingdom of darkness there is the trinity of evil (father–Satan, son–Antichrist, and the helper–False Prophet).

The devil is always imitating the holy things of God. Although chapter 13 of Revelation will present a more extensive discussion of the dragon, the Antichrist, and the False Prophet, let us see what chapter 12 shows, in general terms, about this great dragon.

"And another sign appeared in heaven: behold, a fiery red dragon having seven heads and ten horns, and seven diadems on his heads. His tail drew a third of the stars of heaven" (v. 12:3; see figure 13: The Dragon).

> Here is the mind which has wisdom: The seven heads are seven mountains on which the woman sits.
> There [They, as per translation from RV60] are also seven kings. Five have fallen, one is, and the other has not yet come. And when he comes, he must continue a short time.
>
> Revelation 17:9–10

The seven heads with the diadems (crowns) mean seven kings, of whom five had already reigned, the sixth reigned in the apostle John's time, and the last one will reign in the future. The kingdoms of the first six kings extended through the Middle East region, including Israel. Unlike these previous, the seventh king shall have dominion over the entire world.

Figure 13: The Dragon
(Satan or Devil)

The ten horns are ten kings or nations who will receive authority for a time, together with the Antichrist. "The ten horns which you saw are ten kings who have received no kingdom as yet, but they receive authority for one hour as kings with the beast" (v. 17:12). It has been already mentioned that these ten nations or kingdoms, represented by the ten horns, are the integration of the European Union, which will be the highest collaborator of the Antichrist.

> And war broke out in heaven: Michael and his angels fought with the dragon; and the dragon and his angels fought, but they did not prevail, nor was a place found for them in heaven any longer.
>
> So the great dragon was cast out, that serpent of old, called the Devil and Satan, who deceives the whole world; he was cast to the earth, and his angels were cast out with him.
>
> Then I heard a loud voice saying in heaven, 'Now salvation, and strength, and the kingdom of our God, and the power of His Christ have come, for the accuser of our brethren, who accused them before our God day and night, has been cast down.'
>
> Revelation 12:7–10

The third part of the stars drawn by the dragon are the angels deceived by Satan (then called Lucifer—Isaiah 14:12–14) when he was cast out from heaven. In Revelation 1:20, the angels of God are represented by stars. The dragon is a deceiver and liar, who accuses the servants of the Lord before the throne of God (Job 1:9–11). In Luke 22:31–32, the Lord Jesus warns of the indictment of the devil to try to cause Peter to stumble:

> And the Lord said, 'Simon, Simon! Indeed, Satan has asked for you, that he may sift you as wheat.
>
> But I have prayed for you, that your faith should not fail; and when you have returned to Me, strengthen your brethren.'

The devil deceived a large army of angels who served God, and turned them against the Son of God. For this reason, all of them were thrown from heaven and they are now servants and ministers of evil. "And it grew up to the host of heaven; and it cast down some of the host and some of the stars to the ground, and trampled them" (Dan. 8:10).

In the passage of Revelation under consideration, we see an unusual battle—angels against angels. The passage says that "they did not prevail, nor was a place found for them in heaven any longer;" therefore, from this time forth (middle of the Great Tribulation), the access Satan had to heaven in the past is now restricted.

There will be no more accusations by the father of lies, who has never ceased to accuse faithful men before the throne of God. The time has come when that liar will be thrown down to the earth, bringing with him all the attributes which describe what he has been from his beginning, that is, the dragon, the serpent of old, the devil, and Satan.

"Woe to the inhabitants of the earth and the sea! For the devil has come down to you, having great wrath, because he knows that he has a short time" (v. 12:12).

Oh, dear reader, what will come upon the earth from this time forward is not a game or a fiction film with alien characters. The devil is very angry with both God and His servants. Enlist on God's side on time, be brave, and do not lose heart, for the Lord has already prepared a place together with Him in heaven for those who love and serve Him with all their mind, soul, heart, and strength. "Be faithful until death, and I will give you the crown of life" (v. 2:10).

Our God is great in mercy and does not forget His promises, so He will have mercy on the people of Israel again. Although many Jews and inhabitants of other nations will suffer much, and will even die, the Lord will keep and nourish those chosen believing people, the remnant, for the last period of the Great Tribulation.

In verses 12:6 and 14, the Lord shows how He will deal with the people of Israel for a time, times, and half a time. This means one year, two years, and a half year, respectively; added all together, we get three and a half years, equal to 1,260 days (Dan. 7:25; 12:7).

> Then the woman fled into the wilderness, where she has a place prepared by God, that they should feed her there one thousand two hundred and sixty days.
>
> Revelation 12:6

> Now when the dragon saw that he had been cast to the earth, he persecuted the woman who gave birth to the male Child.
> But the woman was given two wings of a great eagle, that she might fly into the wilderness to her place, where she

is nourished for a time and times and half a time, from the presence of the serpent.

So the serpent spewed water out of his mouth like a flood after the woman, that he might cause her to be carried away by the flood.

But the earth helped the woman, and the earth opened its mouth and swallowed up the flood which the dragon had spewed out of his mouth

And the dragon was enraged with the woman, and he went to make war with the rest of her offspring, who keep the commandments of God and have the testimony of Jesus Christ.

Revelation 12:13–17

The prophetic clock which tracks the fulfillment of the apocalyptic prophecies related to the nation of Israel stopped after the death of Jesus and His ascension into heaven. From that time forward, God has worked in the people of all nations, saving and blessing many, and in this way building His church.

While the work of redemption and salvation is taking place within God's plan, Jesus connects His ascension with the events of the Great Tribulation without even mentioning the period of the church, as we have said several times. Thereby, after the church is taken away to heaven, God will deal again with the people of Israel one last time, in the Great Tribulation. That is why, once the child is born and is taken to heaven (Jesus' ascension), Israel is fiercely persecuted by the devil from the middle of the Great Tribulation.

In short, for the purposes of this prophecy in Revelation 12, the next scenario after the ascension of Jesus will be the desperate pursuit of Israel by Satan, as exactly stated in verses 12:4–6 and 13–17. But according to the perfect plan of God, the remnant of Israel (the *woman*) shall flee into the wilderness, where she will be fed for the last three and a half years.

Since the beginning of Israel's history, there have been examples very similar to what will happen in the time of the Great Tribulation. The event experienced by the prophet Noah and his family, when they were saved by God from the judgment of the flood, is a picture of what will come to pass soon in the Great Tribulation. The instrument used by God to save them was a wooden ark. But let us look at how wonderful God is.

We can say that Noah and his family went through the trial, but they were victorious, being still within the ark. God nourished them even being in the midst of that judgment. Therefore, Noah and his family represent the people that will remain through the Great Tribulation, whom after believing and serving God, will be able to pass through the judgment, up to the very end. The remnant of Israel is that people who will be separated and saved, although they will be living in the place that will undergo the greatest trials in the world's history.

In the days of Joseph, son of Jacob, the people lived in a piece of land in Egypt called Goshen. After 400 years, in the time of Moses, a series of judgments and signs came upon all the land of Egypt, without touching the land of Goshen. God protected them, even though a lot of calamities took place in surrounding territories.

> And in that day I will set apart the land of Goshen, in which My people dwell, that no swarms of flies shall be there, in order that you may know that I am the Lord in the midst of the land.
>
> Exodus 8:22

> Only in the land of Goshen, where the children of Israel were, there was no hail.
>
> Exodus 9:26

While all these trials came over all the land of Egypt, Israel enjoyed peace and blessing from God.

> So Moses stretched out his hand toward heaven, and there was thick darkness in all the land of Egypt three days. They did not see one another; nor did anyone rise from his place for three days. But all the children of Israel had light in their dwellings.
>
> Exodus 10:22–23

God is great and makes possible what for the man is impossible. At the end of the trials, God declared a categorical affirmation for the last judgment in Egypt, the death of the firstborn:

> Then there shall be a great cry throughout all the land of Egypt, such as was not like it before, nor shall be like it again.

But against none of the children of Israel shall a dog move
its tongue, against man or beast, that you may know that
the Lord does make a difference between the Egyptians
and Israel.

Exodus 11:6–7

If God has done so in the past, why will He not do it again? Yes, He
will do it again in the time of the Great Tribulation, with the presence of
Moses again, as one of His witnesses.

Shall all Israelites be saved and nourished by God in the most crucial
time of the Great Tribulation? I do not believe that all Israel will be saved,
but only a remnant chosen by God. Romans 9:27 says, "Though the number
of the children of Israel be as the sand of the sea, the remnant will be saved
[... only the remnant will be saved—RV60]." Joel and Obadiah also say,

And it shall come to pass that whoever calls on the name
of the Lord shall be saved. For in Mount Zion and in
Jerusalem there shall be deliverance, as the Lord has said,
among the remnant whom the Lord calls.

Joel 2:32

For the day of the Lord upon all the nations is near ...
But on Mount Zion there shall be deliverance, and there
shall be holiness; the house of Jacob shall possess their
possessions.

Obadiah, verses 15 and 17

There should be no doubt, God is great in mercy and truth; He will
remember His covenant and promises to this chosen people. It seems
unusual that this remnant of Israel is protected in the time of greatest
trouble and distress on the earth, but so is it. This is the plan of God, not
of men.

Let us look at some other passages related to the salvation and
nourishment of the remnant of Israel in the distressing times that they
shall experience at the end times. Isaiah 10:20–23 says,

And it shall come to pass in that day that the remnant of
Israel, and such as have escaped of the house of Jacob,
will never again depend on him who defeated them, but
will depend on the Lord, the Holy One of Israel, in truth.

The remnant will return, the remnant of Jacob, to the
Mighty God.
For though your people, O Israel, be as the sand of the sea,
a remnant of them will return; the destruction decreed
shall overflow with righteousness.
For the Lord God of hosts will make a determined end in
the midst of all the land.

On the other hand, the prophet Ezekiel specifies that the remnant of
this people will be brought out (to the desert), there to be saved.

For thus says the Lord God: "How much more it shall be
when I send My four severe judgments on Jerusalem—the
sword and famine and wild beasts and pestilence—to cut
off man and beast from it?
Yet behold, there shall be left in it a remnant who will
be brought out, both sons and daughters; surely they
will come out to you, and you will see their ways and
their doings. Then you will be comforted concerning the
disaster that I have brought upon Jerusalem, all that I have
brought upon it.

Ezekiel 14:21–22

The four trials referred to in this passage—sword, famine, wild
beasts, and pestilence—are the main trials to be manifested in the Great
Tribulation. When the openings of the seals in Revelation chapter 6 were
discussed, these four types of trials to come upon the nations were also
described. God has a plan to keep the remnant of Israel from these trials
which shall come upon the whole world.

The Antichrist will tread the city of Jerusalem for forty-two months (v.
11:2). He will try to eliminate all Israelites, but God will intervene, bringing
them somewhere else. This is why Jesus warns them, saying,

But when you see Jerusalem surrounded by armies, then
know that its desolation is near.
Then let those who are in Judea flee to the mountains, let
those who are in the midst of her depart, and let not those
who are in the country enter her.
For these are the days of vengeance, that all things which
are written may be fulfilled.

But woe to those who are pregnant and to those who are nursing babies in those days! For there will be great distress in the land and wrath upon this people.
And they will fall by the edge of the sword, and be led away captive into all nations. And Jerusalem will be trampled by Gentiles until the times of the Gentiles are fulfilled.

Luke 21:20–24

This is the time to flee from Jerusalem to the place that God has prepared in the desert. This people coming out from Jerusalem, who worshiped the Lord in the temple (v. 11:1), are the remnant chosen by God to be saved from the trials to come.

But where is this place in the desert? There are several passages in the Scriptures by which the location of this place can be identified. Daniel 11:41 says that the Antichrist "shall also enter the Glorious Land, and many countries shall be overthrown; but these shall escape from his hand: Edom, Moab, and the prominent people of Ammon."

It seems that a portion of the territory of Edom (not its inhabitants, as we will see later) is part of those cities that will be kept from the hands of Satan, the dragon, to be used then as the refuge of the people fleeing from Jerusalem. Everything seems to indicate that the desert chosen by God to protect the remnant of Israel is in Edom, located to the south of the Dead Sea in Israel (see figure 14: Map of Israel).

Although the inhabitants of Edom will see how God, with His power, will save the remnant of Israel, these, deceived by the Antichrist, shall mock and betray Israel, also taking part in the persecution against the remnant gathered in the wilderness of Edom. But at the end of the three and a half years, God will intervene again to deliver His chosen people. Obadiah, verses 1 and 10–14 describe the behavior of the people of Edom against the Israelites, which displeased God very much:

The vision of Obadiah. Thus says the Lord God concerning Edom (We have heard a report from the Lord, and a messenger has been sent among the nations, saying, 'Arise, and let us rise up against her for battle').
For violence against your brother Jacob, shame shall cover you, and you shall be cut off forever.

173

Figure 14: Map of Israel

In the day that you stood on the other side—in the day
that strangers carried captive his forces, when foreigners
entered his gates and cast lots for Jerusalem—even you
were as one of them.

'But you should not have gazed on the day of your brother
in the day of his captivity; nor should you have rejoiced
over the children of Judah in the day of their destruction;
nor should you have spoken proudly in the day of distress.
You should not have entered the gate of My people in the
day of their calamity. Indeed, you should not have gazed
on their affliction in the day of their calamity, nor laid
hands on their substance in the day of their calamity.
You should not have stood at the crossroads to cut off those
among them who escaped; nor should you have delivered
up those among them who remained in the day of distress.'

The prophet Ezekiel prophesied about what will happen to Edom for
his multiple actions of contempt against the remnant of Israel. The entire
chapter 35 of Ezekiel describes these judgments, but I will only quote
verses 35:5–6 and 15.

'Because you have had an ancient hatred, and have shed the
blood of the children of Israel by the power of the sword at
the time of their calamity, when their iniquity came to an
end, therefore, as I live,' says the Lord God, 'I will prepare
you for blood, and blood shall pursue you; since you have
not hated blood, therefore blood shall pursue you.'
As you rejoiced because the inheritance of the house
of Israel was desolate, so I will do to you; you shall be
desolate, O Mount Seir, as well as all of Edom—all of it!
Then they shall know that I am the Lord.

According to these prophecies, Edom will be totally destroyed.
Obadiah 18 says that the "house of Esau [Edom] shall be stubble; they
shall kindle them and devour them, and no survivor shall remain of the
house of Esau, for the Lord has spoken." God is indignant forever against
the people of Edom (Mal. 1:3–5), so their destruction will occur directly
by the hands of the Lord.

The prophet describes in Isaiah 63:1–4 what will happen to King Jesus

175

when He faces with the Antichrist's army which has the remnant of Israel besieged in the wilderness of Edom.

> Who is this who comes from Edom, with dyed garments from Bozrah, this One who is glorious in His apparel, traveling in the greatness of His strength?—'I who speak in righteousness, mighty to save.'
> Why is Your apparel red, and Your garments like one who treads in the winepress?
> 'I have trodden the winepress alone, and from the peoples no one was with Me. For I have trodden them in My anger, and trampled them in My fury; their blood is sprinkled upon My garments, and I have stained all My robes.
> For the day of vengeance is in My heart, and the year of My redeemed has come.'

Bozrah was the capital of Edom (1 Chron. 1:43–44). The God of Abraham, Isaac, and Jacob will not forget His promises, so He will come against the Antichrist's army and the people of Edom, and will destroy all of them with His power.

These passages reveal that the remnant of Israel, stationed in the territory of Edom, will be saved from the Antichrist's army; and second, it is in Edom where the garments of the Lord Jesus will be splashed with blood—this being the first site that He will visit in His second coming. More details on these events will be provided later in the section of Revelation 14:14–20, *Order to Reap the Earth*.

Everything seems to indicate that the first place that the Lord will judge in His coming will be Edom, that is, its inhabitants, and certainly too, the portion of the Antichrist's army that has besieged the remnant of Israel. This is why Isaiah says that the Lord comes from Edom with His garments sprinkled with their blood. Similarly, Revelation 19:11–21 describes Jesus' garments stained with blood at the beginning of the battle of Armageddon: "He was clothed with a robe dipped in blood ..."

Chapter 34 of Isaiah mentions the trial to come on Edom; I will specifically make reference to verses 5 and 6,

> For My sword shall be bathed in heaven; indeed it shall come down on Edom, and on the people of My curse, for judgment.

> The sword of the Lord is filled with blood … For the Lord
> has a sacrifice in Bozrah, and a great slaughter in the land
> of Edom.

The prophet Jeremiah also mentions the total destruction of Edom in chapter 49:

> But I have made Esau [Edom] bare; I have uncovered his
> secret places, and he shall not be able to hide himself. His
> descendants are plundered, his brethren and his neighbors,
> and he is no more.
> 'For I have sworn by Myself,' says the Lord, 'that Bozrah
> shall become a desolation, a reproach, a waste, and a curse.
> And all its cities shall be perpetual wastes.'
> Jeremiah 49:10, 13

Therefore, the Lord Jesus, with His heavenly hosts, will firstly come to the wilderness of Edom to liberate the remnant of Israel, besieged in that place (where His clothes are sprinkled with blood). He then continues His attack against the other part of the Antichrist's army, all the way from Edom to the Valley of Armageddon (Megiddo), where the remainder and greatest part of that army will be located.

As will be discussed later in the section of chapter 14 of Revelation, this journey from Edom to Megiddo has an approximate distance of 180 miles, equal to 1,600 furlongs, according to verse 14:20 (see figure 14).

Zechariah 12:7–9 also mentions that the Lord will come first to release the Jews captive in Edom and will then continue His battle against the other nations' armies, located in the Valley of Armageddon.

> The Lord will save the tents of *Judah first [the remnant]*,
> so that the glory of the house of David and the glory of
> the inhabitants of Jerusalem shall not become greater than
> that of Judah.
> In that day the Lord will defend the inhabitants of
> Jerusalem; the one who is feeble among them in that day
> shall be like David, and the house of David shall be like
> God, like the Angel of the Lord before them.
> It shall be in that day that I will seek to destroy all the
> nations that come against Jerusalem.

After these battles in Edom and Armageddon are over, Jesus will go to Jerusalem and stand on the Mount of Olives. From here He will begin to judge the nations, separating the "goats" from the "sheep," to then establish His millennial kingdom, reigning from the new plain in Jerusalem. This chronology of events is confirmed in Zechariah's prophecy when he said,

> Behold, the day of the Lord is coming, and your spoil will be divided in your midst.
> For I will gather all the nations to battle against Jerusalem; the city shall be taken, the houses rifled, and the women ravished. Half of the city shall go into captivity, but the remnant of the people shall not be cut off from the city.
> Then the Lord will go forth and fight against those nations, as He fights in the day of battle.
> And in that day His feet will stand on the Mount of Olives, which faces Jerusalem on the east. And the Mount of Olives shall be split in two, from east to west, making a very large valley; half of the mountain shall move toward the north and half of it toward the south.
> And the Lord shall be King over all the earth. In that day it shall be—"The Lord is one," and His name one.
> Zechariah 14:1–4, 9

Revelation 12:14 has a great similarity to the departure of the people of Israel from Egypt. This passage says, "But the woman was given two wings of a great eagle, that she might fly into the wilderness to her place." Exodus 19:4 says, "You have seen what I did to the Egyptians, and how I bore you on eagles' wings and brought you to Myself." The wings of eagles speak about the power of God delivering the Israelites from Egypt—what we expect to occur in the same way in the Great Tribulation.

Now then, I think the people that will be preserved and nourished in the desert will not comprise all the remnant of the Israelites to be saved, but only a part of them. It seems that the people to be besieged in Edom's desert are Jews who are living in Judah at that time. We can see this in Luke 21:20–21, mentioned before, when Jesus warns the Jews, saying,

> But when you see Jerusalem surrounded by armies, then know that its desolation is near.
> Then let those who are in Judea flee to the mountains, let those who are in the midst of her depart ...

As mentioned in chapter 11 of Revelation, the apostle John was commanded to "measure the temple of God, the altar, and those who worship there" (v. 11:1). The Lord gives special importance to the number of people who were worshiping in the temple. It could be that these are faithful Israelites in whom there is no deception, who will believe in Jesus as the Messiah. This group of faithful whom John sees worshiping in the temple will definitely be part of the remnant that will be protected in the desert for the last three and a half years.

The other part of the remnant consists of those whom the devil (in the person of the Antichrist), failing to destroy the woman (Israel), "... went to make war with the rest of her offspring, who keep the commandments of God and have the testimony of Jesus Christ" (v. 12:17).

This passage suggests that not all the remnant of Israel to be saved will be exempt from the tribulation and persecution of the devil. In other words, many Jews, although they have believed in the Lord, will suffer much, and many will even die, but they will be saved too.

In short, the total of the remnant of Jewish root to be saved shall consist of the group in Edom's desert, plus those who are persecuted and may even suffer death, but who "keep the commandments of God and have the testimony of Jesus Christ."

Verses 7:1–8, already discussed, refers to a group of 144,000 chosen by God from all the tribes of the children of Israel, who will have a special mission at the time of the Great Tribulation. These 144,000 servants might also be part of the chosen remnant, but they will not be located in the desert of Edom. These servants will also be persecuted by the Antichrist's army; however, they shall be protected from the attacks of the Antichrist (v. 9:4), until they complete their mission to spread the Gospel of the Kingdom up to the end of the Great Tribulation.

In verse 12:15 we read that the dragon spewed water like a river (flood) out of his mouth, so the women (Israel) would be carried away. Waters like rivers mean armies of soldiers. Isaiah 59:19 says, "... when the enemy comes in like a flood ..." Jeremiah 46:7–8 shows armies of men like waters of a river:

> Who is this coming up like a flood, whose waters move like the rivers?
> Egypt rises up like a flood, and its waters move like the rivers; and he says, 'I will go up and cover the earth, I will destroy the city and its inhabitants.'

Therefore, we must understand what the devil will send against Israel is part of his army, prepared for that hour and for that purpose. Similar to what happened when Pharaoh sent his army against the people of Israel in their departure from Egypt, and the entire Egyptian army perished when the water of the Red Sea covered them (Ex. 14:22–28). So it will also happen with the events mentioned in Revelation, when the earth will open its "mouth" and swallow the army sent against Israel. Similarly, we find another event in the history of Israel when God judged the men of Korah by opening the earth and swallowing them all.

> But if the Lord creates a new thing, and the earth opens its mouth and swallows them up with all that belongs to them, and they go down alive into the pit, then you will understand that these men have rejected the Lord.
> Now it came to pass, as he finished speaking all these words, that the ground split apart under them, and the earth opened its mouth and swallowed them up, with their households and all the men with Korah, with all their goods.
> So they and all those with them went down alive into the pit; the earth closed over them, and they perished from among the assembly.
>
> Numbers 16:30–33

If this happened in the past, why may it not recur in the future?

The Beast from the Sea

Revelation 13:1–10

As with the prophet Daniel, God shows the apostle John who the Antichrist and his ministers of evil truly are. Both prophets saw them as beasts or nasty creatures, representing the kind of beings these "leaders" will be and the work of destruction they will do, especially from the halfway point of the Great Tribulation onward.

By describing them as beasts, God shows many aspects of these characters and their evil and cruel actions. They can no longer be seen as attractive and pleasant people, but as something horrible and despicable. All this clearly shows that from the halfway point of the Great Tribulation onward, the earth and its inhabitants will receive the cruelest and most terrible judgments they have ever been subjected to.

> Then I stood on the sand of the sea. And I saw a beast rising up out of the sea, having seven heads and ten horns, and on his horns ten crowns, and on his heads a blasphemous name.
>
> Now the beast which I saw was like a leopard, his feet were like the feet of a bear, and his mouth like the mouth of a lion. The dragon gave him his power, his throne, and great authority.
>
> And I saw one of his heads as if it had been mortally wounded, and his deadly wound was healed. And all the world marveled and followed the beast.
>
> So they worshiped the dragon who gave authority to the beast; and they worshiped the beast, saying, 'Who is like the beast? Who is able to make war with him?'
>
> And he was given a mouth speaking great things and blasphemies, and he was given authority to continue for forty-two months.
>
> Then he opened his mouth in blasphemy against God, to blaspheme His name, His tabernacle, and those who dwell in heaven.
>
> It was granted to him to make war with the saints and to overcome them. And authority was given him over every tribe, tongue, and nation.
>
> All who dwell on the earth will worship him, whose names have not been written in the Book of Life of the Lamb slain from the foundation of the world.
>
> If anyone has an ear, let him hear. He who leads into captivity shall go into captivity; he who kills with the sword must be killed with the sword. Here is the patience and the faith of the saints.
>
> Revelation 13:1–10

Before continuing with the description of this beast, I would like to comment on the book mentioned at the end of this passage. This book, called the Book of Life, contains the names of the saved ones, and is also mentioned in Daniel 12:1:

> At that time Michael shall stand up, the great prince who stands watch over the sons of your people; and there shall be a time of trouble, such as never was since there was a nation, even to that time. And at that time your people shall be delivered, every one who is found written in the book.

So this book contains names of people from the beginning of the world. That is why the passage in Revelation says that the Book of Life is "of the Lamb slain from the foundation of the world." This means that Jesus is the owner and author of that book.

But where do we see Jesus as "the Lamb slain from the foundation of the world"? Let us go back to the beginning of mankind. The Scriptures say that after Adam and Eve sinned, "the eyes of both of them were opened, and they knew that they were naked; and they sewed *fig leaves* together and made themselves coverings" (Gen. 3:7).

They tried to cover their sin using a kind of cloth with fig leaves made by themselves, which did not please God. Man can do nothing for his own redemption. The source of the great blessing of redemption comes directly from God, and according to His own method. Hebrews 9:22 says that "without shedding of blood there is no remission."

So God the Father, in His eternal love, is the One who sacrificed the first lamb to cover the sin of the first man and woman. Genesis 3:21 says, "Also for Adam and his wife the LORD God made tunics of skin, and clothed them." In the mind and purpose of God, this sacrifice to take the skin for the tunics of Adam and Eve represented His Son Jesus, "the Lamb slain from the foundation of the world."

In addition, the fig tree represents the ancient Israel under the law. Therefore, the *fig leaves* can represent the law (works from themselves), by means of which no one can be justified, and least redeemed. Only by the blood of Christ we can be reconciled to God and our sins forgiven.

The beast that John saw rising up out of the sea had "seven heads and ten horns, and on his horns ten crowns, and on his heads a blasphemous name." See figure 15: Beast Rising up from the Sea.

The sea is a symbol of peoples, crowds, and nations. "Then he said to me, 'The waters which you saw, where the harlot sits, are peoples, multitudes, nations, and tongues'" (v. 17:15).

Figure 15: Beast Rising up from the Sea
(Antichrist)

This beast, which represents the Antichrist, is a very charismatic man who will be greatly supported by many people during the first three and a half years; for this reason he is coming out of the sea, that is, from among the crowds or nations. As the Antichrist has been described previously, he will be a leader with understanding in riddles, who can move the multitudes with great convincing ability and shrewdness.

The seven heads represent seven kings or kingdoms.

> Here is theq mind which has wisdom: The seven heads are seven mountains on which the woman sits.
> There are also seven kings. Five have fallen, one is, and the other has not yet come. And when he comes, he must continue a short time.
>
> Revelation 17:9–10

The ten horns with crowns symbolize ten kings or nations who emerge from the territory ruled by the ancient Roman Empire, which will reign together with the beast during the Great Tribulation.

> The ten horns are ten kings who shall arise from this kingdom ...
>
> Daniel 7:24

> The ten horns which you saw are ten kings who have received no kingdom as yet, but they receive authority for one hour as kings with the beast.
>
> Revelation 17:12

This beast that rose up out of the sea "was like a leopard, his feet were like the feet of a bear, and his mouth like the mouth of a lion. The dragon gave him his power, his throne, and great authority" (v. 13:2). These beasts (leopard, bear, and lion) symbolize three of the ancient kingdoms (Greece, Media-Persia and Babylon, respectively) which ruled in the Middle East region, Asia, and part of Europe, including Israel, before the Roman Empire (Dan. 7:4–7, 17).

In order to describe in more detail what this beast represents, let us review again what the Book of Daniel says about this topic. Daniel 2:26–45 describes the dream of Nebuchadnezzar, king of Babylon, and the interpretation from God through the prophet Daniel. This passage shows that the dream is a revelation of "what will be in the latter days."

The king saw in his dream an image composed of four parts: the head of gold representing the kingdom of Babylon; the chest and arms of silver representing Media-Persia, the kingdom that followed the Babylonian; then the belly and thighs of bronze depicting the kingdom of Greece; and lastly, the legs of iron and feet partly of iron and partly of clay, which identify the kingdom of Rome, which was the last kingdom.

By noting the materials of each part of the image, we see the deterioration or decline in the quality of the kingdoms—from gold to iron mixed with clay. The Scriptures say that the fourth and last kingdom of Rome "shall be as strong as iron, inasmuch as iron breaks in pieces and shatters everything; and like iron that crushes, that kingdom will break in pieces and crush all the others" (Dan. 2:40).

Also, as the feet of iron are mixed with clay, likewise this kingdom will be partly strong and partly fragile, mingling with other kingdoms or nations through human alliances (see Daniel 2:41–43).

The Roman kingdom, which ruled in Jesus' lifetime will continue ruling at the time of the Great Tribulation, but this time as a divided kingdom shared with the Antichrist and the great harlot. This Roman kingdom will be a political-religious kingdom.

On the political side, it will be represented by the ten kingdoms or nations of the European Union (symbolized by the ten toes of Nebuchadnezzar's image, the ten horns of the fourth beast seen by the prophet Daniel, and the ten horns of the beast which rises from the sea in Revelation). On the religious side it will be represented, as we shall see in details later, by the institution of the Catholic Church, the great harlot.

Another passage that brings great clarity concerning the four kingdoms mentioned above is chapter 7 of Daniel (see the section that comments on this chapter). This passage has great similarity to the verses we are considering in chapter 13 of Revelation. The prophet Daniel saw four beasts which rose from the sea: the first was like a lion with wings of eagles (kingdom of Babylon); the second was similar to a bear, which was raised up on one side (kingdom of Media-Persia).

The side that lifted more than the other represented the kingdom of Persia, which prevailed more than the kingdom of Media. The third beast was like a leopard with four heads and four wings (kingdom of Greece), where the four heads and four wings represented the four kingdoms into which the kingdom of Greece was divided—Egypt, Syria, Phrygia (old Europe), and Macedonia.

The fourth beast (kingdom of Rome) seen by Daniel was

dreadful and terrible, exceedingly strong. It had huge iron teeth; it was devouring, breaking in pieces, and trampling the residue with its feet. It was different from all the beasts that were before it, and it had ten horns.

I was considering the horns, and there was another horn, a little one, coming up among them, before whom three of the first horns were plucked out by the roots. And there, in this horn, were eyes like the eyes of a man, and a mouth speaking pompous words.

Daniel 7:7–8

Thus he said: 'The fourth beast shall be a fourth kingdom on earth, which shall be different from all other kingdoms, and shall devour the whole earth, trample it and break it in pieces.

The ten horns are ten kings who shall arise from this kingdom. And another shall rise after them; he shall be different from the first ones, and shall subdue three kings. He shall speak pompous words against the Most High, shall persecute the saints of the Most High, and shall intend to change times and law. Then the saints shall be given into his hand for a time and times and half a time.'

Daniel 7:23–25

Those great beasts, which are four, are four kings which arise out of the earth.

Daniel 7:17

The fourth beast is the most dreadful and terrible of all. This shows the kind of government that will rule in the Great Tribulation. It will be a government led by the small horn, which knocks down the other three, and who will speak against the Most High and will break the believers. This small horn which shall exalt himself exceedingly is the Antichrist, who has a mouth speaking great things and will mislead many people.

Turning back to chapter 13 of Revelation, we see that the "the dragon [Satan] gave him [beast, Antichrist] his power, his throne, and great authority." That is why this last earthly king will be so different and more frightening than the previous kings. The power and authority of the Antichrist will not come from his own abilities, but from Satan himself who will equip him with these tools.

186

"His power shall be mighty, but not by his own power; he shall destroy fearfully, and shall prosper and thrive; he shall destroy the mighty, and also the holy people" (Dan. 8:24). So the Antichrist will be a despicable man, totally possessed by demons, under the highest authority of the devil, who will work fiercely for the last three and a half years. 2 Thessalonians clearly describes the Antichrist:

> ... the man of sin is revealed, the son of perdition, who opposes and exalts himself above all that is called God or that is worshiped, so that he sits as God in the temple of God, showing himself that he is God.
> The coming of the lawless one is according to the working of Satan, with all power, signs, and lying wonders, and with all unrighteous deception among those who perish, because they did not receive the love of the truth, that they might be saved.
>
> 2 Thessalonians 2:3–4, 9–10

The character described in these passages refers to the Antichrist, who will receive all his authority and capacity to govern from Satan, who will treat him as his own son. This is an example of how Satan takes control of a person. We must be filled with the Holy Spirit, which is the only way to not be deceived in the midst of this perverse and adulterous generation.

> I beseech you therefore, brethren, by the mercies of God, that you present your bodies a living sacrifice, holy, acceptable to God, which is your reasonable service.
> And do not be conformed to this world, but be transformed by the renewing of your mind, that you may prove what is that good and acceptable and perfect will of God.
>
> Romans 12:1–2

In order to present a more detailed description of the beast, the Antichrist, I will refer to Revelation 17:7–13. For greater understanding, see again the comments provided in the sections *The Antichrist: His Ancestry* and *The Antichrist: His Traits and Actions*. The seven heads of the beast

> are also seven kings. Five have fallen, one is, and the other has not yet come. And when he comes, he must continue a short time.

> The beast that was, and is not, is himself also the eighth,
> and is of the seven, and is going to perdition.
>
> Revelation 17:10–11

The five kings who had already fallen and who had authority over the Middle East region, Asia, and Europe, including Israel, were the five kingdoms which ruled prior to the Roman kingdom, under which the apostle John was living when he received this revelation. These five kingdoms, with which Israel has been involved, are the following: first: Egyptian (1657–1067 BC), second: Assyrian (1365–612 BC), third: Babylonian (606–536 BC), fourth: Media-Persian (536–330 BC), and fifth: Greek (330–30 BC).

Some of these kingdoms, such as the Egyptian, extended for a longer period, interlacing with the next. These five kingdoms are those which John refers to as the five which have fallen (see figure 16: Kingdoms of the Earth).

The *one is* is the sixth kingdom which ruled during the apostle John's lifetime; this is the Roman kingdom (30 BC—AD 364). Remember again that for the purposes of Israel's prophecies, the prophetic clock stopped with Jesus' death, and it will continue moving in the time of the Great Tribulation. The Roman kingdom (the sixth kingdom) was ruling in Israel at the time of Jesus' death, and Israel will again be under that kingdom in the Great Tribulation (more details about this sixth kingdom will be provided later).

Verse 17:10, referring to the seventh kingdom, says, "and the other has not yet come. And when he comes, he must continue a short time." This seventh kingdom is the kingdom of the Antichrist and will be short, because the Antichrist will be wounded with a mortal wound. "And I saw one of his heads as if it had been mortally wounded, and his deadly wound was healed. And all the world marveled and followed the beast" (v. 13:3).

Then, after the Antichrist is healed, he will continue ruling the nations as the eighth king. "The beast that was, and is not, is himself also the eighth, and is of the seven" (v. 17:11). So the seventh and eighth kings are the same, and they are the Antichrist (see figure 16).

Verse 13:14 also says, "to make an image to the beast who was wounded by the sword and lived." Because of this healing, the inhabitants of the world worshiped the dragon (Satan) and the beast (Antichrist), and "marveled and followed the beast." This is a clear imitation of the death and resurrection of Jesus Christ.

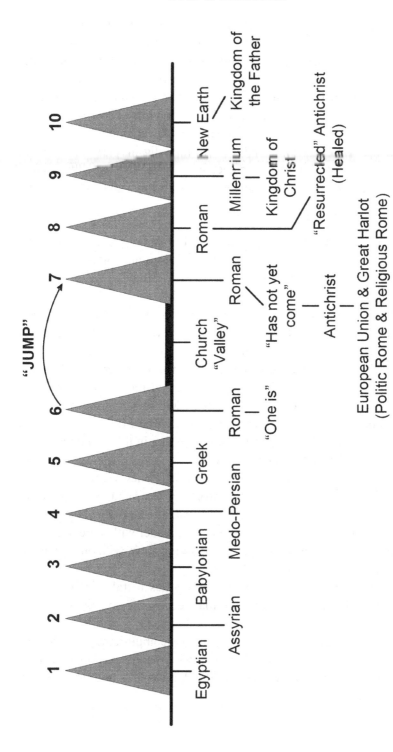

Figure 16: Kingdoms of the Earth

So we see that at some point in the last three and a half years, the Antichrist will be mortally wounded, and then he will be healed. I ask myself, how can the Antichrist be mortally wounded while having total control of the whole world? Who will be able to wound this "king," evading the very tight security around him? I think it most likely to be someone very close to him, who will use a sword to wound him. These queries will be answered in the comments on chapter 17 of Revelation.

After the Antichrist is healed, he will then dig in, planting his roots deeper to seize control of the world even more. From that specific moment of his healing, the majority of the nations will believe and follow him (v. 13:3).

"The ten horns which you saw are ten kings who have received no kingdom as yet, but they receive authority for one hour as kings with the beast" (v. 17:12). These ten kings, which shall rise with authority over the earth, are ten nations who will join by human alliances to monopolize and control the economy and politic worldwide, especially in the regions close to Israel. As discussed before, these ten horns (nations) refer to the European Union (EU), which now has a very important role throughout the Middle East and nearby nations.

The EU will take control, with the Antichrist as leader, of all kinds of trade, currency, entry and exit of people, and the armies of the regions that make up the partner nations. The Antichrist will seek control in all areas of life (economic, political, social, health, etc.). The EU will be the most valuable tool for the Antichrist's purpose, starting in the Middle East and spreading to dominate the entire world.

When I was working on this book (end of 2011), news from the Vatican began to spread throughout the entire world. A clear and public directive concerning the global government was spread: as a summary, the Vatican is promoting one global government with one leader with enough teeth to rule all nations. One bank in charge of all money flow, with one currency, is also proposed by the Vatican (Ref. 10).

The time is ready for the Antichrist's allies to take their position in support of the global empire commanded by the son of Satan, the Antichrist.

The Antichrist is a wicked man, chosen to accomplish the last judgment over the nations. He is a despicable man, who insults even God without any fear. Verses 13:5–7 describe what the Antichrist is and what he will do on the earth:

> And he was given a mouth speaking great things and blasphemies, and he was given authority to continue for forty-two months.
> Then he opened his mouth in blasphemy against God, to blaspheme His name, His tabernacle, and those who dwell in heaven.
> It was granted to him to make war with the saints and to overcome them. And authority was given him over every tribe, tongue, and nation.

There is no other word coming out from the mouth of the Antichrist but blasphemies and insults against the God Almighty and the faithful saints of the Lord.

Who are these "who dwell in heaven," mentioned in this passage, whom the Antichrist blasphemes day and night? In addition to God and the Lamb Jesus, these inhabitants of heaven are composed of the angels, the four heavenly creatures, the conquerors coming out of the Great Tribulation, and of course, the church that was taken away in the rapture before the Great Tribulation began. The Antichrist is full of hate against all those who are in heaven, the place of his past dwelling.

While the judgments of God upon the earth are being consummated, all these heavenly inhabitants do not cease to worship the One who lives forever, the God Almighty who reigns forever and ever; and the devil cannot stand this. The devil and his servant the Antichrist are very angry, because they know they have only a short time before the final defeat. Therefore, henceforth they come with all their forces against the saints, having full authority over all the inhabitants of the earth.

> I was watching; and the same horn was making war against the saints, and prevailing against them.
>
> Daniel 7:21

> If anyone has an ear, let him hear.
> He who leads into captivity shall go into captivity; he who kills with the sword must be killed with the sword. Here is the patience and the faith of the saints.
>
> Revelation 13:9–10

191

The Beast from the Earth and the Mark of the Beast

Revelation 13:11–18

> Then I saw another beast coming up out of the earth, and
> he had two horns like a lamb and spoke like a dragon.
> And he exercises all the authority of the first beast in his
> presence, and causes the earth and those who dwell in it to
> worship the first beast, whose deadly wound was healed.
> He performs great signs, so that he even makes fire come
> down from heaven on the earth in the sight of men.
> And he deceives those who dwell on the earth by those
> signs which he was granted to do in the sight of the beast,
> telling those who dwell on the earth to make an image to
> the beast who was wounded by the sword and lived.
> He was granted power to give breath to the image of the beast,
> that the image of the beast should both speak and cause as
> many as would not worship the image of the beast to be killed.
> He causes all, both small and great, rich and poor, free
> and slave, to receive a mark on their right hand or on their
> foreheads, and that no one may buy or sell except one who has
> the mark or the name of the beast, or the number of his name.
> Here is wisdom. Let him who has understanding calculate
> the number of the beast, for it is the number of a man: His
> number is 666.
>
> Revelation 13:11–18

This passage describes another beast that John saw coming out of the
earth (see figure 17: Beast Coming up from the Earth). This second beast
causes the people to worship the Antichrist. It commands an image of
the Antichrist to be made, and the inhabitants of the earth are required to
worship and bow before it. The mark of the beast, the number 666, shall
also be implemented at that time.

These two commands will take place after the Antichrist is healed
of his mortal wound. This beast with horns of a lamb (a gentle and good
animal), but speaking like a dragon (an evil and cunning beast), comes on
the scene to glorify the Antichrist. In this way it imitates the work of the
Holy Spirit who glorifies Jesus. In John 16:14–15, Jesus, speaking of the
Holy Spirit, says,

Figure 17: Beast Coming up from the Earth
(False Prophet)

He will glorify Me, for He will take of what is Mine and
declare it to you.
All things that the Father has are Mine. Therefore I said
that He will take of Mine and declare it to you.

This is what the second beast will clearly try to do—glorify the
Antichrist. This second beast, called in verses 16:13 and 19:20 the False
Prophet, performs great signs to convince the inhabitants of the earth to
believe and serve the Antichrist. He is a messenger of Satan, a greatly
corrupt and deceitful man, one who

causes all, both small and great, rich and poor, free and slave,
to receive a mark on their right hand or on their foreheads,
and that no one may buy or sell except one who has the mark
or the name of the beast, or the number of his name.
Revelation 13:16–17

The person who does not have this seal or mark cannot perform any
kind of transaction, nor buy or sell any product. All kinds of trade will be
100% controlled by the Antichrist. This requirement will be for all kinds
of persons, regardless of their social level, since "He causes all, both small
and great, rich and poor, free and slave, to receive a mark."

This mark is also an imitation of the seal mentioned in Ephesians 1:13,
"In Him you also trusted, after you heard the word of truth, the gospel of
your salvation; in whom also, having believed, you were sealed with the
Holy Spirit of promise." Remember that once someone is sealed, he is
owned by the one who sealed him, whether by God to eternal life, or by
the devil to perpetual doom. The person who resists the seal of the mark
will suffer much, and many will die.

Do not be deceived by interpretations without basis in the word of God.
Many people interpret this number 666 as having a symbolic meaning. But
the Scriptures are clear: they say that it is a number of man; there is nothing
complex to be misunderstood. This is the method the Antichrist will use
to control all kinds of business transactions throughout the nations. This
will not be too difficult for that time, when computer technology will be at
its maximum development.

I firmly believe that currency will no longer flow as it circulates today.
There will be no more cash flow. Purchases and sales transactions will
be carried out through electronic devices or credit cards, which will only
give access to those who are identified with the mark of the beast. Even if

a person has a million dollars in cash, he will not be able to use it unless he subjects to the electronic procedures governing at that time.

At the time of Nebuchadnezzar, king of Babylon, those who did not fall down and worship his image were cast into a burning fiery furnace (Daniel chapter 3). Now in the Great Tribulation, the punishment for those who do not worship the image of the beast and do not receive his mark will be the death by beheading.

> ... Then I saw the souls of those who had been beheaded for their witness to Jesus and for the word of God, who had not worshiped the beast or his image, and had not received his mark on their foreheads or on their hands. And they lived and reigned with Christ for a thousand years.
>
> Revelation 20:4

> He was granted power to give breath to the image of the beast, that the image of the beast should both speak and cause as many as would not worship the image of the beast to be killed.
>
> Revelation 13:15

This is part of the tricks and lies that these experts of evil will do in the sight of all mankind. With the help of advanced technology, it is not difficult to make an object or image to speak and move. This is not new in this "electronic age." Today there are electronic devices (robots) used to do cleaning jobs in homes, and they are programmed even to speak.

Dear reader, this is not a game or a fiction film. This is the manifestation of the work of Satan to trap the mankind forever. This mark, to be imposed by the Antichrist's government, will be the ticket of a sure entrance to hell, where there will be weeping and gnashing of teeth forever.

Verses 14:9–11 show what shall come to pass for those who receive the mark of the devil and worship his image. It says that they will drink of the wrath of God and will be tormented with fire and brimstone. Also it says that "the smoke of their torment ascends forever and ever; and they have no rest day or night, who worship the beast and his image, and whoever receives the mark of his name."

Your life is worth much more than you think; you were created for God's glory—to exalt the beauty of His holiness. Jesus Christ paid a great price to give us the opportunity to be delivered from the trial which shall come upon all nations, and to be found without blame by means of the redemptive work of Christ and the filling of the Holy Spirit. The Lord Jesus already paid the price so that we may now receive the inheritance of God, that is, eternal life with Him.

The Proclamations of Three Angels

Revelation 14:1–13

Verses 14:1–5 were already discussed in the passage 7:1–8 (please refer to this).

Hebrews 1:14, speaking of the work of angels in our favor, says, "Are they not all ministering spirits sent forth to minister for those who will inherit salvation?" There are millions of angels in heaven, created and instructed to minister according to the commands of God. At this time in the Great Tribulation, God sends three angels to proclaim certain messages to the worldwide population.

> Then I saw another angel flying in the midst of heaven, having the everlasting gospel to preach to those who dwell on the earth—to every nation, tribe, tongue, and people— saying with a loud voice, 'Fear God and give glory to Him, for the hour of His judgment has come …'
> Revelation 14:6–7

The everlasting gospel to be preached by the angels at the end time is not the same preaching that introduces us now to the body of Christ, the church. It is the gospel of entrance to the millennial kingdom.

The first angel announces that men should fear God, because the hour of His judgment has come. This angel is responsible for the declaration of one of the last warnings that the inhabitants of the earth might repent of their ways and believe in God.

God, in His great mercy, does not cease to warn men, so they have a chance to fear Him and be saved. I believe that this angel will not preach for many days, but his message will be short and specific. The continuous and complete preaching of the Gospel of the Kingdom in the Great Tribulation will mainly be charged to the 144,000 chosen Jews (vv. 7:1–8) and the two witnesses (vv. 11:1–12).

The message of the second angel (v. 14:8) will be discussed later in Revelation chapter 18 (please refer to this).

In verses 14:9–11, the third angel brings a warning to all those who yield before the pressure of the Antichrist to receive his mark. This angel warns of the punishment they will receive for eternity: "... shall also drink of the wine of the wrath of God ... shall be tormented with fire and brimstone ... have no rest day or night ..."

With the entry of the mark of the beast, the pressure on the faithful believers of the Lord will multiply and become extreme. The apostle John receives a message of encouragement to the saints who remain in the Great Tribulation, to withstand to the end:

> Here is the patience of the saints; here are those who keep the commandments of God and the faith of Jesus.
> Then I heard a voice from heaven saying to me, 'Write: "Blessed are the dead who die in the Lord from now on."'
> 'Yes,' says the Spirit, 'that they may rest from their labors, and their works follow them.'
>
> Revelation 14:12–13

Order to Reap the Earth

Revelation 14:14–20

"Then I looked, and behold, a white cloud, and on the cloud sat One like the Son of Man, having on His head a golden crown, and in His hand a sharp sickle" (v. 14:14). This is Christ, prepared for the hour that has come to punish the earth. The harvest of the earth is ripe, ready to be reaped. These grapes are not the saints who believe in God, but a crowd of people who belong to the largest army that has ever existed on the earth.

This army is composed of 200 million soldiers who come to fight against the saints in Jerusalem. "Now the number of the army of the horsemen was two hundred million; I heard the number of them" (v. 9:16). Although this subject will be considered in more detail in Revelation chapter 19, due to the direct relationship with chapter 14, I will refer here to verses 19:15–19.

Now out of His mouth goes a sharp sword, that with it He should strike the nations. And He Himself will rule them with a rod of iron. He Himself treads the winepress of the fierceness and wrath of Almighty God.
And He has on His robe and on His thigh a name written:

KING OF KINGS AND LORD OF LORDS.

Then I saw an angel standing in the sun; and he cried with a loud voice, saying to all the birds that fly in the midst of heaven, 'Come and gather together for the supper of the great God,
that you may eat the flesh of kings, the flesh of captains, the flesh of mighty men, the flesh of horses and of those who sit on them, and the flesh of all people, free and slave, both small and great.'
And I saw the beast, the kings of the earth, and their armies, gathered together to make war against Him who sat on the horse and against His army.

We see here that the armies of the ten nations (ten horns of the beast) will be part of the army of 200 million prepared to fight against the Lord, who will overcome them (vv. 17:12–14).

This great army will meet in a place outside the city of Jerusalem called Armageddon.

For they are spirits of demons, performing signs, which go out to the kings of the earth and of the whole world, to gather them to the battle of that great day of God Almighty. And they gathered them together to the place called in Hebrew, Armageddon.

Revelation 16:14, 16

Armageddon is a valley also known by other names, such as Valley of Megiddo, Valley of Jezreel, Valley of Esdraelon, Valley of Jehoshaphat, and the valley of decision (Joel 3:1–2, 11–14). The Valley of Armageddon, a name that only appears in Revelation chapter 16, has been the scene of many battles in biblical and non-biblical times.
This valley is located between Galilee and Samaria, and comprises

several mountains and valleys, such as Mount Tabor, Mount Carmel, and Mount Gilboa (see figure 14: Map of Israel).

The grapes (the soldiers) will be thrown into the great winepress of the wrath of God. A winepress is an enclosure where the grapes are trodden or squeezed to extract their juice. In this passage, the winepress means the lands that the soldiers will occupy, from which "blood came out of the winepress, up to the horses' bridles, for one thousand six hundred furlongs" (v. 14:20),

This harvest or gathering refers to the battle which will start at the Edom's wilderness and will extend along the strip of 1,600 furlongs, up to the great Battle of Armageddon. Here the loyal soldiers of the Antichrist will face off against the army of angels, who come with the Lord to end the evil of this world forever (vv. 19:14–15).

The entire army of 200 million soldiers of the Antichrist will be killed in such a way that their blood will cover the Valley of Armageddon and a strip of 1,600 furlongs, that is, about 288 kilometers (180 miles). (A furlong is a linear measure equivalent to approximately 180 meters—Ref. 11.)

> And the kings of the earth, the great men, the rich men, the commanders, the mighty men, every slave and every free man, hid themselves in the caves and in the rocks of the mountains, and said to the mountains and rocks, 'Fall on us and hide us from the face of Him who sits on the throne and from the wrath of the Lamb!
> For the great day of His wrath has come, and who is able to stand?'
>
> Revelation 6:15–17

In the section covering Revelation 12:1–17, *The Woman Persecuted by the Dragon*, the siege of Israel in Edom is described in detail. That section describes what will happen with the Lord in His coming to the land of Edom, as His first place of attack, along with His angels. There are 180 miles from the northern part of the Valley of Megiddo (Armageddon) to the wilderness of Edom, where the remnant of Israel will be besieged—and this distance is not incidental.

Many people say that this distance (1,600 furlongs) is symbolic. But we must ask ourselves why the Scriptures describe this measure with such accuracy. It is definitely not symbolic, and it is not a coincidence.

Therefore, according to verse 14:20, everything seems to indicate that the blood of the 200 million soldiers shall be spread from Edom to the

Valley of Megiddo, that is, from the two ends where the biggest battle will take place, and where the largest army of evil will be gathered together (see figure 14).

This means that after the Lord destroys the army assembled in Edom, along with its inhabitants, He will then continue His course to Megiddo, killing all the soldiers found along the distance of 180 miles, until His final victory against the remaining army in Armageddon. This massacre will produce a "strip" of blood 180 miles long. So many will be the dead of the enemy in this strip of land, that their blood will reach up to the horses' bridles—about four to five feet high.

This will be the great banquet prepared for the birds of prey (vv. 19:17–18, 21). "For wherever the carcass is, there the eagles will be gathered together" (Matt. 24:28). After the Lord Jesus and His angels defeat the great army of the Antichrist in Armageddon, they will then continue to the Mount of Olives in Jerusalem, where Jesus will place His feet and establish His millennial kingdom.

The events described in verses 14:14–20 refer to the battle in the wilderness of Edom, including the 1,600 furlongs strip. Verses 19:11–21 refer to the Battle of Armageddon. There are several passages directly related to the events mentioned in Revelation chapter 14. I will just mention a couple of them.

> For behold, in those days and at that time, when I bring back the captives of Judah and Jerusalem,
> I will also gather all nations, and bring them down to the Valley of Jehoshaphat; and I will enter into judgment with them there on account of My people, My heritage Israel, whom they have scattered among the nations; they have also divided up My land.
> Assemble and come, all you nations, and gather together all around. Cause Your mighty ones to go down there, O Lord.
> 'Let the nations be wakened, and come up to the Valley of Jehoshaphat; for there I will sit to judge all the surrounding nations.
> Put in the sickle, for the harvest is ripe. Come, go down; for the winepress is full, the vats overflow—for their wickedness is great.'

Multitudes, multitudes in the valley of decision! For the day of the Lord is near in the valley of decision.

Joel 3:1–2, 11–14

The prophet Isaiah also reveals the events to occur from Edom to Armageddon, when he says in verses 34:1–5,

> Come near, you nations, to hear; and heed, you people! Let the earth hear, and all that is in it, the world and all things that come forth from it.
> For the indignation of the Lord is against all nations, and His fury against all their armies; He has utterly destroyed them, He has given them over to the slaughter.
> Also their slain shall be thrown out; their stench shall rise from their corpses, and the mountains shall be melted with their blood.
> All the host of heaven shall be dissolved, and the heavens shall be rolled up like a scroll; all their host shall fall down as the leaf falls from the vine, and as fruit falling from a fig tree.
> 'For My sword shall be bathed in heaven; indeed it shall come down on Edom, and on the people of My curse, for judgment.'

The Seven Angels with the Seven Bowls of the Wrath of God

Revelation 15:1–8

John saw seven angels who had the seven last plagues by which God will show His final wrath upon the inhabitants of the earth. Seven golden bowls were given to these angels, full of the wrath of God.

We must understand that what is presented in chapter 15 will not be chronologically fulfilled after the events described in the preceding chapters. On the contrary, the events to take place through the seven bowls will be fulfilled before the "harvest" described at the end of chapter 14.

Verses 15:2–4 were already discussed in the comments on verses 7:1–8.

The Seven Bowls of the Wrath of God

Revelation 16:1–21

The plagues and signs to be manifested at this time are similar to those identified with the seven trumpets in chapters 8, 9, and 11, and with the two witnesses in chapter 11 of Revelation. All these judgments are the same, described in different ways. These plagues and signs are also similar to those performed through God's servant Moses at the time of Israel's exodus from Egypt. If these signs were a reality in that time, they shall also be real (not symbolic) in the time of the Great Tribulation.

There is a direct connection between the works and signs through the two witnesses and all the judgments described to occur after the halfway point of the Great Tribulation. In other words, at the same time God announces a judgment from heaven, the two witnesses pray to God for that judgment to fall on the earth.

This is why, after the death of the two witnesses at the end of the Great Tribulation, "those who dwell on the earth will rejoice over them, make merry, and send gifts to one another, because these two prophets tormented those who dwell on the earth" (v. 11:10). These two witnesses are always active, carrying out the signs under God's command.

In this passage, we see now seven angels pouring out seven bowls of the wrath of God upon the earth. Through these trials, we clearly see that those who received the mark of the Antichrist shall not escape from the plagues and signs to come over the entire earth. Although they think that they have the "privilege" of obtaining food and are qualified for marketing, they will certainly suffer the deserved punishment of their bad deeds.

As we will see below, many of these trials will fall exclusively "upon the men who had the mark of the beast and those who worshiped his image" (v. 16:2). We will also see that the majority of the worldwide population in the last days will not repent of their sins, although the judgment of God falls upon them. They are rebel and sinners, as the apostle Paul well describes them in his second letter to Timothy:

> But know this, that in the last days perilous times will come:
> For men will be lovers of themselves, lovers of money, boasters, proud, blasphemers, disobedient to parents, unthankful, unholy, unloving, unforgiving, slanderers,

without self-control, brutal, despisers of good, traitors, headstrong, haughty, lovers of pleasure rather than lovers of God, having a form of godliness but denying its power. And from such people turn away!
But evil men and impostors will grow worse and worse, deceiving and being deceived.

2 Timothy 3:1–5, 13

First Bowl

With the pouring out of the first bowl, foul and loathsome sores come upon the people who have the mark of the beast. This plague will produce irresistible pain. This will be an exclusive trial for non-believers, servants of Satan, who already "signed" their sentence of condemnation as they were sealed with the number 666.

Similarly, this was one of the plagues that fell upon the unbelieving Egyptians at the time of Moses. "Then they took ashes from the furnace and stood before Pharaoh, and Moses scattered them toward heaven. And they caused boils that break out in sores on man and beast" (Ex. 9:10).

These sores are not simple and small eruptions on the skin, since verse 16:11 says that men "blasphemed the God of heaven because of their pains and their sores, and did not repent of their deeds." Exodus 9:11 also says that "the magicians could not stand before Moses because of the boils, for the boils were on the magicians and on all the Egyptians."

As stated before, the judgments mentioned in the Book of Revelation are shown through four different points of view: the seven seals, the seven trumpets, the seven bowls, and the two witnesses. These four groups of judgments occur simultaneously. For example, with the command of the two witnesses who "have power ... to strike the earth with all plagues, as often as they desire" (v. 11:6), this sign of sores shall happen.

Second and Third Bowls

When the second and third bowls are poured, the water bodies (sea, rivers, and springs of water) become blood as of a dead man, and every living creature in them dies. The sea referenced in this passage could be the Mediterranean Sea, located to the west of Israel. Let us remember that the emergence of these plagues and signs will mainly be in Israel and its surrounding regions, although they will also affect the inhabitants of all the other nations.

This plague also fell on Egypt when the Pharaoh, by his stubbornness, did not let the people of Israel go to worship God on Mount Sinai.

> Thus says the Lord: 'By this you shall know that I am the Lord. Behold, I will strike the waters which are in the river with the rod that is in my hand, and they shall be turned to blood.
> And the fish that are in the river shall die, the river shall stink, and the Egyptians will loathe to drink the water of the river.'
> Then the Lord spoke to Moses, 'Say to Aaron, "Take your rod and stretch out your hand over the waters of Egypt, over their streams, over their rivers, over their ponds, and over all their pools of water, that they may become blood. And there shall be blood throughout all the land of Egypt, both in buckets of wood and pitchers of stone."' ...
>
> Exodus 7:17–21

It is commonly known that dead marine creatures, after they become rotten, produce a stench so unpleasant that it is very difficult to tolerate. The blood in the water bodies will aggravate the situation even more, contaminating the waters so that they cannot be used. The angel announces (and Isaiah also talks about this),

> For they have shed the blood of saints and prophets, and You have given them blood to drink. For it is their just due.
>
> Revelation 16:6

> For behold, the Lord comes out of His place to punish the inhabitants of the earth for their iniquity; the earth will also disclose her blood, and will no more cover her slain.
>
> Isaiah 26:21

Because the unbelieving Jews killed the saints and prophets sent by God, and even Jesus, these plagues will come upon them.

> Therefore, indeed, I send you prophets, wise men, and scribes: some of them you will kill and crucify, and some of them you will scourge in your synagogues and persecute

from city to city, that on you may come all the righteous
blood shed on the earth, from the blood of righteous Abel
to the blood of Zechariah, son of Berechiah, whom you
murdered between the temple and the altar.
Assuredly, I say to you, all these things will come upon
this generation.

Matthew 23:34–36

This sign of blood in the water bodies occurs when the second and third
bowls are poured out. This sign is performed similarly when the second
trumpet is sounded and with the two witnesses:

Then the second angel sounded: And something like a
great mountain burning with fire was thrown into the sea,
and a third of the sea became blood.
And a third of the living creatures in the sea died ...
... and they [witnesses] have power over waters to turn
them to blood ...

Revelation 8:8–9; 11:6

Fourth Bowl

Then the fourth angel poured out his bowl on the sun, and
power was given to him to scorch men with fire.
And men were scorched with great heat, and they
blasphemed the name of God who has power over these
plagues; and they did not repent and give Him glory.

Revelation 16:8–9

Verse 7:16 says that the believers emerging from the Great Tribulation
shall not have heat anymore, which leads us to understand that they were
present at the time of the fourth bowl plague. Isaiah 13:13 says, "Therefore
I will shake the heavens, and the earth will move out of her place, in the
wrath of the Lord of hosts and in the day of His fierce anger."

It is possible that as the earth moves from its place, its orbit changes
around the sun and then approaches closer to the sun, producing such
intense heat on the earth that it burns a lot of people. The earth is surrounded
by a chemical substance called ozone, which protects human beings from
the ultraviolet rays emitted by the sun. This ozone is an unstable triatomic

molecule called resonance hybrid, which in the presence of certain volatile chemicals reacts, then changing to oxygen molecules.

It may happen by that time that because there is so much pollution on the earth, chemicals will reach the ozone layer, deteriorating it significantly. Thus, the ozone layer will cease to have one of its wonderful functions—protecting us from solar rays.

Whether one way or another, at the time of the fourth bowl the sun will produce a heat so intense that it will burn up human beings. Thousands of children and elderly will die due to this plague. Even so, men will continue blaspheming God and will not repent of their wrongdoings.

Fifth Bowl

The fifth bowl was poured

> on the throne of the beast, and his kingdom became full of darkness; and they gnawed their tongues because of the pain.
> They blasphemed the God of heaven because of their pains and their sores, and did not repent of their deeds.
>
> Revelation 16:10–11

This plague will fall on Jerusalem, where the throne of the Antichrist will be. 2 Thessalonians 2:4, speaking of the Antichrist, says, "who opposes and exalts himself above all that is called God or that is worshiped, so that he sits as God in the temple of God, showing himself that he is God" (see also Matthew 24:15 and Daniel 11:31).

So far, these plagues have produced great suffering for all who have the mark of the beast (although as we have said before, all the inhabitants of the earth will also be affected). They suffer so greatly from these plagues, that after the death of the two witnesses, by whom these plagues occur, "those who dwell on the earth will rejoice over them, make merry, and send gifts to one another, because these two prophets tormented those who dwell on the earth" (v. 11:10).

This fifth plague is targeted to the Antichrist and his "staff." I have no idea how long this dense darkness upon the city of Jerusalem will last, but I think the Antichrist will not be happy with this plague on his throne. No matter what power or authority this minister of the devil has, he shall not dissipate this dense darkness which will make his life very difficult.

This darkness is similar to the one occurred in Egypt. The darkness in Egypt was so dense that a person could not see his partner even if they were face to face.

> Then the Lord said to Moses, 'Stretch out your hand toward heaven, that there may be darkness over the land of Egypt, darkness which may even be felt.'
> So Moses stretched out his hand toward heaven, and there was thick darkness in all the land of Egypt three days.
> They did not see one another; nor did anyone rise from his place for three days. But all the children of Israel had light in their dwellings.
>
> Exodus 10:21–23

At the same time this sign of darkness happens, similar signs are occurring with the sound of the fourth trumpet ("Then the fourth angel sounded: And a third of the sun was struck, a third of the moon, and a third of the stars, so that a third of them were darkened. A third of the day did not shine, and likewise the night"—v. 8:12), and with the two witnesses (v. 11:6).

Sixth Bowl

> Then the sixth angel poured out his bowl on the great river Euphrates, and its water was dried up, so that the way of the kings from the east might be prepared.
> And I saw three unclean spirits like frogs coming out of the mouth of the dragon, out of the mouth of the beast, and out of the mouth of the false prophet.
> For they are spirits of demons, performing signs, which go out to the kings of the earth and of the whole world, to gather them to the battle of that great day of God Almighty.
> 'Behold, I am coming as a thief. Blessed is he who watches, and keeps his garments, lest he walk naked and they see his shame.'
> And they gathered them together to the place called in Hebrew, Armageddon.
>
> Revelation 16:12–16

With the pouring out of the sixth bowl, the great river Euphrates, located in the modern Iraq, is dried up. This provides to the kings of the east, with their armies, to go across and move together with other coalition countries to the Valley of Armageddon, where they will gather for the great battle against the people of God.

The military forces who meet in this valley come from all over the world, to fight by the side of the dragon (Satan) and the beast (Antichrist). This great army composed of 200 million soldiers will all be killed in the battle against Jesus and His angels (see comments on passages 9:13–16 and 14:14–20).

Three spirits of demons coming out of the mouths of the three beasts (dragon—Satan, beast which emerges from the sea—Antichrist, and the beast coming out of the earth—False Prophet) have the task of going throughout the world to bring together the biggest army ever to exist on the earth, for the final battle against Jesus and His heavenly hosts.

It is important to note that Satan, shown to the apostle John as the dragon, will be present in person, together with the Antichrist and the False Prophet, on the earth at the time of these final events.

At the same time this sign related to the gathering of this great army of the Antichrist is happening, a similar sign is occurring with the sound of the sixth trumpet:

> … 'Release the four angels who are bound at the great river Euphrates.'
> So the four angels, who had been prepared for the hour and day and month and year, were released to kill a third of mankind.
> Now the number of the army of the horsemen was two hundred million; I heard the number of them.
> Revelation 9:14–16

Seventh Bowl

> Then the seventh angel poured out his bowl into the air, and a loud voice came out of the temple of heaven, from the throne, saying, *'It is done!'*
> And there were noises and thunderings and lightnings; and there was a great earthquake, such a mighty and great

earthquake as had not occurred since men were on the earth.

Now the great city was divided into three parts, and the cities of the nations fell. And great Babylon was remembered before God, to give her the cup of the wine of the fierceness of His wrath.

Then every island fled away, and the mountains were not found.

And great hail from heaven fell upon men, each hailstone about the weight of a talent. Men blasphemed God because of the plague of the hail, since that plague was exceedingly great.

Revelation 16:17–21

What a great and frightening spectacle we see now on the face of the earth! I imagine the apostle John shocked by this scenario: noises, thunders, lightnings, voices, a great earthquake, division of Jerusalem into three parts, the cities of the nations destroyed, islands fleeing away or moving out of their places, the mountains falling, and huge hailstones from heaven.

When in the history of mankind has anything been seen akin to this, even on a smaller scale? The time has come for the Lord Jesus to finally fulfill every word uttered by Him through the prophets and apostles; that is why we hear the utterance, *It is done!*

This statement marks the completion of *this generation*, which covers the time from Jesus' birth to His second coming, as Mathew 24:34 says, "Assuredly, I say to you, this generation will by no means pass away till all these things take place."

The apostle John saw many things never seen by any other human being, such as the disappearance of islands, mountains fading, the division of Jerusalem into three parts, and the destruction of nations. Jesus will fight against those nations gathered in the Valley of Armageddon. He will then stand on the Mount of Olives in Jerusalem, and all the earth will experience in that moment the greatest and most devastating earthquake in all its history.

This geological phenomenon will transform the topography of many cities, including Jerusalem—and this region will become a valley. These events to happen at the latter time were prophesied by several prophets, such as Zechariah and Isaiah, who wrote in their books the following:

> And in that day His feet will stand on the Mount of Olives, which faces Jerusalem on the east. And the Mount of Olives shall be split in two, from east to west, making a very large valley; half of the mountain shall move toward the north and half of it toward the south.
>
> All the land shall be turned into a plain from Geba to Rimmon south of Jerusalem. Jerusalem shall be raised up and inhabited in her place from Benjamin's Gate to the place of the First Gate and the Corner Gate, and from the Tower of Hananel to the king's winepresses.
>
> Zechariah 14:4, 10

> Therefore I will shake the heavens, and the earth will move out of her place, in the wrath of the LORD of hosts and in the day of His fierce anger.
>
> Isaiah 13:13

These same signs are described with the sixth and seventh seals, and finally with the seventh trumpet:

> Then the sky receded as a scroll when it is rolled up, and every mountain and island was moved out of its place.
>
> And the kings of the earth, the great men, the rich men, the commanders, the mighty men, every slave and every free man, hid themselves in the caves and in the rocks of the mountains, and said to the mountains and rocks, 'Fall on us and hide us from the face of Him who sits on the throne and from the wrath of the Lamb!
>
> For the great day of His wrath has come, and who is able to stand?'
>
> Revelation 6:14–17

> When He opened the seventh seal ...
>
> Then the angel took the censer, filled it with fire from the altar, and threw it to the earth. And there were noises, thunderings, lightnings, and an earthquake.
>
> Revelation 8:1, 5

> Then the seventh angel sounded: And there were loud voices in heaven, saying ...

Then the temple of God was opened in heaven, and the ark of His covenant was seen in His temple. And there were lightnings, noises, thunderings, an earthquake, and great hail.

Revelation 11:15, 19

The Great Harlot

Revelation 17 and 18

Because the events described in chapters 17 and 18 refer to the same subject, these two chapters will be considered together, since the word contained in one enhances the other. Verses 17:7–13 will not be considered here because they were already discussed in the passage 13:1–10.

Then one of the seven angels who had the seven bowls came and talked with me, saying to me, 'Come, I will show you the judgment of the great harlot who sits on many waters, with whom the kings of the earth committed fornication, and the inhabitants of the earth were made drunk with the wine of her fornication.'
So he carried me away in the Spirit into the wilderness. And I saw a woman sitting on a scarlet beast which was full of names of blasphemy, having seven heads and ten horns.
The woman was arrayed in purple and scarlet, and adorned with gold and precious stones and pearls, having in her hand a golden cup full of abominations and the filthiness of her fornication.
And on her forehead a name was written:

MYSTERY, BABYLON THE GREAT,
THE MOTHER OF HARLOTS AND OF THE
ABOMINATIONS OF THE EARTH.

> I saw the woman, drunk with the blood of the saints and
> with the blood of the martyrs of Jesus. And when I saw
> her, I marveled with great amazement.
>
> Revelation 17:1–6

It is my full understanding that the great harlot depicted in these passages represents the largest religious institution in the world, the so-called Roman Catholic Church. These two chapters reveal the characteristics that identify her as the great harlot, in a spiritual sense, and also describe how her destruction will come. Some expositors think that the name Babylon in these chapters refers to the ancient Babylon, modern-day Iraq.

In order to provide the most clarity possible on this matter, a list of the characteristics which distinguish the Catholic Church as "Babylon the great" and "the great harlot" is provided.

1. Underline: She is called a harlot

> ... Come, I will show you the judgment of the great harlot
> who sits on many waters.
> And on her forehead a name was written: Mystery, Babylon
> the great, the mother of harlots and of the abominations
> of the earth.
>
> Revelation 17:1, 5

A harlot is a woman who has continuous sexual relations with many men, resulting in adulteries. We can mention three types of harlots: one acting for remuneration, either money or something else of value or interest; another acting for delight; and a third who combines the two previous types. The case here does not refer to a woman, but to a religious institution.

As a matter of example, the nation of Israel was called an adulteress when she left God to serve another gods or idols. Ezekiel 23:37 says, "For they have committed adultery, and blood is on their hands. They have committed adultery with their idols, and even sacrificed their sons whom they bore to Me, passing them through the fire, to devour them."

The woman whom the apostle John saw is called the great harlot, mother of harlots; therefore, she is not a common harlot, but a special one of great influence and authority, the chief and mother of all other harlots. This woman is the Catholic Church, the largest religious institution that has ever existed on earth, which teaches how to worship and serve idols of wood, iron, and other materials.

This religious institution also teaches its followers to worship and serve creatures like us, such as the apostles and other saints of God. One of her major practices is to pay special homage to Mary, Jesus' mother, even using an object called rosary to in her name intercede for the dead and to ask petitions to God.

This so-called church chooses servants and faithful men of her organization who have died, to canonize (declare them saints), to then pay them reverence and veneration. This has been a practice which yields much fruit to that institution, because this type of activity attracts many people from the communities, especially from their birth' countries.

Therefore, as this religious institution worships (they would say "venerates") images or idols and pays homage and spiritual services to the dead, she is, in God's eyes, a spiritual adulteress or harlot. There is no other like her worldwide.

Moreover, as the Catholic Church is called *mother of harlots*, we understand that she has many daughters who imitate her and take part in her actions. She has also been called by many people *the Mother and Mistress of all churches of Rome and the world.*

These daughters might be all those religious institutions which in one way or another have also made its followers to prostitute, obeying the words of men and not serving God with all obedience and fear to His word. Many of these religions, daughters of the great harlot, have leaders serving for money, fame, power, or something else that does not honor the name of God. The apostle Paul warned about these deceivers, when he said,

> For I know this, that after my departure savage wolves will come in among you, not sparing the flock.
> Also from among yourselves men will rise up, speaking perverse things, to draw away the disciples after themselves.
>
> Acts 20:29–30

> Not everyone who says to Me, 'Lord, Lord,' shall enter the kingdom of heaven, but he who does the will of My Father in heaven.
>
> Matthew 7:21

The true children of God are those redeemed by the blood of Christ, filled with the Holy Spirit, and living a life in holiness, pleasing the Lord in everything.

Verse 17:2 says that kings and inhabitants of the earth have fornicated with this woman. Verses 18:3 and 9 also say,

> For all the nations have drunk of the wine of the wrath of her fornication, the kings of the earth have committed fornication with her.
> The kings of the earth who committed fornication and lived luxuriously with her will weep and lament for her, when they see the smoke of her burning.

This is a religious fornication, from which many leaders of nations have not been able to escape, for in seeking the favor of this institution, they have surrendered to the idolatry which she promotes.

Ancient Babylon had authority and influence only on regional areas (the Middle East, part of Africa and Europe, and Israel), not worldwide as the Catholic Church has had for many centuries. These passages above describe how the kings (leaders) of the nations of the earth were subject to the powerful actions of this "woman," committing fornication and living a lustful life with her.

2. She is seated on many waters

> Come, I will show you the judgment of the great harlot who sits on many waters.
> Then he said to me, 'The waters which you saw, where the harlot sits, are peoples, multitudes, nations, and tongues'
> Revelation 17:1, 15

> O you who dwell by many waters, abundant in treasures, your end has come, the measure of your covetousness.
> Jeremiah 51:13

By this interpretation offered by the same Scriptures, it is clearly understood that this woman, that is, the Catholic Church, is present in all places worldwide, which is an indisputable fact. She exerts authority and influence over all nations.

What person, institution, kingdom, or government (including the ancient and actual Babylon) do you know, apart from the Catholic Church, is present in all places on earth and has so much authority and influence over the rulers of the nations? Such is her authority that the headquarters of this institution in Rome, known as the Holy See or Vatican City, is considered by all nations as a sovereign city-state, having her own embassies for official worldwide representation.

History tells us that in ancient times the Roman Catholic Church placed and took away kings, so they obeyed her ordinances. Remember that by the time of the apostle John, Rome controlled politically all this region, including Israel.

Rome will play a dual role in the Great Tribulation, having authority over the nations in both religious and political points of view. Rome will reign from the Vatican from the religious point of view, represented in the prophecy by the great harlot.

I will not go into detail about the origin of the Catholic Church, but it is commonly known that this religious institution emerged from a direct relationship with the Roman Empire. Even her official name is the Roman Catholic Church.

On the other hand, Rome will rule politically again through the European Union, represented in the prophecy by the ten horns of the beast.

The beast mentioned in verse 17:3 with seven heads and ten horns is the same beast mentioned in chapter 13, which represents the Antichrist, who along with the ten nations and the great harlot, will govern the entire world for a short time.

Christ has a wife, His church, which is virgin, holy, and spotless. The Antichrist will emulate this; so he will have his wife too, but this one is not without spot, but a harlot (in spiritual sense), the Roman Catholic Church.

That is why she says of herself that she is not a widow and lives in delights. "In the measure that she glorified herself and lived luxuriously, in the same measure give her torment and sorrow; for she says in her heart, 'I sit as queen, and am no widow, and will not see sorrow'" (v. 18:7).

3. She is a great city, settled on seven mountains

> Here is the mind which has wisdom: The seven heads are
> seven mountains on which the woman sits.
> And the woman whom you saw is that great city which
> reigns over the kings of the earth.
>
> Revelation 17:9, 18

The city of Rome is notorious for being settled among seven hills. There are, of course, other cities that were established on seven hills, such as Jerusalem and Rio de Janeiro in Brazil. But none of these two match the description found in the Book of Revelation. Even with this affirmation, we need more characteristics to limit the identification to Rome as the city of the great harlot of Revelation.

Rome, capital of Italy, is seated on seven hills named as follows: Capitoline, Quirinal, Viminal, Esquiline, Caelian, Aventine, and Palatine (Ref. 12). Rome is located approximately 24 kilometers (15 miles) from the Tyrrhenian Sea, which connects with the Mediterranean Sea. This city, including the Vatican, has also been called for a long time *the Eternal City* and *the Queen of Nations*.

Pursuant to this last name, verse 18:7 says: "... for she says in her heart, 'I sit as queen, and am no widow, and will not see sorrow.'" How accurate and true is the word of God!

The design and construction of the Vatican has no parallel. There is great wealth (gold, precious stones, etc.) on the walls, ceilings, floors, and in different rooms of the Vatican's structures. Verses 18:16–19 say,

> ... 'Alas, alas, that great city that was clothed in fine linen,
> purple, and scarlet, and adorned with gold and precious
> stones and pearls!
> For in one hour such great riches came to nothing.' ...
> ... 'What is like this great city?'
> ... 'Alas, alas, that great city, in which all who had ships
> on the sea became rich by her wealth! For in one hour she
> is made desolate.'

As the Catholic Church is also called a city, it is a clear imitation of the true church of God, which is called *the holy city, the New Jerusalem* (v. 21:2).

4. She uses a particular clothing

"The woman was arrayed in purple and scarlet, and adorned with gold and precious stones and pearls, having in her hand a golden cup full of abominations and the filthiness of her fornication" (v. 17:4; see also v. 18:16). This clothing is very similar to that used by Catholic priests—intense colors such as red, violet, and green.

They also use a golden chalice in their religious services. The Vatican, where the so-called pope resides as prince of all Catholic priests in the world, is built and adorned with gold and precious stones. It is a place full of idols, wealth, and much splendor. The buildings have walls covered with gold. The wealth accumulated in this place is so vast that it cannot even be estimated.

5. She carries a very particular name

"And on her forehead a name was written: Mystery, Babylon the Great, the Mother of Harlots and of the Abominations of the Earth" (v.17:5). The word Babylon comes from the word *babel*, which means confusion (Genesis 11:9). Here the great harlot is called "Babylon the great," that is, the great confusion.

The Catholic Church has misled many kings, rich and poor people, free and slaves. The doctrines preached in this religious institution do not conform to the teachings of God's word, resulting in much confusion and deception. Both the content and the method of their religious ceremonies are based on writings of men, not subject to biblical teachings.

This institution is also called *Mother of the Abominations of the Earth*, for many inhabitants of the earth have sinned and corrupted their lives through its idolatry and exercise of questionable rituals, very similar to spiritualist activities: for example, lighting candles to dead. Therefore, says the Lord,

Come out of her, my people, lest you share in her sins, and lest you receive of her plagues.

Revelation 18:4

Therefore

> "Come out from among them
> And be separate, says the Lord.
> Do not touch what is unclean,
> And I will receive you.
> I will be a Father to you,
> And you shall be My sons and daughters,
> Says the Lord Almighty."
>
> 2 Corinthians 6:17–18

6. <u>She has a history of homicide</u>

"I saw the woman, drunk with the blood of the saints and with the blood of the martyrs of Jesus. And when I saw her, I marveled with great amazement" (v. 17:6).

What does it mean that this woman is drunk with the blood of the saints and martyrs of Jesus? Many believers in God have lost their lives through criminal operations led by this religious institution. Clear examples of this are the events of the so-called Holy Inquisition.

The Holy Inquisition was an ecclesiastical tribunal created by the Catholic Church at the beginning of the Middle Age (AD 1231), under the rule of Pope Gregory IX. The purpose of this tribunal was to punish the "violators" of the Catholic faith. The judges or inquisitors (usually priests belonging to the Catholic Dominican Order, founded AD 1216) worked in the investigation, persecution, and judgment of those who were identified as heretics.

If the accused ones did not relinquish what they believed (that which was contrary to Catholic teachings), they were found guilty of heresy against the Catholic faith and sentenced to death at the bonfire.

Many kinds of torture were also used to obtain confessions from the defendants (Ref. 13). That is why, in addition to verse 17:6, the passage in 18:24 says that "in her was found the blood of prophets and saints, and of all who were slain on the earth."

Much has been written of the agreements between the Catholic Church and leaders of the Nazi army during World War II. It has even been said that this religious institution worked to help many Nazis escape at the end of this cruel and disastrous war.

7. <u>She produces religious merchandise and idolatry</u>

> And the merchants of the earth will weep and mourn over
> her, for no one buys their merchandise anymore:
> merchandise of gold and silver, precious stones and pearls,
> fine linen and purple, silk and scarlet, every kind of citron
> wood, every kind of object of ivory, every kind of object
> of most precious wood, bronze, iron, and marble; and
> cinnamon and incense, fragrant oil and frankincense,
> wine and oil, fine flour and wheat, cattle and sheep, horses
> and chariots, and bodies and souls of men.
> The fruit that your soul longed for has gone from you, and
> all the things which are rich and splendid have gone from
> you, and you shall find them no more at all.
> The merchants of these things, who became rich by her,
> will stand at a distance for fear of her torment, weeping
> and wailing.
>
> Revelation 18:11–15

This passage describes the merchants crying when they see
the Vatican City in Rome (here called Babylon) burning in fire.
They weep and lament because no one shall buy their merchandise
anymore. Among these goods are articles and idols (images) of
gold, precious stones, and other materials and products. These
businesses produced large profits (vv. 18:3, 19) to many people
and companies.

Acts 19:23–27 describe an event that happened in Ephesus.
Certain craftsmen of images lost substantial earnings because
many people stopped buying their idols as the consequence of the
apostle Paul's preaching. The craftsmen said, "Men, you know that
we have our prosperity by this trade."

There are many articles and products (candles, ornaments,
crucifixes, etc.) which are manufactured to meet a great demand
for Catholic religious rites and activities. Thousands of people
profit much from the sale of these things. Romans 1:22–25 says:

> Professing to be wise, they became fools, and changed the
> glory of the incorruptible God into an image made like
> corruptible man—and birds and four-footed animals and
> creeping things.

Therefore God also gave them up to uncleanness, in the lusts of their hearts, to dishonor their bodies among themselves, who exchanged the truth of God for the lie, and worshiped and served the creature rather than the Creator, who is blessed forever. Amen.

Another thing that produces large profits for this religious institution is the merchandising of slaves and souls of men, as it appears in the above-mentioned passage: "... and bodies and souls of men" (v 18:13).

A very particular characteristic of the Catholic Church is that many people pay this institution a large quantity of money to intercede for the souls of dead people so that they can be "saved." This is why the passage says that she markets "bodies and souls of men."

The doctrine of the Catholic Church provides that through the intercession of Catholic priests, the souls of dead people, who are supposedly in what they call purgatory, can be saved and go to heaven. According to their teaching, purgatory is a place of penitence where souls incompletely purified will purge their faults.

8. She is creator of rites and questionable activities

The sound of harpists, musicians, flutists, and trumpeters shall not be heard in you anymore. No craftsman of any craft shall be found in you anymore, and the sound of a millstone shall not be heard in you anymore.
The light of a lamp shall not shine in you anymore, and the voice of bridegroom and bride shall not be heard in you anymore. For your merchants were the great men of the earth, for by your sorcery all the nations were deceived.

Revelation 18:22–23

There are many unscriptural practices which are an integral part of the activities of this religious institution. The craftsmen are those who make images and idols, by which the followers of this religion are greatly deceived.

Lighting candles and making intercession for the souls of dead people are similar to the activities of those who practice sorcery and spiritualism. All these are part of doubtful rites that have misled many people.

Precisely when this book was being completed (September 2013), The New York Times newspaper quoted a recent interview with Pope Francis in *America* magazine, relating to his position on remarried people and homosexuals (Ref. 14). He talked about his vision of the church, and why he has chosen not to spend much time talking about abortion, gay marriage, and contraception.

He explained what he meant by the headline-grabbing remark he made about gay people: "Who am I to judge?" The Pope said that in response to a question once posed to him, he replied: "Tell me: when God looks at a gay person, does he endorse the existence of this person with love, or reject and condemn this person? We must always consider the person."

The pope articulated his vision of an inclusive church—a "home for all." "We have to find a new balance; otherwise even the moral edifice of the church is likely to fall like a house of cards, losing the freshness and fragrance of the Gospel." Dear reader, what do you think about these comments?

God has declared His punishment against this religious institution which has most confused the world, so He says: "And great Babylon was remembered before God, to give her the cup of the wine of the fierceness of His wrath" (v. 16:19). The Lord will use the Antichrist's hosts to destroy the great harlot, the Catholic Church. Verses 17:16–17 indicate that

> the ten horns which you saw on the beast, these will hate
> the harlot, make her desolate and naked, eat her flesh and
> burn her with fire.
> For God has put it into their hearts to fulfill His purpose,
> to be of one mind, and to give their kingdom to the beast,
> until the words of God are fulfilled.

This passage offers a clear picture of how the European Union (ten horns) will hate the Catholic Church to the extent that they will destroy her, burning her See in Rome with fire. The explanation of why the European Union will destroy the Catholic Church is found in the next paragraphs. This judgment will come to pass sometime before the end of the Great Tribulation, with the announcement of the seventh trumpet.

The apostle John saw an angel descending from heaven, crying mightily with a loud voice saying, "Babylon the great is fallen, is fallen, and has become a dwelling place of demons, a prison for every foul spirit, and a cage for every unclean and hated bird!" (v. 18:2). Such will be the city of Rome, including the Vatican, after her destruction. As she has glorified herself and lived in delights, so she will be given torments and crying.

> Therefore her plagues will come in one day—death and mourning and famine. And she will be utterly burned with fire, for strong is the Lord God who judges her.
> The kings of the earth who committed fornication and lived luxuriously with her will weep and lament for her, when they see the smoke of her burning,
> standing at a distance for fear of her torment, saying, 'Alas, alas, that great city Babylon, that mighty city! For in one hour your judgment has come.'
>
> Revelation 18:8–10

All those who work on the sea will stop and look from afar with regret for this city, as they see the smoke from her fire.

> 'For in one hour such great riches came to nothing.' Every shipmaster, all who travel by ship, sailors, and as many as trade on the sea, stood at a distance and cried out when they saw the smoke of her burning, saying, 'What is like this great city?'
>
> Revelation 18:17–18

Let us remember that Rome is a city located about 24 kilometers (15 miles) from the coast of the Mediterranean Sea, so that at least the smoke from her fire will be visible. God says, "Rejoice over her, O heaven, and you holy apostles and prophets, for God has avenged you on her!" (v. 18:20).

Verses 19:1–3 show a great multitude in heaven exalting and worshiping God with a loud voice, saying,

> 'Alleluia! Salvation and glory and honor and power belong to the Lord our God!
> For true and righteous are His judgments, because He has judged the great harlot who corrupted the earth with her fornication; and He has avenged on her the blood of His servants shed by her.'
> Again they said, 'Alleluia! Her smoke rises up forever and ever!'

Apparently the fire that will consume the Vatican in Rome will continue burning in such a way that it will be seen even at the time of the Millennium.

As mentioned before, some expositors understand that the Babylon mentioned in these chapters refers to the ancient Babylon, that majestic city ruled by Nebuchadnezzar. This interpretation does not fit with the whole content of chapters 17 and 18.

Firstly, the ancient Babylon, now Iraq, is not located near the shore of a sea or ocean, to be viewed by merchants and people who work on ships on the sea when she is burnt (vv. 18:17–18). The nearest seacoast (Persian Gulf) is located approximately 500 kilometers (300 miles) southeast of Baghdad (capital city of Iraq). I think it would not be possible to see the smoke from her fire at that distance.

Secondly, the judgment announced by God here is against the great harlot, also called a city (v. 17:18), which will be destroyed and burnt; whereas Iraq (ancient Babylon) is a nation, which in the past was a great empire covering a large area of land.

Furthermore, the Mediterranean Sea was and is the most important maritime transportation medium throughout that region, because it provides access to all nations and countries around Europe, Africa, Israel, and toward the Middle East. Therefore, I believe that the sea which is indirectly referenced in these passages is the Mediterranean Sea, not the Persian Gulf; and it is the city of Rome which is located near the coast of the Mediterranean Sea.

Thirdly, the region from the river Euphrates in Babylon up to the coast of the Mediterranean Sea is the land promised by God to the patriarch Abraham as an inheritance for his generation after him (Gen. 15:18). This is the land chosen by God to establish the kingdom of the Millennium. Therefore, this is a land that will remain and be inhabited by those entering the kingdom.

The Babylon to be judged will be desolated and burned "and shall not be found anymore" (v. 18:21), and "her smoke rises up forever and ever!" (v. 19:3). Therefore, this one cannot be part of the Millennium's land.

I definitely believe that the city called "Babylon" here is Rome, see of the Catholic Church, the great harlot.

The ten nations will exalt the Antichrist as the sole sovereign king over all the earth. On the other hand, it is possible that sometime before the end of the Great Tribulation, the Catholic Church will be no longer in agreement with the Antichrist's dictates, and want to take absolute power of the world by herself. This kind of authority has been shown in this religious institution since its foundation. This is why she is shown in verse 17:3 seated on the beast (Antichrist), trying to exert leadership or authority on it.

Another issue which could bring great controversy between the Catholic Church and the Antichrist is who will take control of Jerusalem. The Vatican has always wanted and tried to have authority of this capital and the "sacred" places in Israel. After many efforts, this religious institution has achieved part of their desires.

In an article in *Arutz Sheva* newspaper of February 1, 2013 (Ref. 15), it was published that "An historic agreement has been drafted between Israel and the Vatican," in which "the Israeli authorities have granted the Pope an official seat in the room where the Last Supper is believed to have taken place, on Mount Zion in Jerusalem."

The Vatican has been looking to gain sovereignty over Mount of Zion and many other sites in Jerusalem for a long time. It has called for Jerusalem to be designated as an "international zone," for them to have control of this city.

The so-called pope seeks to sit in Jerusalem as sovereign and sole authority. In the Great Tribulation, this Vatican's goal will create a huge controversy with the Antichrist, who will also seek that place of control and authority, "so that he sits as God in the temple of God, showing himself that he is God" (2 Thess. 2:2).

For these reasons, the Catholic Church may then secretly send some of her criminal agents to kill the Antichrist, which could be why the Antichrist is mortally wounded with a sword (vv. 13:3, 14)—which seems to be an individual attack, not a battle. It could be that this assault is what causes the ten nations to hate the great harlot and to raid Rome after the Antichrist is healed.

> The ten horns which you saw on the beast, these will hate the harlot, make her desolate and naked, eat her flesh and burn her with fire.
> For God has put it into their hearts to fulfill His purpose, to be of one mind, and to give their kingdom to the beast, until the words of God are fulfilled.
>
> Revelation 17:16–17

The purpose of God is that all the power to rule the whole world is given only to the Antichrist, without sharing it with the Catholic Church. So although at the beginning of chapter 17 we see the woman seated on the beast, as a clear representation of shared government between the Catholic

Church and the Antichrist, the time shall come to suppress the woman's power and influence (because of her treacherous act), and give them exclusively to the Antichrist. Even the ten nations recognize that absolute power will be for the Antichrist, because thus it has been determined by God Himself. Verses 17:12–13 show that the great harlot is excluded from the power shared with the Antichrist, because her destruction is already determined.

> The ten horns which you saw are ten kings who have received no kingdom as yet, but they receive authority for one hour as kings with the beast.
> These are of one mind, and they will give their power and authority to the beast.

The devil is always imitating God and His work. Following a summary of some of those imitations:

Item	God's working	Imitations of the devil
Trinity	God, Jesus Christ, Holy Spirit	Satan, Antichrist, False Prophet
Seal	Holy Spirit (Ephesians 1:13)	666 or name of the beast (Rev. 13:18)
Wife	The church of Christ: virgin	Catholic Church: the great harlot
City	Holy City, New Jerusalem	Rome (Vatican)

Preparation of the Lamb's Wedding

Revelation 19:1–9

Some of the most outstanding scenes we see in the Book of Revelation are the many times the angels, the four heavenly creatures, and the twenty-four elders are praising and glorifying God. It is wonderful to see the expressive joy of all these beings serving around God's throne. Especially at this crucial moment, when the judgments of God upon the earth are to be consummated, all the heavenly inhabitants do not cease to worship the One who lives forever, the God Almighty who reigns forever and ever, amen.

The apostle John sees a great crowd giving glory and praises to God, saying,

> Let us be glad and rejoice and give Him glory, for the marriage of the Lamb has come, and His wife has made herself ready.
> And to her it was granted to be arrayed in fine linen, clean and bright, for the fine linen is the righteous acts of the saints.
>
> Revelation 19:7–8

What a wonderful exclamation this is! These words produce a great joy and excitement in my life. This is something extremely great; it is the completion of our faith and hope. This has been the purpose of God the Father since the foundation of the world—to prepare the wife of His Son.

If all heavenly beings rejoice and worship God all the time, how much more now with the preparation of the wedding of the Lamb—they will do so with greater impetus and jubilation! The most expected moment in heaven has come: the time to prepare for the permanent union of Christ and His church.

It is very clear that the wife mentioned in this passage is the true church of the Lord; there is no doubt about this. What it is not thoroughly explicit is when this wedding will take place.

I would like to stop here to consider three points of view related to this subject. I am not of those who echo any interpretation of the Scriptures where there is no certainty or sound biblical evidence. For this reason, I will try to present the points of view which I believe are most often heard, in the most impartial way possible. My intention is to present the truth with the greatest possible clarity.

Wedding in Heaven after the Rapture

The first option is that the wedding shall be conducted in heaven, immediately after the rapture of the church. While the earth is preparing for two great events, the attack of Russia against Israel and the Great Tribulation, the church will be at her wedding ceremony with Christ. This thought has several weaknesses.

It is important to note that through the entire period of the Great Tribulation, we see the twenty-four elders seated on their thrones around the throne of God and the Lamb—even up to the end of the Great Tribulation. "And the twenty-four elders and the four living creatures fell down and worshiped God who sat on the throne, saying, 'Amen! Alleluia!'" (v. 19:4).

These twenty-four elders, representing the church, are not seen prepared with wedding attire; instead, they have continued praising and worshiping God from their places around the throne of God. In addition, Christ is not seen preparing for marriage to the church; He has been very active with the events happening on earth.

Jesus, the Savior of the world, has not yet completed His work of salvation, and has yet to complete the events outlined by God for the time of the Great Tribulation. God made His Son Jesus Christ judge over the earth, so it is Jesus Himself who will command each of the different events to be fulfilled during this period of seven years.

This is why Jesus is the One opening the seven seals of the scroll, which cover all the timespan of the Great Tribulation. Will the Lord leave His bride behind, to lead all these events? Furthermore, the Lord will continue in His position of intercessor for humanity in this time of greatest need and tribulation upon the inhabitants of the earth.

The Great Tribulation ends with the coming of Christ to the earth. Jesus comes with His angels to fight against the Antichrist's military forces. Will the Lord leave His new bride behind, to come to wage war on the earth? There are even some who say that the church will come with Him to the battles—the "bride" will leave her place in heaven to join the warriors of the battle.

This is not possible, because once the marriage of Jesus with the church is consummated, they will be together and united for eternity. Even the law in the Old Testament provided for the newly married not to go to war or to be busy in other matters—they were to avoid them and stay together. "When a man has taken a new wife, he shall not go out to war or be charged with any business; he shall be free at home one year, and bring happiness to his wife whom he has taken" (Deut. 24:5).

Considering all that is mentioned above, it does not seem accurate to place the wedding of the Lamb and the church in heaven, after the rapture.

Wedding at the Beginning of the Millennium

Although there are many references of the millennial kingdom in the Scriptures, these do not describe in detail what will happen in that period of a thousand years on this earth. I cannot find any clear word which locates the church in the Millennium, or accompanying Jesus in His second coming.

Many people say that when Jesus returns in His second coming, the church which is in heaven will come along with Him to reign with Him. They think so because they understand that the promise to be kings and priests will be accomplished in the Millennium. They use verses 1:6 and 5:10 of Revelation for this purpose, which say:

> and has made us kings and priests to His God and Father,
> to Him be glory and dominion forever and ever. Amen.
> And have made us kings and priests to our God; and we
> shall reign on the earth.

All this sounds good, but the fact that the word of God declares us kings and says that we will reign on the earth does not necessarily mean that this will happen in the millennial kingdom. I believe that these promises will be fulfilled on the new earth. (What I am looking for is biblical clarity, and not just to repeat what others say.)

There are several passages which have been used to place the church as coming with Christ in His second coming. Jude, verses 14 and 15 say,

> Behold, the Lord comes with ten thousands of His saints,
> to execute judgment on all, to convict all who are ungodly
> among them of all their ungodly deeds which they have
> committed in an ungodly way, and of all the harsh things
> which ungodly sinners have spoken against Him.

We previously saw in Matthew 13:36–42; 24:30–31, and 25:31–46 that the angels are those who will come up with Jesus in His second coming to judge the inhabitants of the earth. They have a great job: to separate the *goats* from the *sheep*. The angels are also identified as the heavenly armies (v. 19:14) coming with Jesus for the great battles in Edom and Armageddon. I have never seen any biblical passage identifying the church as taking swords to kill or wage war against the enemies of God; this work has been charged to the angels, rather than to a bride.

The church is not part of God's army; she is the bride of Christ. This is not a question of logic or whether it sounds good, but of what the written word of God clearly shows. I have no doubt that the "ten thousands of His saints" mentioned in this passage refer to the angels of the Lord, who will accompany Him to complete the work of judgment upon the nations. This is not the work of the members of the church, the bride of the Lamb of God.

Another passage is found in Zechariah 14:4–5, which says, "And in that day His feet will stand on the Mount of Olives ... Thus the Lord my God will come, and all the saints with you." This passage clearly refers to the second coming of Christ, when the Lord stands His feet on the Mount of Olives. However, I do not see that the saints mentioned here are the church.

There is a great revelation in this passage. The saints here refer to the faithful of the old covenant who died before Christ, together with those believers who die in the Great Tribulation. All these will be resurrected at the time of the coming of the Lord Jesus to the Mount of Olives, to then inherit the kingdom prepared for them. Note the last phrase of this passage: "Thus the Lord my God will come, and *all the saints with you.*"

This prophecy mentions all the saints, including the prophet Zechariah. This was the promise for them, and our faithful God shall fulfill it in the person of Jesus. These saints will not go to the battle in Armageddon, but will rise from the dead at the moment Jesus comes to the Mount of Olives, after the battle.

As stated before, the return of Jesus to the Mount of Olives will happen after He finishes the battle of Armageddon. More details about the resurrection of these saints are found in Revelation 20:4 section. This verse says as follows:

> And I saw thrones, and they sat on them, and judgment was committed to them. Then I saw the souls of those who had been beheaded for their witness to Jesus and for the word of God, who had not worshiped the beast or his image, and had not received his mark on their foreheads or on their hands. And they lived and reigned with Christ for a thousand years.
>
> Revelation 20:4

These saints were before the presence of God prior to the return of Christ (vv. 7:9, 13). To the faithful who come out of the Great Tribulation,

God has promised that "the Lamb who is in the midst of the throne will shepherd them and lead them to living fountains of waters. And God will wipe away every tear from their eyes" (v. 7:17).

Like the passages mentioned in Jude, the passage of Zechariah does not refer to the church. The promise to be shepherded is not for the church—since she is the bride of Christ—but for the people of God on earth entering into the Millennium.

The other passage frequently cited is found in 1 Thessalonians 3:12–13, which says,

> And may the Lord make you increase and abound in love to one another and to all, just as we do to you, so that He may establish your hearts blameless in holiness before our God and Father at the coming of our Lord Jesus Christ with all His saints.

I agree that this passage is somewhat difficult to understand. Paul urges and encourages the brothers of the church in Thessalonica to bear fruit so that their hearts are strengthened and established blameless in holiness, at the coming of Jesus with all His saints. When I read this passage, I do not clearly see that the saints of this church are included with the saints who come with Jesus at His coming.

In other words, Paul urges the believers to be in an attitude of holiness before the Father when Jesus comes with His saints. So it seems that the believers in Thessalonica are not part of the saints who come with Jesus.

I consulted several Bible versions, including a Greek version (IGNT, see *References*). The verse is similar in all the consulted versions. The referenced verse 3:13 in the IGNT, translated into English, says, "to establish your hearts blameless in holiness before our God and Father in the *presence* of our Lord Jesus with all his saints."

The Greek word (παρουσια) used for *presence* is the same word used for *coming*. If the correct word is presence, the verse is more easily interpreted, as exhorting the believers to remain in holiness before the presence of our Lord Jesus.

I do not want to push any interpretation to accommodate a possible personal opinion concerning this verse. Nor do I want to create a conflict with only one verse from the Scriptures. Therefore, I leave the reader to form his own conclusion.

Another very important element, previously discussed in the chapter on the Gospel of Matthew, is that the Millennium is a promise for the people of Israel and not for the church. Christ will come to His own for the second time to fulfill this promise prophesied since the time of the patriarch Abraham. God has purposed that Jesus will reign in the Promised Land. He is the Messiah and King of Israel and other nations.

The church will not be on earth in the Millennium, because that was not the promise for her. As will be covered in detail in the section on Revelation 21, the promise for the church is the Kingdom of the Father, which will be in the new earth. Therefore, after seeing God's purpose for the church and for the people of Israel, my understanding tells me that the wedding of the Lamb will not be in the Millennium.

Wedding on the New Earth

In order to better explain the subject of this section, several passages of Revelation 21 will be advanced, where the "fiancée" of the Lamb is shown:

> Then I, John, saw the holy city, New Jerusalem, coming down out of heaven from God, prepared as a bride adorned for her husband.
> … 'Come, I will show you the bride, the Lamb's wife.'
> And he carried me away in the Spirit to a great and high mountain, and showed me the great city, the holy Jerusalem, descending out of heaven from God, having the glory of God. …
>
> Revelation 21:2, 9–11

These passages locate the church, the Lamb's wife, in a specific place and time, that is, coming from heaven with God the Father to the new earth, after the final judgment. Jesus does not come with her, because He is waiting for her in the new city of Jerusalem which He built on the new earth. This assertion will be explained in more detail later.

The church is described here with splendor and great glory, as one prepared for her wedding. This majesty, splendor, and glory in the church have never been seen before. After the church descends on the new earth, we see Christ, the Lamb and Husband, in a place with her and in the midst of her.

> But I saw no temple in it [the city—the church], for the Lord God Almighty and the Lamb are its temple.

> The city had no need of the sun or of the moon to shine
> in it, for the glory of God illuminated it. The Lamb is its
> light.
>
> Revelation 21:22–23

We do not see Christ leaving the church to go to war or to punish wicked men who were on the earth when He returned in His second coming. As Husband, He is now with the church forever.

In Matthew 26:29, Jesus said, "But I say to you, I will not drink of this fruit of the vine from now on until that day when I drink it new with you in My Father's kingdom." I have no doubt that the Lord has reserved that great event of communion with His chosen, the church, to be consummated at the wedding ceremony.

The fulfillment of this glorious prophecy will evoke the death and resurrection of Christ, and will proclaim the culmination of God's purpose and plan of redemption and salvation for mankind. With this permanent union with the church, Jesus completes all the work to which He was called—now Jesus can enter into His Father's Kingdom on the new earth.

Jesus established the "Supper of the Lord" when He took it with His disciples that first time. He will partake of it again, the second and last time, with His bride in His wedding ceremony in His Father's Kingdom. This last supper will seal the final victory of Jesus and the church for all eternity.

Verse 21:6 says, "And He said to me, '*It is done!* I am the Alpha and the Omega, the Beginning and the End.'" The phrase *It is done!* marks the completion of the work of Christ as He joins with the church forever. The wedding could not be performed before the creation of the new heaven and new earth, because Jesus had not completed all His work before then. The wedding will be the reward for the completion of His whole work. How great is the love of God!

Continuing in Revelation 19, verse 9 says, "Blessed are those who are called to the marriage supper of the Lamb!" Who are *those who are called*? There are two points of view on this. Let us first consider the *called* as the members of the church. They will partake directly in the wedding supper as the bride.

If this is so, at that great and wonderful time of the wedding of the Lamb with the church, where will all the other faithful who were saved during the Millennium be? Shall they be excluded from participation in that majestic ceremony? If we choose this point of view, these questions will remain unanswered. Therefore, I think that the "called" of this passage does not refer to the members of the church.

The other point of view is to consider these *called* to refer to the guests at the wedding ceremony, specifically the marriage supper; this means that they are not part of the bride, the church. If this is the case, who these guests are? They might be the victorious who come out from the Millennium, who are called the people of God.

Because this is the wedding of His Son, God Himself will invite them to partake of the ceremony, where the prophesied supper will take place. Representatives of all saved nations with their kings, including the ancient patriarchs and prophets, will be present at this ceremony. In this way, other prophecies shall be fulfilled.

> And the nations of those who are saved shall walk in its
> light, and the kings of the earth bring their glory and honor
> into it.
> And they shall bring the glory and the honor of the nations
> into it.
>
> Revelation 21:24, 26

> There will be weeping and gnashing of teeth, when you
> see Abraham and Isaac and Jacob and all the prophets in
> the kingdom of God, and yourselves thrust out.
> They will come from the east and the west, from the north
> and the south, and sit down in the kingdom of God.
>
> Luke 13:28–29

It will be a glorious day, greatly anticipated even by our Lord Jesus Christ. I believe the previously described second point of view is the more accurate interpretation.

In chapter 20 of Revelation, which speaks of the Millennium, we do not see the Father physically present with Jesus, reigning over the nations (although within the mystery of the divine trinity, the Father and Christ are one). Neither I see the bride with Christ.

On the other hand, the Father, Christ, and the church shall be present together on the new earth, where the Father will reign together with His Son Jesus. The Father's throne will be located in the middle of the Holy City, the New Jerusalem—where the church will also be dwelling (vv. 21:3, 22–23; 22:1, 3).

This kingdom on the new earth will be called the Kingdom of the Father, as Jesus also called it: "I will not drink of this fruit of the vine from now on until that day when I drink it new with you in My *Father's kingdom*." Due to all that has been described above, I believe that the wedding of Jesus to the church will be consummated on the new earth.

Now, who will be part of the victorious church, the bride of the Lord? If you ask anyone on the street if he is a Christian, the response is obvious; he will probably say yes. I think that more than 80 percent of the worldwide population will respond that they profess the Christian faith, because they attend a congregation where the word of God is preached.

Indeed, the devil has deceived many people into thinking that they are saved and part of the church, because they visit a "temple" and "try" to do the best they can. The phrase "I do not do anything wrong" is heard everywhere.

But what do the Scriptures say about those who are active members of the church of the Lord? "For I am jealous for you with godly jealousy. For I have betrothed you to one husband, that I may present you as a *chaste virgin* to Christ" (2 Cor. 11:2). This is the bride, a pure virgin. She does not have the appearance of sheep—she is a true sheep. She is a church without spot or wrinkle, subject to Christ in everything.

> Therefore, just as the church is subject to Christ, so let the wives be to their own husbands in everything.
> Husbands, love your wives, just as Christ also loved the church and gave Himself for her, that He might sanctify and cleanse her with the washing of water by the word,
> that He might present her to Himself a glorious church, not having spot or wrinkle or any such thing, but that she should be holy and without blemish.
>
> Ephesians 5:24–27

The true testimony of God is expressed by the union of the members of the church with Christ. The marriage is defined by the union, not by written or spoken agreements or covenants. The church that will be married to Christ must have the same qualities that He has—she must be holy and spotless. This is not a work to be done by God in heaven—this is the condition in which the Lord shall find the church on the earth at the time of the rapture.

It is not a church which will be struggling to be holy and trying to overcome. It is a church that is holy and victorious now, one whose members live committed to the truth and righteousness of God. She is saved by the life given by Jesus through the Holy Spirit. She has the testimony of God and lives according to His word.

"And to her it was granted to be arrayed in fine linen, clean and bright, for the fine linen is the righteous acts of the saints" (v. 19:8). This fine linen and clean dress of the church represent the righteousness of the saints; its whiteness and beauty represent purity (1 Peter 3:3–4) and good works (1 Tim. 2:9–10).

This dress contrasts greatly with the dress of the Antichrist's "wife," the great harlot, who dresses in purple and scarlet (deep red color). There is no righteousness or purity in the great harlot, but evil and sin.

The Final Battle

Revelation 19:10–21

John was so excited about what he was seeing in regard to the preparation of the bride for her wedding that he even tried to worship the angel who was showing him the vision. But the angel did not allow it. Then the angel says to him: "Worship God! For the testimony of Jesus is the spirit of prophecy" (v. 19:10).

What can we say about this special statement? I think the answer is simple; all prophecy is fulfilled in Christ. He is the beginning and end of every word of God that is fulfilled. His testimony, that is, what He is, speaks for itself and reveals God to us. The substance of all revelation is Christ Himself. Jesus Christ is the revealed word.

> In the beginning was the Word, and the Word was with God, and the Word was God.
> And the Word became flesh and dwelt among us, and we beheld His glory, the glory as of the only begotten of the Father, full of grace and truth.
>
> John 1:1, 14

> For all the promises of God in Him are Yes, and in Him Amen, to the glory of God through us.
>
> 2 Corinthians 1:20

All the plan of God is based on what Christ is and on His work (what He has done and what He will do).

The apostle John describes the descent of Jesus to the Valley of Megiddo, Armageddon, in verses 19:11–16. John sees Jesus seated on a white horse, with His clothes dipped in blood and with a written name, *The Word of God.* He also sees a sharp sword coming out of His mouth to strike the nations, and on His thigh a name written, *King of kings and Lord of lords.*

We see Jesus here as we have never seen Him before. When Jesus was on earth with His disciples, although He was the Messiah and Savior, we see Him meek and lowly, one who suffered unto death. Then, after His ascension to heaven, we see Him like a Lamb, interceding for us before the throne of God, full of mercy, and forgiving the sins of those who believe in Him.

Now, on His return to the earth, we see Him as a warrior, one determined to finish with evil, destroying and killing the unfaithful.

The fact that John sees Jesus coming seated on a horse does not mean that it is really a horse. Like chapter 6 of Revelation, where the four horses represent different tactics or strategies, this horse can signify that Jesus comes to fight or comes from a fight, accompanied by His heavenly army, His angels, also seated on horses.

The white color means peace. Jesus comes to bring peace to the world forever—but this time He brings it through war. "… and in righteousness He judges and makes war" (v. 19:11). On the other hand, if this white horse is real, not symbolic, I would not have any problem accepting it.

Verse 19:13 mentions that Christ "was clothed with a robe dipped in blood." Where did Jesus dip His clothes in blood? It cannot be on the throne in heaven. He was dipped in blood somewhere before coming to the Mount of Olives. This place is the wilderness of Edom.

In the comments on Revelation 12:1–17, *The Woman Persecuted by the Dragon*, a more detailed explanation about this place in Edom and how Jesus was dipped in blood is provided. I strongly urge you to review that section.

"Now out of His mouth goes a sharp sword, that with it He should strike the nations." Although this sword can be spiritually seen as the power of God according to Ephesians 6:17, it could be a physically real sword.

In the battle at Edom, Jesus' clothes are stained with blood by His fighting with His sword. Then He continues His path to Armageddon where "the rest were killed with the sword which proceeded from the mouth of Him who sat on the horse" (v. 19:21). In this last battle, both the Antichrist and the False Prophet are finally defeated, and Satan is cast into a bottomless pit.

The prophet Daniel prophesied likewise when he said, "He shall even rise against the Prince of princes; but he shall be broken without human means" (Dan. 8:25). The Antichrist will finally fall forever.

The apostle Paul also prophesied the downfall of this evil and cruel man, when in his second letter to the Thessalonians he said, "And then the lawless one will be revealed, whom the Lord will consume with the breath of His mouth and destroy with the brightness of His coming" (2 Thess. 2:8).

This passage of Revelation 19 describes what it is known as the Battle of Armageddon (v. 16:16). More details concerning this battle are included in the comments on passages 9:13–21; 14:14–20, and 16:12–21.

This is a very special battle, in which the angels of God will have a very active part. "And the armies in heaven, clothed in fine linen, white and clean, followed Him on white horses" (v. 19:14). Matthew 25:31 also mentions the angels of God accompanying the sovereign King in His return to the earth. "When the Son of Man comes in His glory, and all the holy angels with Him, then He will sit on the throne of His glory."

Thousands of angels will kill the enemies of God and will deliver them to the birds of prey, as the greatest banquet ever known on earth.

> Then I saw an angel standing in the sun; and he cried with a loud voice, saying to all the birds that fly in the midst of heaven, 'Come and gather together for the supper of the great God, that you may eat the flesh of kings, the flesh of captains, the flesh of mighty men, the flesh of horses and of those who sit on them, and the flesh of all people, free and slave, both small and great.'
> And the rest were killed with the sword which proceeded from the mouth of Him who sat on the horse. And all the birds were filled with their flesh.
>
> Revelation 19:17–18, 21

The beast (Antichrist) and the False Prophet will be caught, and both will be thrown alive into the lake of fire burning with brimstone.

> Then the beast was captured, and with him the false prophet who worked signs in his presence, by which he deceived those who received the mark of the beast and those who worshiped his image. These two were cast alive into the lake of fire burning with brimstone.
>
> Revelation 19:20

This place of continual torment is real—it is not a tale—and it is prepared for all those who will be sentenced in the final judgment (vv. 20:15; 21:8). This is the most terrible place ever known, which will be inaugurated by the Antichrist and the False Prophet.

We do not know with certainty where the lake of fire will be located, but we do know that it will already exist in the time of the Great Tribulation. The Scriptures locate hell at the center of the earth. In Numbers 16:28–33, we see how the earth was opened and Korah with his family went down alive to Hades (hell).

I have no doubt that the lake of fire and brimstone is the "latest version" of hell—a place of much more torment than hell, located also at the center of the earth. Scientists assert that, according to their studies, the temperature of the center of the earth is equal to the temperature of the surface of the sun, which reaches about 5,000 degrees Celsius. According to them, the center of the earth is composed of melted iron, among other metals.

What shall happen when Jesus comes down to the Mount of Olives? We already said that He will judge all the remaining inhabitants of the entire world. The parable of the wheat and tares shows how this judgment will be done.

> The Son of Man will send out His angels, and they will gather out of His kingdom all things that offend, and those who practice lawlessness, and will cast them into the furnace of fire. There will be wailing and gnashing of teeth.
> Then the righteous will shine forth as the sun in the kingdom of their Father. He who has ears to hear, let him hear!
> Matthew 13:41–43

Chapter 25 of Matthew also speaks about this judgment:

> When the Son of Man comes in His glory, and all the holy angels with Him, then He will sit on the throne of His glory.
> All the nations will be gathered before Him, and He will separate them one from another, as a shepherd divides his sheep from the goats.
> And He will set the sheep on His right hand, but the goats on the left.

Then the King will say to those on His right hand, 'Come, you blessed of My Father, inherit the kingdom prepared for you from the foundation of the world.'

Matthew 25:31–34

Then He will also say to those on the left hand, 'Depart from Me, you cursed, into the everlasting fire prepared for the devil and his angels.'
And these will go away into everlasting punishment, but the righteous into eternal life.

Matthew 25:41, 46

The angels, not the church, will be responsible to collect the *tares* or *goats* which remain on the earth after the victory of Jesus in Armageddon. These wicked who are alive at the end of the Great Tribulation are those individuals who received the mark of the Antichrist, plus the unfaithful who, although did not have the mark, they did not believe in the Lord to be saved.

After these people are cast into hell, the remaining earth's population (*wheat* or *sheep*) will be ready to start a new life in the kingdom of Christ, the Millennium.

As a summary, let us see the chronological events to occur in Christ's second coming:

1. Preparation for the departure of Christ from heaven (Rev. 11:15–19).
2. First stop of Jesus in the wilderness of Edom, where He shall liberate the remnant of Israel besieged in that place. This is the place where Jesus' clothes are sprinkled with blood, in His first battle with the Antichrist's army and the people of Edom (Rev. 14:14–20; Isa. 63:1–4).
3. Jesus, along with His angels, continues destroying the Antichrist's military forces throughout a strip of 1,600 furlongs (180 miles), between Edom and the Valley of Megiddo (Rev. 14:14–20).
4. The great Battle of Armageddon takes place. The Antichrist and the False Prophet are captured and cast into the lake of fire (Rev. 19:11–21).
5. After the great victory in Armageddon, Satan, the dragon, is bound and cast into an abyss for a thousand years (Rev. 20:1–3).
6. Christ descends as King to the Mount of Olives (Zech. 14:2–5) and the faithful who lived and died before Christ's lifetime, together

239

with those believers who died during the Great Tribulation, are resurrected from the dead—this is the "first resurrection" (Rev. 20:4–6).

7. The judgment of the Lord on the remaining inhabitants of all the earth is accomplished. The *goats* are separated from the *sheep*, and cast into hell (Matt. 25:31–46).

8. Jesus, the King of kings, establishes His millennial kingdom on this earth (Rev. 20:4–6).

The Millennium

Revelation 20:4–6

John saw an angel catching the dragon, who is also known as the "old serpent," "the devil," and Satan, and tying and locking him into an abyss for a thousand years. From this time forward, the devil shall not deceive the nations any more until the thousand years are completed. Then the devil will be released, but only for a little while.

The time has come to have true peace among all nations; no more wars. This is the promise of God to the people of Israel, and they will inherit the Promised Land. The throne of the King and Lord Jesus will be in Jerusalem. Israel and all the other saved nations will be in peace and shall bring their offerings and thanksgivings to Christ. Before Jesus was born, God announced to Mary through an angel that Jesus

> will be great, and will be called the Son of the Highest; and the Lord God will give Him the throne of His father David. And He will reign over the house of Jacob forever, and of His kingdom there will be no end.
>
> Luke 1:32–33

> Afterward the children of Israel shall return and seek the Lord their God and David [Jesus] their king. They shall fear the Lord and His goodness in the latter days.
>
> Hosea 3:5

Revelation 20:4–6 describes what the believers who enter the Millennium will do:

> And I saw thrones, and they sat on them, and judgment was committed to them. Then I saw the souls of those who had been beheaded for their witness to Jesus and for the word of God, who had not worshiped the beast or his image, and had not received his mark on their foreheads or on their hands. And they lived and reigned with Christ for a thousand years.
>
> But the rest of the dead did not live again until the thousand years were finished. This is the first resurrection.
>
> Blessed and holy is he who has part in the first resurrection. Over such the second death has no power, but they shall be priests of God and of Christ, and shall reign with Him a thousand years.

In Genesis 15:18, we find the promise of God to Abraham, extended to all the people of Israel: "On the same day the LORD made a covenant with Abram, saying: 'To your descendants I have given this land, from the river of Egypt to the great river, the River Euphrates.'"

How great is God! When Abraham left his land in Ur of the Chaldeans in Babylon, he did not know that even his own land in Babylon would be included in the land promised to him by God. God spoke to Abraham about the specific land with its extension up to the River Euphrates, when he was already living in the land of Canaan. So on his entire journey to Canaan, Abraham was contemplating the Promised Land without knowing it.

In the time of the prophet Moses, God remembered again His promise to the people of Israel, after they came out from the land of Egypt:

> And I will set your bounds from the Red Sea to the sea, Philistia [Mediterranean], and from the desert to the River [Euphrates]. For I will deliver the inhabitants of the land into your hand, and you shall drive them out before you.
> Exodus 23:31

> Every place on which the sole of your foot treads shall be yours: from the wilderness and Lebanon, from the river,

the River Euphrates, even to the Western Sea, shall be
your territory.

Deuteronomy 11:24

History speaks for itself; in the time of King Solomon, he reigned over
this Promised Land:

> So Solomon reigned over all kingdoms from the River
> [Euphrates] to the land of the Philistines, as far as the
> border of Egypt. They brought tribute and served Solomon
> all the days of his life.
> For he had dominion over all the region on this side of
> the River from Tiphsah even to Gaza, namely over all the
> kings on this side of the River; and he had peace on every
> side all around him.
>
> 1 Kings 4:21, 24

This was the land promised to Israel, and it is the same land where the
Millennium shall be established (see figure 18: Map of the Millennium's
Land).

There must be no doubt that the territory of the kingdom which Christ
will establish on the earth after the Great Tribulation is the same territory
God promised to Israel. There are many biblical references (Isaiah,
Jeremiah, Ezekiel, Daniel, Zechariah, and others) mentioning this promise
of God to the people of Israel. I will only mention some of them.

Daniel chapter 7 provides some details about the saints entering or
possessing the kingdom.

> I was watching; and the same horn was making war
> against the saints, and prevailing against them, until the
> Ancient of Days came, and a judgment was made in favor
> of the saints of the Most High, and the time came for the
> saints to possess the kingdom.
> Then the kingdom and dominion, and the greatness of the
> kingdoms under the whole heaven, shall be given to the
> people, the saints of the Most High. His kingdom is an
> everlasting kingdom, and all dominions shall serve and
> obey Him.
>
> Daniel 7: 21–22, 27

Millennium's Land
Genesis 15:8 "from Egypt to River Euphrates"
Exodus 23:31 "from Red Sea to the sea, Philistia, and from the desert to the River (Euphrates)"
Deuteronomy 11:24 "from the wilderness and Lebanon, from River Euphrates to Western Sea"

Figure 18: Map of the Millennium's Land

Chapter 37 of Ezekiel provides a wonderful revelation about the restoration of the people of Israel and their place in the millennial kingdom, of which I quote the passage 37:21–25 (I suggest that the reader reads the entire chapter):

> Then say to them, 'Thus says the Lord God: "Surely I will take the children of Israel from among the nations, wherever they have gone, and will gather them from every side and bring them into their own land; and I will make them one nation in the land, on the mountains of Israel; and one king shall be king over them all; they shall no longer be two nations, nor shall they ever be divided into two kingdoms again.
>
> They shall not defile themselves anymore with their idols, nor with their detestable things, nor with any of their transgressions; but I will deliver them from all their dwelling places in which they have sinned, and will cleanse them. Then they shall be My people, and I will be their God.
>
> David [Jesus] My servant shall be king over them, and they shall all have one shepherd; they shall also walk in My judgments and observe My statutes, and do them.
>
> Then they shall dwell in the land that I have given to Jacob My servant, where your fathers dwelt; and they shall dwell there, they, their children, and their children's children, forever; and My servant David shall be their prince forever."'

Revelation 20:4–6 speaks of the believers killed in the Great Tribulation, who will be resurrected in the so-called first resurrection. Then they will enter into the Promised Land, where they shall dwell with Christ for a thousand years. In this way the Scriptures will be fulfilled. Verses 7:13–14, 16–17 also say:

> Then one of the elders answered, saying to me, 'Who are these arrayed in white robes, and where did they come from?' And I said to him, 'Sir, you know.' So he said to me, 'These are the ones who come out of the great tribulation, and washed their robes and made them white in the blood of the Lamb.

They shall neither hunger anymore nor thirst anymore; the sun shall not strike them, nor any heat; for the Lamb who is in the midst of the throne will shepherd them and lead them to living fountains of waters. And God will wipe away every tear from their eyes.'

This people who go into the Millennium is now comforted by his King—different from the church, which no longer needs this consolation because her position in heaven is assured as the bride of Christ, not as people to be shepherded.

These resurrected believers, together with those believers remaining alive on the earth at the end of the Great Tribulation, constitute a part of the people over whom the King and Lord Jesus will reign for a thousand years.

In addition to these two groups of believers, there will be another group. This third group is composed of all those servants who believed and served God before Christ's birth, that is, the faithful servants of the time of the law and the prophets of the old covenant. These believers of the old covenant died in hope, without receiving what was promised to them. Following some passages referring to the ancient servants:

And all these, having obtained a good testimony through faith, did not receive the promise, God having provided something better for us, that they should not be made perfect apart from us.

Hebrews 11:39–40

And I say to you that many will come from east and west, and sit down with Abraham, Isaac, and Jacob in the kingdom of heaven.

Matthew 8:11

… And at that time your people shall be delivered, every one who is found written in the book.

And many of those who sleep in the dust of the earth shall awake, some to everlasting life, some to shame and everlasting contempt.

But you, go your way till the end; for you shall rest, and will arise to your inheritance at the end of the days.

Daniel 12:1–2, 13

This last verse spoken by God to the prophet Daniel will be fulfilled when the Lord resurrects him in His second coming, and so he will enter into the Promised Land, where he will receive his promised inheritance.

Revelation 11:18 says that the time has come: "the time of the dead, that they should be judged, and that You should reward Your servants the prophets and the saints, and those who fear Your name, small and great." When these resurrected faithful enter the Millennium, the promise of receiving the land by inheritance will be fulfilled. "Blessed are the meek, for they shall inherit the earth" (Matt. 5:5).

Although the issue of the souls of those who were beheaded was discussed in the passage 7:9–17, some additional comments will now be added in this section. Those who receive faculty to judge shall sit on thrones to judge the nations in the millennial kingdom. Who could these be, who will have authority to judge and be leaders of nations?

The passage says that they shall reign with Christ a thousand years (v. 20:6). In accordance with what I have seen through all the Scriptures, I deduce that these future leaders will emerge from two groups: those victorious who come out from the Great Tribulation and those faithful who belonged to the era before Christ's lifetime. From these two groups, God will choose those who in their lifetime exercised some degree of responsibilities in God, which qualify them to be useful and good administrators of the grace of God—so they have faculty or power to judge.

To present some examples, I will mention some ancient prophets who lived before Christ's time and exercised great responsibility and authority: Abraham, Joseph, Isaiah, Jeremiah, Daniel, and many others. God made a promise to the prophet Daniel to raise (resurrect) him, so that he could receive his inheritance. God said the same to Zechariah (Zech. 14:5).

God also said that the patriarch Abraham, his son, and his grandson would be present in the millennial kingdom. "And I say to you that many will come from east and west, and sit down with Abraham, Isaac, and Jacob in the kingdom of heaven" (Matt. 8:11). The phrases "kingdom of heaven" and the "kingdom of God" are used in the Bible referring to heaven or earth, depending on the passage. The *kingdom of heaven* here is the Millennium, where Jesus will be the King.

The passage of Revelation 20 talks about the first resurrection and second death. As it was with the body of Lazarus when he was resurrected by Jesus, so it will be with those who experience the first resurrection.

This first resurrection will include (as mentioned above) two groups of people: those believers who lived at the time of the Great Tribulation, who died because of the testimony of Jesus; and those faithful who lived and died before Christ's time. These two groups shall rise from the dead at the time of the descending of Christ to the Mount of Olives. This was discussed in more detail in the section on verses 7:9–17.

These two groups of saints are blessed, because the *second death* has no power over them (vv. 20:5–6; 21:8). In other words, those who partake of the first resurrection shall never be deceived or condemned, but God will save them forever. This is the promise of God for them, so they shall not experience more death; therefore, they will not be part of the group who will be deceived by Satan at the end of the Millennium. Matthew 22:31–32 says,

> But concerning the resurrection of the dead, have you not read what was spoken to you by God, saying, 'I am the God of Abraham, the God of Isaac, and the God of Jacob'? God is not the God of the dead, but of the living.

By this passage we can understand that these three servants of God were put away in a place of rest, to wait for the great promised day when they shall rise to inherit the Promised Land. "These all died in faith, not having received the promises, but having seen them afar off were assured of them, embraced them and confessed that they were strangers and pilgrims on the earth" (Heb. 11:13).

On the other hand, the second death will be experienced by those who did not believe in God and lived their own lives. This group consists of the wicked of all times, from the time of the first man Adam until the last day of the Millennium. All these will undergo the second death (v. 20:6), which will be a death of condemnation in the lake of fire and brimstone for all eternity. This subject will be expanded a little more in the next section *The Final Judgment*.

The kingdom of a thousand years will bring a new experience for mankind, because the world will be governed by the laws of God and by Jesus Christ as the King—it will be a theocratic kingdom.

After the Great Tribulation, the earth will need to be restored in order to be inhabited by the saved nations. Chapters 60 and 61 of Isaiah describe the life in the Millennium. Isaiah 61:4 speaks about the work of restoration to be carried out in the Millennium: "And they shall rebuild the old ruins, they shall raise up the former desolations, and they shall repair the ruined cities, the desolations of many generations."

With Jesus Christ as King, life will be different—it is like an introduction to life on the new earth, which will be created by the Lord after the final judgment. Jesus will reign with perfect justice, and even the wild animals shall not do harm anymore. Children will play with them. This means that even the behavior of animals will change in this new kingdom, and they will be as they were in the beginning of creation. The Scriptures say that

> The wolf also shall dwell with the lamb, the leopard shall lie down with the young goat, the calf and the young lion and the fatling together; and a little child shall lead them. The cow and the bear shall graze; their young ones shall lie down together; and the lion shall eat straw like the ox. The nursing child shall play by the cobra's hole, and the weaned child shall put his hand in the viper's den.
> They shall not hurt nor destroy in all My holy mountain, for the earth shall be full of the knowledge of the Lord as the waters cover the sea.
>
> Isaiah 11:6–9

God will fulfill His promises to Israel—that they shall be saved and walk as head of the nations. In other words, Israel shall be the closest nation to the throne of Jesus in Jerusalem. The rest of the nations will be beyond Israel, towards the four corners of the earth.

> And the Lord will make you the head and not the tail; you shall be above only, and not be beneath ...
>
> Deuteronomy 28:13

> The word that Isaiah the son of Amoz saw concerning Judah and Jerusalem.
> Now it shall come to pass in the latter days that the mountain of the Lord's house shall be established on the top of the mountains, and shall be exalted above the hills; and all nations shall flow to it.
> Many people shall come and say, 'Come, and let us go up to the mountain of the Lord, to the house of the God of Jacob; He will teach us His ways, and we shall walk in His paths.' For out of Zion shall go forth the law, and the word of the Lord from Jerusalem.
>
> Isaiah 2:1–3

Those who live in the Millennium shall come every year to worship the King in Jerusalem and to celebrate the Feast of Tabernacles. "And it shall come to pass that everyone who is left of all the nations which came against Jerusalem shall go up from year to year to worship the King, the Lord of hosts, and to keep the Feast of Tabernacles" (Zech. 14:16).

This celebration will be held in memory of the second coming of Christ to the earth, which marked the release of Israel and all the other nations from the yoke of Satan. This holiday was celebrated in Israel in ancient times to commemorate the way the Israelites dwelled in tabernacles in the wilderness, when God brought them out from Egypt. This feast was held in the seventh month (Tisri), between September and October of each year.

> Speak to the children of Israel, saying: 'The fifteenth day of this seventh month shall be the Feast of Tabernacles for seven days to the Lord.'
> 'You shall keep it as a feast to the Lord for seven days in the year. It shall be a statute forever in your generations. You shall celebrate it in the seventh month.
> You shall dwell in booths for seven days. All who are native Israelites shall dwell in booths, that your generations may know that I made the children of Israel dwell in booths when I brought them out of the land of Egypt: I am the Lord your God.'
> Leviticus 23:34, 41–43

What shall happen with those nations (through their representatives) which do not come up to Jerusalem to celebrate the Feast of Tabernacles? The Lord Jesus will punish them by stopping the rain in their land.

> And it shall be that whichever of the families of the earth do not come up to Jerusalem to worship the King, the Lord of hosts, on them there will be no rain.
> If the family of Egypt will not come up and enter in, they shall have no rain; they shall receive the plague with which the Lord strikes the nations who do not come up to keep the Feast of Tabernacles.
> This shall be the punishment of Egypt and the punishment of all the nations that do not come up to keep the Feast of Tabernacles.
> Zechariah 14:17–19; see also Isaiah 2:1–3

These actions of the nations show that even when Jesus is present as King and Satan is imprisoned, so that he cannot deceive them, rebellion and sin will still be manifest in many people. This is because these people have not experienced the union with God in the Spirit; so they will be exposed to disobedience.

This rebellion will be seen more in the generations to come after the first inhabitants of the Millennium—these people shall not know the powerful works performed by God in the Great Tribulation. The same happened with the ancient people of Israel when entered Canaan, after the exodus from Egypt.

This is why God will test them once more. The test shall be that after the thousand years, Satan will be let loose and deceive many people of the nations, and will gather them for the last battle on earth. In this way, God will purify His people, as gold is purified with fire.

The Last Rebellion

Revelation 20:1–3, 7–10

> Then I saw an angel coming down from heaven, having the key to the bottomless pit and a great chain in his hand. He laid hold of the dragon, that serpent of old, who is the Devil and Satan, and bound him for a thousand years; and he cast him into the bottomless pit, and shut him up, and set a seal on him, so that he should deceive the nations no more till the thousand years were finished. But after these things he must be released for a little while.
>
> Revelation 20:1–3

> Now when the thousand years have expired, Satan will be released from his prison and will go out to deceive the nations which are in the four corners of the earth, Gog and Magog, to gather them together to battle, whose number is as the sand of the sea.
> They went up on the breadth of the earth and surrounded the camp of the saints and the beloved city. And fire came down from God out of heaven and devoured them.

The devil, who deceived them, was cast into the lake of
fire and brimstone where the beast and the false prophet
are. And they will be tormented day and night forever
and ever.

Revelation 20:7–10

In chapter 19 we see that at the end of the Great Tribulation, with
the coming of the Lord Jesus, the Antichrist and the False Prophet are
thrown into the lake of fire and brimstone, becoming the first inhabitants
of that frightful and gloomy place. Simultaneously, another wonderful and
expected event is happening, that is, an angel, prepared and chosen for that
specific hour, holds and ties Satan with a great and special chain and casts
him into an abyss.

What a wonderful pictures these are! The two false and malevolent
"leaders" are now cast out forever and the great liar and deceiver is
immobilized, and his power suppressed for a thousand years. However,
under God's perfect plan this evil devil "must be released for a little while"
at the end of the thousand years of the reign of Christ.

Many people wonder why this should happen—why there should be a
need again to fight against the forces of evil. The answer to this question
is simple: God wants a holy people, truly faithful to Him, so He will test
them for the last time, so that they are refined as gold is refined with fire.
The same is with many religious people who need to be tested, as Matthew
15:8–9 says,

'These people draw near to Me with their mouth,
And honor Me with their lips,
But their heart is far from Me.
And in vain they worship Me, ...'

God is seeking those who worship, love, and serve Him in spirit and
truth, with all their hearts. This is why He tests our hearts (1 Thess. 2:4).

Who will be deceived by Satan at the end of the Millennium? We find
in Israel's history how the generations after the people who came out from
Egypt, forgot God and the great signs and miracles made by the prophet
Moses.

When all that generation had been gathered to their
fathers, another generation arose after them who did not
know the Lord nor the work which He had done for Israel.

> Then the children of Israel did evil in the sight of the Lord,
> and served the Baals; and they forsook the Lord God of
> their fathers, who had brought them out of the land of
> Egypt; and they followed other gods from among the gods
> of the people who were all around them, and they bowed
> down to them; and they provoked the Lord to anger.
>
> Judges 2:10–12

I think that the same thing will happen in the Millennium; the generations that will arise after that one which came out from the Great Tribulation will forget God, His word, and the great signs performed in that time.

The majority of the people to be deceived by Satan will be those disobedient not coming to Jerusalem to celebrate the Feast of Tabernacles. In the previous section, *The Millennium*, the rebellious attitude and behavior of many inhabitants of the earth are described. Although they are present in a kingdom ruled by Christ, they revel in disobeying His ordinances.

> And it shall come to pass that everyone who is left of all
> the nations which came against Jerusalem shall go up from
> year to year to worship the King, the Lord of hosts, and to
> keep the Feast of Tabernacles.
> And it shall be that whichever of the families of the earth
> do not come up to Jerusalem to worship the King, the Lord
> of hosts, on them there will be no rain.
> This shall be the punishment of Egypt and the punishment
> of all the nations that do not come up to keep the Feast of
> Tabernacles.
>
> Zechariah 14:16–17, 19

We see here that the sinful nature of the *old man* is still in those who are not born again of the Spirit, despite the fact that the deceiver and producer of every evil is out of reach. Even living in a kingdom of peace under the direct rule of the Messiah, these are still rebellious and disobedient.

All those who partake of the first resurrection will not be deceived by Satan; this was the promise of God for them: "Blessed and holy is he who has part in the first resurrection. Over such the second death has no power, but they shall be priests of God and of Christ, and shall reign with Him a thousand years" (v. 20:6).

Once Satan is released after the thousand years, he will make his last effort to snatch the kingdom from the hands of Jesus. He will deceive a large number of people from the nations and will gather them to make war against Christ and His people, who dwell in Jerusalem and surrounding areas. By the phrase "the nations which are in the four corners of the earth" it is clearly stated that the earth will be totally populated again during the thousand years.

This great army of Satan, "whose number is as the sand of the sea," will be stationed in Magog, a place located to the far north of Israel (Ezek. 38:1-16, 22; 39:1-6).

Jesus will obliterate Satan's army, sending fire from heaven to consume those who rebel against Him.

> 'And it will come to pass at the same time, when Gog comes against the land of Israel,' says the Lord God, 'that My fury will show in My face.'
> And I will bring him to judgment with pestilence and bloodshed; I will rain down on him, on his troops, and on the many peoples who are with him, flooding rain, great hailstones, fire, and brimstone.
> And I will send fire on Magog and on those who live in security in the coastlands. Then they shall know that I am the Lord.
>
> Ezekiel 38:18, 22; 39:6

> ... And fire came down from God out of heaven and devoured them.
>
> Revelation 20:9

Who or what Gog and Magog are? Chapters 38 and 39 of Ezekiel describe the location and other characteristics of Gog and Magog, and what they shall try to do against Israel.

> Then you will come from your place out of the far north, you and many peoples with you, all of them riding on horses, a great company and a mighty army.
> You will come up against My people Israel like a cloud, to cover the land. It will be in the **latter days** that I will bring you against My land, so that the nations may know Me, when I am hallowed in you, O Gog, before their eyes.
>
> Ezekiel 38:15-16

It seems that this name (Magog) refers to Russia, which is located to the north of Israel, and its prince or leader Gog.

> Son of man, set your face against Gog, of the land of Magog, the prince of rosh, Meshech, and Tubal, and prophesy against him, and say, 'Thus says the Lord GOD: "Behold, I am against you, O Gog, the prince of rosh, Meshech, and Tubal."'
> And you, son of man, prophesy against Gog, and say, 'Thus says the Lord GOD: "Behold, I am against you, O Gog, the prince of rosh, Meshech, and Tubal; and I will turn you around and lead you on, bringing you up from the far north, and bring you against the mountains of Israel."'
>
> Ezekiel 38:2–3; 39:1–2

When we carefully read these two chapters of Ezekiel, it is not difficult to see that the prophecy shown here will have double fulfillment. The first fulfillment shall be when Russia and her allies attack Israel before the Great Tribulation starts. This battle will be led by Russia's leader (*Gog*). The explanation of this battle is covered in the upcoming chapter of this book called *Russia Will Attack Israel Soon*. More detailed descriptions of Gog, Magog, and their allies are found in that chapter.

The second time the prophecy is accomplished will be at the end of the Millennium (vv. 20:7–10), where Gog and Magog are mentioned. God will consume with fire all rebels of the nations which come against His people. This battle at the end of the Millennium will not be led by the Russia's leader, but by the devil himself.

> Now when the thousand years have expired, Satan will be released from his prison and will go out to deceive the nations which are in the four corners of the earth, Gog and Magog, to gather them together to battle, whose number is as the sand of the sea.
>
> Revelation 20:7–8

Remember that these two different battles will have a separation of approximately one thousand years.

The devil that deceived so many nations will be finally judged and cast into the lake of fire and brimstone, where he will join the Antichrist and the False Prophet. Each of these three will be tormented in this gloomy place forever and ever. Once the devil is thrown into the lake of fire, there will be no more temptation of sin, and no one shall be deceived anymore. The accuser Satan and his evil ministers are eliminated forever.

This is the culmination of the just punishment of God planned for the trinity of evil and for all who rejoiced in injustice and sin and did not serve the Lord of truth. With the completion of these events, the righteous judgment of God is consummated on the earth.

The Final Judgment

Revelation 20:11–15

> Then I saw a great white throne and Him who sat on it, from whose face the earth and the heaven fled away. And there was found no place for them.
> And I saw the dead, small and great, standing before God, and books were opened. And another book was opened, which is the Book of Life. And the dead were judged according to their works, by the things which were written in the books.
> The sea gave up the dead who were in it, and Death and Hades delivered up the dead who were in them. And they were judged, each one according to his works.
> Then Death and Hades were cast into the lake of fire. This is the second death.
> And anyone not found written in the Book of Life was cast into the lake of fire.

The time for God's final judgment and His punishment on all those who delighted in doing wickedness has come! This is the so-called "great white throne final judgment." God also showed the prophet Daniel this great final judgment event.

> I watched till thrones were put in place, and the Ancient of Days was seated; His garment was white as snow, and the hair of His head was like pure wool. His throne was a fiery flame, its wheels a burning fire; a fiery stream issued

and came forth from before Him. A thousand thousands
ministered to Him; ten thousand times ten thousand stood
before Him. The court was seated, and the books were
opened.

Daniel 7:9–10

Two kinds of books will be opened: the Book of Life and the books of
works, through which those who were raised in the "second resurrection"
will be judged. The Book of Life contains the names of the saved, including
the members of the church of the Lord, the faithful who lived before the
time of Jesus, and the overcomers in the Millennium.

For example, Moses, a humble man who loved his people, asked God
to forgive the sins of the people, and if not, then to remove his own name
from the book of saved ones.

'Yet now, if You will forgive their sin—but if not, I pray,
blot me out of *Your book* which You have written.'
And the Lord said to Moses, 'Whoever has sinned against
Me, I will blot him out of *My book.*'

Exodus 32:32–33

He who overcomes shall be clothed in white garments, and
I will not blot out his name from the *Book of Life*; but I will
confess his name before My Father and before His angels.

Revelation 3:5

There are many other references which mention this truth, such as
Revelation 13:8 and 17:8; Philippians 4:3; Psalm 69:28, and others.

In the other books are written the works and behavior of men during
their lifetime on earth. God is so fair that in the final judgment He will
show what everyone did which displeased Him. After the judgment, God
will issue the guilty verdict to each one.

As we have seen, the second resurrection, the resurrection of the
wicked, will happen after the thousand years of the Millennium are
completed. Although the phrase "second resurrection" does not appear in
the Scriptures, it is used to refer to what happens prior to the second death,
which is indeed mentioned in the Scriptures. This second resurrection will
include all those who did not serve or know God, from the first inhabitants
of the earth up to the Millennium.

Do not marvel at this; for the hour is coming in which all who are in the graves will hear His voice and come forth—those who have done good, to the resurrection of life, and those who have done evil, to the resurrection of condemnation.

John 5:28–29

And many of those who sleep in the dust of the earth shall awake, some to everlasting life, some to shame and everlasting contempt.

Daniel 12:2

The resurrection of life pertains to the saved ones and the resurrection of condemnation is the second resurrection, one of shame and perpetual doom. "And anyone not found written in the Book of Life was cast into the lake of fire" (v. 20:15), which is the second death (v. 21:8). They will remain in this place to be tormented, together with the devil, the Antichrist, and the False Prophet, for all eternity. All opportunities are finished and the door of salvation has been closed forever.

During the life of Jesus, the Son of Man, on the earth, the Father gave Him to execute all judgment on the earth.

For the Father judges no one, but has committed all judgment to the Son, that all should honor the Son just as they honor the Father. He who does not honor the Son does not honor the Father who sent Him.

John 5:22–23

Now, in this final judgment, Jesus will not work as the Advocate anymore. He will not be before the throne of His Father interceding for these people, partakers of the second resurrection. Jesus left His word to them and they shall be judged by that word.

And if anyone hears My words and does not believe, I do not judge him; for I did not come to judge the world but to save the world.
He who rejects Me, and does not receive My words, has that which judges him—the word that I have spoken will judge him *in the last day*.

John 12:47–48

God the Father gave all judgment to His Son when He was on the earth, but now it is the Father's turn (*the Ancient of Days*) to conduct this final judgment. The time for Jesus to intercede for others ended in His millennial kingdom.

He actually intercedes to make us free from sin and to save us from the wrath to come, but He will not be supplicating before the Father for the ones to be judged in the final judgment; that is a judgment of condemnation.

The punishment for the guilty is the second death in the lake of fire and brimstone. So I believe that the Lord Jesus will not be present in this last judgment, but God the Father will be leading it by Himself. If this is the case, where will Jesus be? The answer to this possibility is found in the next section, *New Heaven and New Earth.*

If Christ will not be with the Father in the final judgment, then who will be with the Father judging the nations? We can see the following beings in heaven at the end of the Millennium: the Father on His throne, the four living creatures, twenty-four elders sitting on their thrones around the Father (representing the victorious church), and the angels of God. What relation do these heavenly inhabitants have to the final judgment?

Let us see what the prophet Daniel saw in his vision of the final judgment.

> I watched till thrones were put in place, and the Ancient of Days was seated; ...
> ... A thousand thousands ministered to Him; ten thousand times ten thousand stood before Him. The court was seated, and the books were opened.
>
> Daniel 7:9–10

Daniel saw the Father seated on His throne, thrones around Him, and two kinds of crowds. The apostle John also saw these thrones around the Father's throne, but with a little more detail:

> Immediately I was in the Spirit; and behold, a throne set in heaven, and One sat on the throne.
> Around the throne were twenty-four thrones, and on the thrones I saw twenty-four elders sitting, clothed in white robes; and they had crowns of gold on their heads.
>
> Revelation 4:2, 4

The thrones around the Father seen by Daniel are the twenty-four thrones seen by the apostle John. We can therefore say that the church, represented by the twenty-four elders, will be present in the final judgment of all those who will be convicted. This is confirmed when we read in 1 Corinthians 6:2–3,

> Do you not know that the saints will judge the world? And if the world will be judged by you, are you unworthy to judge the smallest matters?
> Do you not know that we shall judge angels? How much more, things that pertain to this life?

Daniel's vision gives to understand that those who sit on the thrones around the Father are the "thousand thousands [who] ministered to Him." I believe that Daniel is watching here the church serving God in the final judgment. We never see the angels of the Lord seated on thrones; this privilege is only given to the Father, the Son Jesus Christ, and the twenty-four elders, the church.

Who could be then the "ten thousand times ten thousand [who] *stood before Him*"? Revelation 20:12 says something very similar to what Daniel saw: "And I saw the dead, small and great, *standing before God*, and books were opened." It seems that these two references speak of the same event: those who will be judged standing before the just Judge to be prosecuted for perpetual damnation.

According to Daniel's reference, the number of wicked to be judged will be 100 times the members of the victorious church. What great sadness to see so many thousands of people going to judgment without the opportunity to be saved. This was prophesied by Jesus when He said: "So the last will be first, and the first last. For many are called, but few chosen" (Matt. 20:16). The time for them to change their lives has passed. All doors are now closed.

This "picture" causes me a great sorrow, but on the other hand, it challenges me to walk seriously and faithfully in His way, and with reverent fear of God. Dear reader, the devil, our enemy, is a thief who "does not come except to steal, and to kill, and to destroy." Jesus came to give us life abundantly.

Who are the angels that will be judged, according to 1 Corinthians 6:3? The Scriptures tell us that God has reserved His *judgment of the great day* for those angels who sinned, rebelling against Him.

And the angels who did not keep their proper domain, but left their own abode, He has reserved in everlasting chains under darkness for the judgment of the great day.

Jude, verse 6

For if God did not spare the angels who sinned, but cast them down to hell and delivered them into chains of darkness, to be reserved for judgment.

2 Peter 2:4

What are the roles of the church, the four living creatures, and the angels of God during the final judgment? How will the church judge the world and the fallen angels?

The church will be present in the final judgment not as a judge, since the Father will be the sole Judge, but as the most important evidence in the court. She will be there to show the living testimony of Christ's work and to present an evident expression of His person. Jesus prepared the church for that special occasion, as it is showed in His last prayer on the earth:

I have manifested Your name to the men whom You have given Me out of the world. They were Yours, You gave them to Me, and they have kept Your word.
Now they have known that all things which You have given Me are from You.
For I have given to them the words which You have given Me; and they have received them, and have known surely that I came forth from You; and they have believed that You sent Me.
That they all may be one, as You, Father, are in Me, and I in You; that they also may be one in Us, that the world may believe that You sent Me.
And the glory which You gave Me I have given them, that they may be one just as We are one:
I in them, and You in Me; that they may be made perfect in one, and that the world may know that You have sent Me, and have loved them as You have loved Me.

John 17:6–8, 21–23

In this way, the church will *judge* the world and the angels—she will be the living evidence of the testimony of the life (person) and word of Jesus Christ.

The four creatures standing before the throne of God show the work and word of Christ (four gospels) by which all convicts will be judged. Read John 12:47–48, as mentioned before. The subsection *The Four Living Creatures* of the section *The Vision of the Throne of God* (Revelation 4:1–11), describes in more detail the meaning of these four creatures in relation to the four gospels and Jesus' work.

The word left by Jesus to all mankind will be the "tool" used by God the Father to judge everyone: "the word that I have spoken will judge him in the *last day*" (John 12:48). The four living creatures represent the four gospels, that is, the word of Jesus.

As for the angels of the Lord, these will serve as witnesses to the just judgment of God. The Scriptures show the angels as witnesses of the works of men and even of Christ.

> For I think that God has displayed us, the apostles, last, as men condemned to death; for we have been made a spectacle to the world, both to angels and to men.
>
> 1 Corinthians 4:9

> I charge you before God and the Lord Jesus Christ and the elect angels that you observe these things without prejudice, doing nothing with partiality.
>
> 1 Timothy 5:21; see also v. 3:16

> He who overcomes shall be clothed in white garments, and I will not blot out his name from the Book of Life; but I will confess his name before My Father and before His angels.
>
> Revelation 3:5

In short, the final judgment will be a just trial, in which the just Judge the Father will present a complete and accurate evidence before each accused one. The sources of evidence are described as follows: bad works recorded in the books opened before them; the word spoken by Jesus, represented by the four living creatures; the testimony of the living word experienced by the life of obedience in love by the victorious church, represented by the twenty-four elders; and the angels, who by their missions around the world, serve as witnesses of the works done by the inhabitants of the earth. There will be no excuse from the accused ones to present before the throne of God.

New Heaven and New Earth

Revelation 21:1

"Now I saw a new heaven and a new earth, for the first heaven and the first earth had passed away. Also there was no more sea." There is a very similar verse in Isaiah 65:17, "For behold, I create new heavens and a new earth; and the former shall not be remembered or come to mind."

These passages speak of a new creation designed by the divine mind. This will be the eternal-dwelling place for all who now remain faithful and holy before God. These are men and women, who even despise their own lives in order to serve the Lord with all love and obedience. To God be the glory and honor forever!

It seems that at the same time the final judgment is being accomplished by God the Father (*the Ancient of* Days—Daniel 7:9) from His throne of glory, the Lord Jesus is working in the creation of the new heaven and new earth. The apostle John says in verse 20:11, "Then I saw a great white throne and Him who sat on it, from whose face the earth and the heaven fled away. And there was found no place for them."

So the current earth and heaven will move from their places and shall be found no more. The Book of Hebrews describes the shock that the earth and heaven will suffer, when it says,

> whose voice then shook the earth; but now He has promised, saying, 'Yet once more I shake not only the earth, but also heaven.'
> Now this, 'Yet once more,' indicates the removal of those things that are being shaken, as of things that are made, that the things which cannot be shaken may remain.'
> Hebrews 12:26–27

Therefore, the Lord Jesus will remove the movable (impermanent) things from the earth and the heaven, that the immovable (permanent) things remain, things created for eternity, which will never be changed or destroyed again.

The apostle Peter says in his second epistle what will happen to the heaven and earth which now exist (movable things): they will be totally burned.

But the heavens and the earth which are now preserved
by the same word, are reserved for fire until the day of
judgment and perdition of ungodly men.

But, beloved, do not forget this one thing, that with the Lord
one day is as a thousand years, and a thousand years as one day.
The Lord is not slack concerning His promise, as some count
slackness, but is longsuffering toward us, not willing that
any should perish but that all should come to repentance.
But the day of the Lord will come as a thief in the night, in
which the heavens will pass away with a great noise, and
the elements will melt with fervent heat; both the earth and
the works that are in it will be burned up.

Therefore, since all these things will be dissolved, what
manner of persons ought you to be in holy conduct and
godliness, looking for and hastening the coming of the day
of God, because of which the heavens will be dissolved,
being on fire, and the elements will melt with fervent heat?
Nevertheless we, according to His promise, look for new
heavens and a new earth in which righteousness dwells.

2 Peter 3:7–13

Romans 8:19–22 declares that the creation cries for a change
(redemption) because of the mankind sins,

For the earnest expectation of the creation eagerly waits
for the revealing of the sons of God.
For the creation was subjected to futility, not willingly,
but because of Him who subjected it in hope; because the
creation itself also will be delivered from the bondage of
corruption into the glorious liberty of the children of God.
For we know that the whole creation groans and labors
with birth pangs together until now.

All of earth and heaven will experience a total transformation. God
wants nothing from old—everything will be made new, and it will be
completed by the Lord Jesus. All things were created through Jesus and for
Him, as it is stated in the epistles to the Colossians and Hebrews:

For by Him all things were created that are in heaven and
that are on earth, visible and invisible, whether thrones

or dominions or principalities or powers. All things were created through Him and for Him.
And He is before all things, and in Him all things consist.

Colossians 1:16–17

... through whom also He made the worlds [universe]; who being the brightness of His glory and the express image of His person, and upholding all things by the word of His power, ...

Hebrews 1:2–3

This means that if Jesus was the one who created the first earth and heaven, then He will be the one who will work on them again, creating a new earth and new heaven as one of His last works.

Let us pause and look, in general terms, at the different transformations that the earth has experienced over the centuries, from its creation until what is prophesied to occur at the end.

In the beginning God created the heavens and the earth. The earth was without form, and void; and darkness was on the face of the deep. And the Spirit of God was hovering over the face of the waters.

Genesis 1:1–2

We all know that what God makes, He makes it good and perfect. He does not make things incomplete or with flaws. We see in this passage that after God created the heavens and earth, everything was disordered and empty. The earth was without form. Jeremiah 4:23 says, "I beheld the earth, and indeed it was without form, and void; and the heavens, they had no light." In the Darby Bible (see *References*), this same passage says, "I beheld the earth, and lo, it was waste and empty; and the heavens, and they had no light."

Would God create something so important as the heavens and earth, without form, desolate, and as waste? I do not think so. God "did not create it in vain, who formed it to be inhabited" (Isa. 45:18). It is possible that after the heavens and the earth were perfectly created, something happened to them.

Without going into details on this topic, because I do not want to blur the purpose of this book, it could be that the heavens and earth were disordered by the devil, when he, as an angel of light, was thrown out of heaven for his rebellion against God.

Ezekiel 28:2–19 describes what could refer to Satan, and specifically it mentions that "You were in Eden, the garden of God; ... You were the anointed cherub who covers; I established you; you were on the holy mountain of God; you walked back and forth in the midst of fiery stones."

So it may be that Satan, together with the army of angels whom he deceived, and in rebellion against God, spoiled the heavens and the earth, creating the chaos shown in the second verse of chapter one of Genesis.

After the destructive work of Satan, God restored everything He had done at the beginning, which we see in the following verses of the first chapter of Genesis. The heavens and the earth returned to normality, as God had created them at the beginning. Psalm 104:5–9 also mentions this fact.

You who laid the foundations of the earth, so that it should not be moved forever, …
They went up over the mountains; they went down into the valleys, to the place which You founded for them.
You have set a boundary that they may not pass over, that they may not return to cover the earth.

This scripture shows how the earth underwent a change from how it was created at the beginning. God then restored it to how it was previously founded (created). We must note that the *beginning* of Genesis 1:1 is not the *first day* of verse five. We can know the time (age) of the first day, but we cannot know the time of the beginning.

Another drastic change experienced by the earth was at the time of the prophet Noah, when the entire earth was flooded with water. In this flood, the earth was totally impacted in such a way that it seems even the continents changed to different shapes and positions, and new islands sprang up. The earth that emerged after the flood was not the same as the one God created (or restored). Indeed, we can affirm that the earth on which we live today is the earth from after the flood.

The current earth will endure another major change, this time very positive. It will enter into rest, in which nature will no more suffer the chaos of war or any other catastrophic phenomenon, at least for the period of a thousand years, when Jesus will reign on earth.

Nature will again have its great splendor as in the time of creation, although not in total perfection. The Scriptures do say that there will be drought in some disobedient nations in the Millennium. This means that a work on the earth needs to be completed to bring it to the place of total perfection.

God prophesied that after the thousand years the earth will be destroyed, not again with water, but with fire. Since the first man sinned, nature "groans and labors with birth pangs," and has been a slave of corruption, although not willingly. It moans waiting for her redemption, that is, a total change where she can grow in peace and rest forever (Rom. 8:19–22).

Although in the Millennium the earth will experience a great rest, its total redemption will only be fulfilled through the creation of the new heaven and the new earth, after the baptism with fire on the present heaven and earth is completed. God revealed this truth through His servant Peter (see 2 Peter 3:7–13, mentioned earlier in this section).

God will not obliterate the actual earth, but will restore it, creating everything new in it. Ecclesiastes 1:4 says that "One generation passes away, and another generation comes; but the earth abides forever." This is the last change the heavens and earth will undergo, because the throne of God and the Lamb will move to the new earth, together with the church, the people of God, and His angels, for all eternity.

Who will be the designer and builder of the new Holy City, the New Jerusalem, which will be located in the new earth? The answer of this question is found in the next section.

Verse one of chapter 21 of Revelation ends by saying that "there was no more sea." I have no certainty of what this means—whether all the seas and oceans of the earth, or only the sea which is close to Israel, the Mediterranean Sea. One thing can indeed be inferred: when the earth is burnt with fire, all water bodies on earth will be dried up. I do not know if God will fill some places with water again, but we can at least deduce that the Mediterranean Sea will exist no more.

The Holy City, the New Jerusalem

Revelation 21:2–27; 22:1–5

> Then I, John, saw the holy city, New Jerusalem, coming down out of heaven from God, prepared as a bride adorned for her husband.
> And I heard a loud voice from heaven saying, 'Behold, the tabernacle of God is with men, and He will dwell with them, and they shall be His people. God Himself will be with them and be their God.

And God will wipe away every tear from their eyes; there shall be no more death, nor sorrow, nor crying. There shall be no more pain, for the former things have passed away.' Then He who sat on the throne said, 'Behold, I make all things new.' And He said to me, 'Write, for these words are true and faithful.'

And He said to me, 'It is done! I am the Alpha and the Omega, the Beginning and the End. I will give of the fountain of the water of life freely to him who thirsts.'

Revelation 21:2–6

As it was said earlier, this holy city, the New Jerusalem, which comes down from heaven, represents the church of the Lord, which is also His wife. God promised a land to Israel, and that promise is fulfilled during the thousand years' kingdom. But that land was not the promise for the church. The church's promise is the dwelling in the new created city, the New Jerusalem, in a permanent union as wife of the Lord Jesus Christ. Revelation 3:12 and 22:4 say that

He who overcomes, I will make him a pillar in the temple of My God, and he shall go out no more. I will write on him the name of My God and the name of the city of My God, the New Jerusalem, which comes down out of heaven from My God. And I will write on him My new name.

They shall see His face, and His name shall be on their foreheads.

This means that the members of the church of the Lord shall be identified by the name of God, the name of the New Jerusalem, and the new name of the Lord Jesus (... *My new name*).

These new names are a sign that shows we are the exclusive property of God, and that we are citizens and permanent members of the holy city, the New Jerusalem. This is a great privilege and honor to all who overcome before the Great Tribulation takes place. The afflictions and testing experienced in our lives on this earth are not comparable with the coming glory to be manifested very soon. Blessed be our God and blessed be His holy name!

We see the church "coming down out of heaven from God." She comes from God and with God, because she was with God.

Jesus will be King and Lord in the Millennium; His throne will be in the current earthly Jerusalem. The church and God the Father are not seen together with Jesus on His throne in the millennial kingdom. The throne in the Millennium is for King Jesus, as mentioned in a previous reference, which says, "my servant David [Jesus] will be king over them."

Therefore, we can understand that the throne of God the Father, together with the church and the thousands of angels, will remain in heaven during the time of the Millennium, while Jesus shall be reigning one thousand years on the earth. After the rapture, the church will serve God the Father before His throne (represented by the twenty-four elders) until her descent to the new earth as the bride, for her wedding with the Lord Jesus Christ.

At the same time God the Father comes down out of heaven with the church, He also moves His throne to the new earth, and places it in the midst of the holy city, the New Jerusalem. This is clearly seen through the following verses or phrases:

> Behold, the tabernacle of God is with men, and He will dwell with them, and they shall be His people. God Himself will be with them and be their God.
> But I saw no temple in it, for the Lord God Almighty and the Lamb are its temple.
> The city had no need of the sun or of the moon to shine in it, for the glory of God illuminated it. The Lamb is its light.
> And he showed me a pure river of water of life, clear as crystal, proceeding from the throne of God and of the Lamb.
> The throne of God and of the Lamb shall be in it.
> For the Lord God gives them light. And they shall reign forever and ever.
> Revelation 21:3, 22–23; 22:1, 3, 5

The Father Himself will be on the new earth as King and God Almighty. The new earth, with its new heaven, will be the perfect place for the abode of God the Father with His Son Jesus Christ. They will be in the middle of the church, reigning over Israel and the other nations. Behold a great revelation: the Millennium can be called the Kingdom of Jesus Christ; however, the new earth can be called the Kingdom of the Father. The following passages strengthen this statement.

But I say to you, I will not drink of this fruit of the vine
from now on until that day when I drink it new with you
in *My Father's kingdom.*

Matthew 26:29

And has made us kings and priests *to His God and Father.*
To him who overcomes I will grant to sit with Me on My
throne, as I also overcame and *sat down with My Father
on His throne.*
And have made us kings and priests *to our God*; and we
shall reign on the earth.

Revelation 1:6; 3:21; 5:10

God the Father has reserved His kingdom to be revealed when
everything is new and perfect—when His Son had completed all the work
committed to Him, including subjecting Himself to God the heavenly
Father. The new earth is the Kingdom of the Father, where the church
and Christ will partake of the fruit of the vine (wine) in their wedding
ceremony. For more details on this topic, please refer to the sections on
Revelation 1:1–8, *The Prophetic Book,* and 19:1–9, *Wedding on the New
Earth.*

The New Jerusalem is a city and it is also the church. Another name
for the New Jerusalem is the "tabernacle of God" (v. 21:3). In Ephesians
2:21–22, the apostle Paul, referring to the church, says,

in whom the whole building, being fitted together, grows
into a holy temple in the Lord, in whom you also are being
built together for a dwelling place of God in the Spirit.

The church is that tabernacle of God, a holy temple and dwelling place
of God in the Spirit. The word of God comes out from her, and faithful
people serve Him there in all truth and obedience. Verse 3:12 says, "He
who overcomes, I will make him a pillar in the temple of My God, and he
shall go out no more."

There is a great revelation in John 14:2–3; the Lord Jesus mentions
many dwelling places where the members of the church will be with the
Father:

In My Father's house are many mansions; if it were not
so, I would have told you. I go to prepare a place for you.

269

> And if I go and prepare a place for you, I will come again
> and receive you to Myself; that where I am, there you may
> be also.

Although we may call the current church the building of God and the dwelling place of the Spirit, those names shall have their full meaning and reality on the new earth. Jesus promised *many mansions* in His Father's house. The passage says that Jesus is the one who will prepare those places for the church (*I go to prepare a place for you*).

When will Jesus "build" these dwelling places? As mentioned in the section *The Final Judgment*, while God the Father is conducting the final judgment on unbelievers from His heavenly throne, Jesus will be working on the new heaven and earth, including the *many mansions*, located in the holy city, the New Jerusalem.

Jesus said in Matthew 16:18, "I will build [*spiritually*] my church;" and now on the new earth, Jesus will be building *physically* the great city, the New Jerusalem, the dwelling place for the church, His wife.

In the middle of that city, Jesus will build the new throne of God His Father. Every detail will be completed as His last work, before His final encounter with His bride. After the final judgment ends, God the Father will then bring the bride, the church, to give her to His Son. "Then I, John, saw the holy city, New Jerusalem, coming down out of heaven from God, prepared as a bride adorned for her husband" (v. 21:2).

Jesus will be waiting for His bride in front of all the marvelous and glorious work He has prepared for her in the New Jerusalem, *that where I am, there you may be also.*

Revelation 21:4 and 6 say,

> ... for the former things have passed away.
> And He said to me, '*It is done!* I am the Alpha and the
> Omega, the Beginning and the End.'

The phrase *It is done!* is used two times in the Book of Revelation and once in the Gospel of John (said by Jesus with a little variation).

John 19:30 says: "So when Jesus had received the sour wine, He said, '*It is finished!*' And bowing His head, He gave up His spirit." With this final exclamation (*It is finished*), Jesus is completing His work as the "Son of Man."

He went to the cross and "nailed" the "man" on it, including everything pertaining to death—sins and sicknesses (Isa. 53:4–6, 10). As a man, although still being the Son of God, He carried on His own body the sins and sicknesses of mankind, and doing this, He "killed" death. In Luke 24:6–7, we find that two angels stood by and said,

> He is not here, but is risen! Remember how He spoke to you when He was still in Galilee, saying, 'The *Son of Man* must be delivered into the hands of sinful men, and be crucified, and the third day rise again '

Mark 15:39 also says: "So when the centurion, who stood opposite Him, saw that He cried out like this and breathed His last, he said, 'Truly this *Man* was the Son of God!'" Hallelujah, Jesus, the Son of Man, finished His work of our justification, dying on the cross as a man! So He could cry out: *It is finished!*, that is, *It is done!*.

The second place the phrase *It is done!* is found is in verse 16:17, where it marks the completion of Jesus' work during "this generation;" which covers from Jesus' birth up to His second coming. Therefore, with the return of Jesus to the earth this generation is completed, as it says in Mathew 24:34, "Assuredly, I say to you, this generation will by no means pass away till all these things take place."

The expression *It is done!* is last used in verse 21:6, but this time it announces the completion of the "last generation," before the perfect and eternal new world comes. The last generation covers the time of the Millennium and the final judgment. The redeeming and saving work of Jesus for all mankind of all time is completed at the end of the last generation. "My food is to do the will of Him who sent Me, and to finish His work" (John 4:34).

Hallelujah, glory to God! This is the most awaited hour of all time, when Jesus is declared the conqueror for all generations. Jesus is the fulfillment of all prophecy, "For the testimony of Jesus is the spirit of prophecy" (v. 19:10). This is the time for the fulfillment of *God's ultimate purpose*, when all things in heaven and on earth gather together in His Son,

> having made known to us the mystery of His will, according to His good pleasure which He purposed in Himself, that in the dispensation of the fullness of the times He might gather together in one all things in Christ, both which are in heaven and which are on earth—in Him.
> Ephesians 1:9–10

The time to celebrate the great victory of the Lord Jesus on the new earth has come. And it is not by chance that this great celebration will coincide with the consummation of the Lord Jesus' wedding with the church. The wedding will be the final reward of our Lord Jesus Christ after the completion of all His work; *"I am the Alpha and the Omega, the Beginning and the End."*

It is after His whole work is finished and everything gathers together in Him, that Jesus then delivers everything into the hands of His Father. 1 Corinthians 15:24–28 describes this great and glorious event which marks the end of Jesus' work:

> Then comes the end, when He delivers the kingdom to God the Father, when He puts an end to all rule and all authority and power.
> For He must reign till He has put all enemies under His feet.
> The last enemy that will be destroyed is death.
> For 'He has put all things under His feet.' But when He says 'all things are put under Him,' it is evident that He who put all things under Him is excepted.
> Now when all things are made subject to Him, then the Son Himself will also be subject to Him who put all things under Him, *that God may be all in all.*

This is within the plan and purpose of God that this prophecy of Corinthians will be fulfilled. Jesus Christ has overcome, and as Son, He will deliver everything to His Father, so that the Father has all the supremacy in His new kingdom located in the new creation. God Himself will be there, along with Jesus and the church, reigning from His throne in the New Jerusalem.

In short, in the Millennium Jesus Christ shall be King over people that have not yet reached perfection; that is why we see at the end of that period many nations rebelling against Jesus.

On the other hand, when God the Father is the King on the new earth, everything in His kingdom will be new and perfect. The Father shall not reign in a disobedient and rebellious kingdom, but in one perfected through the finished work of His Son. Everything will be new ("for the former things have passed away")—the earth, the heaven, and everything in them, including the church. The members of the church and even Jesus will have new names, as verses 2:17 and 3:12 say,

... To him who overcomes I will give some of the hidden manna to eat. And I will give him a white stone, and on the stone a *new name* written which no one knows except him who receives it.

He who overcomes, I will make him a pillar in the temple of My God, and he shall go out no more. I will write on him the name of My God and the name of the city of My God, the New Jerusalem, which comes down out of heaven from My God. And I will write on him *My new name.*

The name Jesus, as the Son of Man, will change; not so the Father's. The Name of the Father will not change on the new earth, because His Name is eternal; HE IS and WILL BE forever.

And God said to Moses, *"I AM WHO I AM."* And He said, "Thus you shall say to the children of Israel, '*I AM* has sent me to you.'"

... This is *My name forever,* and this is *My memorial to all generations.*

Exodus 3:14–15

The twenty-four elders, who were around the throne in heaven, are seen no more on the new earth. They had a special and unique meaning which is finally fulfilled when the church comes down from heaven as the Lamb's wife.

Likewise, neither the four heavenly creatures which were around the throne of God are seen on the new earth, because what they represented is now fully manifested in the victorious person of Christ. There will be no more symbols or representations on the new earth, but everything will be real and true.

The members of the church, joint heirs with Christ, will have a special place in the Kingdom of the Father. They shall reign together with Christ over Israel and all the other nations.

But you are those who have continued with Me in My trials.

And I bestow upon you a kingdom, just as My Father bestowed one upon Me, that you may eat and drink at My table in My kingdom, and sit on thrones judging the twelve tribes of Israel.

Luke 22:28–30

In Matthew 19:28, Jesus put it this way: "So Jesus said to them, 'Assuredly I say to you, that in the *regeneration*, when the Son of Man sits on the throne of His glory, you who have followed Me will also sit on twelve thrones, judging the twelve tribes of Israel.'" Regeneration is a term that denotes and identifies the genuine new era to be established on the new earth, where *God is all in all*. The Father will be there as the *Supreme King* and *God Almighty*.

Israel will be the people of God who will occupy the nearest place around the New Jerusalem; then all the other nations shall be located around Israel, towards the four corners of the earth. The angels of God will also be present on the new earth, as servants of God and the holy city (v. 21:12).

Summarizing, on the new earth, in addition to God the Father and Jesus Christ, there will be four types of inhabitants: the church (inside the city), Israel (around the city), the other nations (around Israel), and the angels in every place.

Let us see what the above-referenced passages reveal about the church. The New Jerusalem is the city where the church shall dwell exclusively, together with the Father on His throne and our Lord Jesus Christ, and the angels. The apostle John describes the church as a wife adorned for her husband, prepared and splendidly arranged, having the glory of God. Never before have this majesty, splendor, and glory been seen in the church.

We see Christ, the Lamb and Husband, in the midst of the church (vv. 21:22–23). This is the church that came out of heaven from God:

> ... 'Come, I will show you the bride, the Lamb's wife.'
> And he carried me away in the Spirit to a great and high mountain, and showed me the great city, the holy Jerusalem, descending out of heaven from God.
> Revelation 21:9-10

Verses 21:11–21 describe that splendor and glory of the church. This passage describes its walls, gates, and foundations—all built of precious metals and stones.

The city will be established as a square shape, with a high wall around it. This wall has twelve gates, three on each side, with the names of the twelve tribes of Israel, and twelve angels at the gates (v. 21:12). The wall of the city will be built on twelve foundations, on which will be written the names of the twelve apostles of Jesus (v. 21:14).

The names of the twelve tribes of Israel and the twelve apostles identify two peoples, both Jewish and Gentile believers, united now in only one holy nation—the New Jerusalem. This picture greatly resembles the twenty-four elders before the throne of God, in which from two peoples Christ made one. This picture was seen by the apostle Paul, when he wrote to the church in Ephesus:

> For He Himself is our peace, who has made both one, and has broken down the middle wall of separation, having abolished in His flesh the enmity, that is, the law of commandments contained in ordinances, so as to create in Himself one new man from the two, thus making peace, and that He might reconcile them both to God in one body through the cross, thereby putting to death the enmity.
>
> Ephesians 2:14–16

Ephesians 2:20, speaking about the church, says, "having been built on the foundation of the apostles and prophets, Jesus Christ Himself being the chief cornerstone." The prophets mentioned here are not those of the Old Testament, but the prophets of the new covenant era (see Ephesians 3:5).

As the apostles are described as the foundation of the church in this passage of Ephesians, they are also described as the foundation of the New Jerusalem in the Book of Revelation.

In Ephesians 2:11–16, we see that the Gentiles (non-Jewish people) were strangers to the covenants of promise to Israel (the Jews). The Lord Jesus Christ reconciled both peoples (Gentiles and Jews) to God in one body (the church) through His cross, bringing them together now into their eternal dwelling place on the new earth, that is, the New Jerusalem.

Revelation 21:16–17 shows the measures and shape the city and its walls shall have.

> The city is laid out as a square; its length is as great as its breadth. And he measured the city with the reed: twelve thousand furlongs. Its length, breadth, and height are equal.
>
> Then he measured its wall: one hundred and forty-four cubits, according to the measure of a man, that is, of an angel.

One furlong is a linear Greek measure equivalent to approximately 180 meters; and a cubit is equivalent to approximately 45 centimeters (Ref. 16). Therefore, we obtain the following equivalents:

12,000 furlongs = 2,160 kilometers = 1,342 miles
144 cubits = 64.8 meters = 212 feet (equal to a building of approximately 22 stories)

In figure 19: The Holy City, the New Jerusalem, the shape and approximate measures of the city are shown.

In order to better visualize the area which this city will cover, let me compare this city with the United States. The area that the New Jerusalem will occupy is approximately 4,665,600 square kilometers. The area occupied by the continental United States is 7,828,391 square kilometers (Ref. 17). Therefore, the holy city will occupy approximately 60% of the total area of the United States, or to visualize it another way, from the western coast to the Mississippi River.

There is no temple in the holy city because God Himself and the Lamb are her temple. The city does not need sun or moon, for the glory of God illuminates her and the Lamb is her light (vv. 21:23; 22:5). Isaiah also talks about the holy city:

> The sun shall no longer be your light by day, nor for brightness shall the moon give light to you; but the Lord will be to you an everlasting light, and your God your glory. Your sun shall no longer go down, nor shall your moon withdraw itself; for the Lord will be your everlasting light, and the days of your mourning shall be ended.
>
> Isaiah 60:19–20

So in the new city there shall be no more night, since there will be light always. But not so in the other nations of the world, which will continue receiving the glow of the sun and the moon.

The city will have only one street built of pure gold and located in the middle of the city (vv. 21:21; 22:2). This street will end at the throne of God. The kings of the saved nations which came out of the Millennium will enter into this city and walk on the street to bring their glory and honor to God.

> And the nations of those who are saved shall walk in its light, and the kings of the earth bring their glory and honor into it. And they shall bring the glory and the honor of the nations into it.
>
> Revelation 21:24, 26

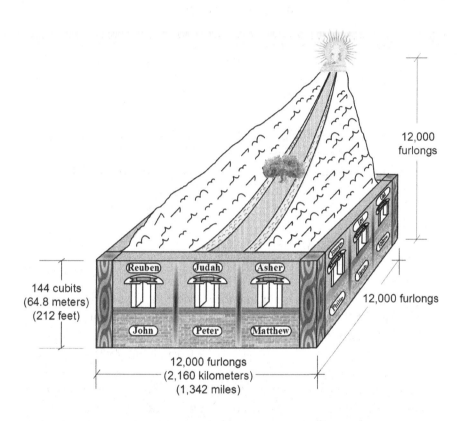

Figure 19: The Holy City, the New Jerusalem

"And God will wipe away every tear from their eyes [from nations, not the church]; there shall be no more death, nor sorrow, nor crying. There shall be no more pain, for the former things have passed away" (v. 21:4). Everything will be rejoicing, life, and salvation in this new earth. No more pain, no more suffering, no more death.

Sin is a poison which ensures death, both physically and spiritually. Remember that sin is the source of all evil, including death.

> Therefore, just as through one man sin entered the world, and death through sin, and thus death spread to all men, because all sinned.
>
> Romans 5:12

> But each one is tempted when he is drawn away by his own desires and enticed.
> Then, when desire has conceived, it gives birth to sin; and sin, when it is full-grown, brings forth death.
>
> James 1:14–15

> 'O Death, where is your sting?
> O Hades, where is your victory?'
>
> The sting of death is sin, and the strength of sin is the law. But thanks be to God, who gives us the victory through our Lord Jesus Christ.
>
> 1 Corinthians 15:55–57

Christ came to overcome and destroy death forever; therefore, on the new earth there will be no more death. "He will swallow up death forever, and the Lord God will wipe away tears from all faces; the rebuke of His people he will take away from all the earth; for the Lord has spoken" (Isa. 25:8).

We must remember two things about the new earth: first, everyone will be new in everything, including their bodies, which shall no longer be corruptible; second, the provoker and tempter to sin is Satan, and he will be in the lake of fire and brimstone for all eternity.

> He who overcomes shall inherit all things, and I will be his God and he shall be My son.

But the cowardly, unbelieving, abominable, murderers, sexually immoral, sorcerers, idolaters, and all liars shall have their part in the lake which burns with fire and brimstone, which is the second death.

Revelation 21:7–8

Dear reader, while the door is open, you can enter and find green pastures; enter now through His door because you do not know when it will be closed. You can become a son of God now, and be delivered from all the torments that shall come upon the whole world, including the lake of fire and brimstone. This word is faithful and true. "... I will give of the fountain of the water of life freely to him who thirsts" (v. 21:6).

And he showed me a pure river of water of life, clear as crystal, proceeding from the throne of God and of the Lamb.
In the middle of its street, and on either side of the river, was the tree of life, which bore twelve fruits, each tree yielding its fruit every month. The leaves of the tree were for the healing of the nations.
And there shall be no more curse, but the throne of God and of the Lamb shall be in it, and His servants shall serve Him.

Revelation 22:1–3

See the river, the tree of life, and the golden street in figure 19.

The tree produces twelve fruits, one each month, which means that each year continues having twelve months. The leaves of the tree will be for the health of the nations. What I understand is that these leaves from the tree of life will be to preserve the health of the inhabitants of the nations; but this does not mean that there will be diseases in their midst. Verse 21:4 confirms this statement, saying that "there shall be no more death, nor sorrow, nor crying. There shall be no more pain."

So there will not be any kind of disease in the nations that causes these types of suffering. It is important to note that these leaves are for the nations and not for the church. The church is the wife of Christ and she is immersed in the whole presence and glory of God, being partaker of His fullness; so she does not require anything to preserve her health. However, in accordance with verses 2:7 and 22:14, it is possible that the church eats the fruits produced by the tree of life:

279

He who has an ear, let him hear what the Spirit says to the churches. To him who overcomes I will give to eat from the tree of life, which is in the midst of the Paradise of God.
Blessed are those who do His commandments, that they may have the right to the tree of life, and may enter through the gates into the city.

The passage ends with the phrase, *And they shall reign forever and ever.* What a wonderful picture and what great glory and splendor are prepared for those who belong to the church of the Lord! It is a great privilege, merged also with much responsibility for those who have given their lives to the Lord in body, soul, and spirit. To Him be the glory and honor forever.

The Last Exhortation

Revelation 22:6–21

This passage provides the last written exhortation of the Lord Jesus to all mankind. The Lord emphasizes again that the things written in this Book of Revelation are

> to show His servants the things which must shortly take place.
> 'Behold, I am coming quickly! Blessed is he who keeps the words of the prophecy of this book.'
> Revelation 22:6–7

It is time to practice justice and to sanctify ourselves even more to produce the fruits that please God. "Every branch in Me that does not bear fruit He takes away; and every branch that bears fruit He prunes, that it may bear more fruit" (John 15:2). We cannot cease to bear fruits for God; it is necessary to finish the race pleasing Him in everything and obeying His word. There is no guarantee in the Lord apart from keeping His word with all our hearts.

'And behold, I am coming quickly, and My reward is with
Me, to give to every one according to his work.
I am the Alpha and the Omega, the Beginning and the
End, the First and the Last.'
Blessed are those who do His commandments, that they
may have the right to the tree of life, and may enter through
the gates into the city.

Revelation 22:12–14

"But outside are dogs and sorcerers and sexually immoral and
murderers and idolaters, and whoever loves and practices a lie" (v. 22:15).
Definitely the dogs mentioned in this verse do not refer to animals, many
of whom are pets in our homes. Deuteronomy 23:17–18 brings light on
this word,

There shall be no ritual harlot of the daughters of Israel,
or a perverted one of the sons of Israel.
You shall not bring the wages of a harlot or the price of
a dog to the house of the Lord your God for any vowed
offering, for both of these are an abomination to the Lord
your God.

Therefore, the word *dog* refers to a sodomite or sexually perverse man
(homosexual). Also, Philippians 3:2 says, "Beware of dogs, beware of evil
workers, beware of the mutilation!"

When God revealed to the prophet Daniel the things that would happen
in the end times, He said him, "But you, Daniel, shut up the words, and
seal the book until the time of the end" (Dan. 12:4). Then, He said again,
"Go your way, Daniel, for the words are closed up and sealed till the time
of the end" (Dan. 12:9).

To Daniel was not given to know the true meaning of everything that
God showed him. But now the end time has come, and consequently also
comes the time to open the prophecy to all who have ears to hear. The Lord
says to John, "Do not seal the words of the prophecy of this book, *for the
time is at hand*" (v. 22:10).

Dear reader, the Lord has opened the book that was closed; now you
can clearly receive the message that God has for you. Just open your heart,
because He is faithful to save you and make you one of the conquerors who
will live for eternity in the light of Christ.

Do not be deceived with the many doctrines and messages which do not have a true basis in the word of God. Salvation is a light thing for many people, and they think that with the mere fact of accepting the Lord and attending a congregation they are saved. But it is not so; God demands holiness and obedience to His word.

> Pursue peace with all people, and holiness, without which no one will see the Lord.
>
> Hebrews 12:14

> Because you have kept My command to persevere, I also will keep you from the hour of trial which shall come upon the whole world, to test those who dwell on the earth.
>
> Revelation 3:10

The Book of Revelation ends with a last warning of the Lord to all of us:

> If anyone adds to these things, God will add to him the plagues that are written in this book; and if anyone takes away from the words of the book of this prophecy, God shall take away his part from the Book of Life, from the holy city, and from the things which are written in this book.
>
> Revelation 22:18–19

You have to know Jesus Christ. He is revealed through the Holy Spirit; therefore, receive Him into your heart. It is time to seek God and surrender our lives to Him, and to love Him with all our heart, with all our soul, with all our mind, and with all our strength.

> *He who testifies to these things says,*
> *SURELY I AM COMING QUICKLY. AMEN.*
> *EVEN SO, COME, LORD JESUS!*

CHAPTER 6

Russia Will Attack Israel Soon

Has God forgotten the people of Israel and rejected this nation forever? We see that the conflicts with Israel in that part of Middle East become more complex and countless every day. News about Israel continuously goes around the world. This will not stop until all prophecies related to Israel are fulfilled.

What do the Scriptures say about the last events to be performed in that Eastern portion of land? Let us start seeing a little about what God thinks in relation to Israel. Romans 11:25–31 says,

> For I do not desire, brethren, that you should be ignorant of this mystery, lest you should be wise in your own opinion, that blindness in part has happened to Israel until the fullness of the Gentiles has come in.
> And so all Israel will be saved, as it is written:

> > "The Deliverer will come out of Zion,
> > And He will turn away ungodliness from Jacob;
> > For this *is* My covenant with them,
> > When I take away their sins."

> Concerning the gospel they are enemies for your sake, but concerning the election they are beloved for the sake of the fathers.
> For the gifts and the calling of God are irrevocable.
> For as you were once disobedient to God, yet have now obtained mercy through their disobedience, even so these

also have now been disobedient, that through the mercy
shown you they also may obtain mercy.

No, God has not forgotten Israel; His plan and purpose with Israel
remain in force, and they will be fulfilled soon. It seems that the time for
the fulfillment of these prophecies is at hand, but everything shall come to
pass in accordance with the Lord's plan and method.

Why has God preserved Israel in spite of its vicissitudes throughout
its history? Chapters 36 to 39 of the Book of Ezekiel provide great light to
find the answer to this question. We can answer in a simple way as follows:
to make known the name of the Lord throughout the earth.

These chapters of Ezekiel provide a tremendous word of revelation
about the last days of Israel. Since Israel's religious leaders rejected their
Messiah Christ, this country has undergone great distresses, scattered
throughout many other nations. However, although Israel has sinned
against the Lord, His mercy has been extended to them. This is the great
love and righteousness of God.

Chapters 36 and 37 of Ezekiel show the restoration of Israel as a nation,
as God brings them again to their land.

For I will take you from among the nations, gather you out
of all countries, and bring you into your own land.
Then you will remember your evil ways and your deeds
that were not good; and you will loathe yourselves in your
own sight, for your iniquities and your abominations.
Ezekiel 36:24, 31

Chapter 37 of Ezekiel speaks about a valley full of dry human bones,
which after the command from God received life and stood upon their feet.

Then He said to me, 'Son of man, these bones are the
whole house of Israel. They indeed say, "Our bones are
dry, our hope is lost, and we ourselves are cut off!"
Therefore prophesy and say to them, "Thus says the Lord
God: 'Behold, O My people, I will open your graves and
cause you to come up from your graves, and bring you into
the land of Israel.
Then you shall know that I am the Lord, when I have
opened your graves, O My people, and brought you up
from your graves.

I will put My Spirit in you, and you shall live, and I will place you in your own land. Then you shall know that I, the Lord, have spoken it and performed it,' says the Lord.'"

Ezekiel 37:11–14

God has not forgotten His promise for Israel. Through the establishment of the State of Israel in 1948, a new hope was brought to the Jews; tired and overwhelmed by the scattering abroad. These bones represent the people of Israel. God opened their "graves" and brought them up, restoring them to their own land. God knows how and when to do things.

I understand that this prophecy of chapter 37 has double fulfillment. The first was partially completed in 1948. The second will be fully accomplished with the entering of the remnant of Israel into the millennial kingdom, after the Great Tribulation. I encourage you, dear reader, to read carefully the details of this prophecy to see for yourself this double fulfillment affirmation.

But the time has come for God to complete His work. Chapters 38 and 39 of Ezekiel describe a prophecy not yet fulfilled that *will be in the latter days* (Ezek. 38:8, 16). The first fulfillment shall be when Russia, led by its leader "Gog," and its allies, as explained below, shall attack Israel before the commencement of the Great Tribulation.

The second accomplishment of the prophecy will be at the end of the Millennium (see comments on Revelation 20:7–10). The battle against Israel in this second fulfillment will be led by the devil himself, and God will consume all rebel nations with fire. These two different attacks against Israel will be approximately one thousand years apart.

Russia has been preparing military equipment of the most advanced and state-of-the-art technology. It is public knowledge that this nation has signed many types of agreements with other nations, including Arab/Islamic nations, such as Iran. Syria is another of these nations, which has its borders to the north of Israel.

Russia will plan a massive attack on Israel, to occur in a quick and surprising way. But God will not allow Israel to be destroyed. There are several passages in Ezekiel that make us think seriously that an attack of Russia against Israel will be performed soon; I will mention two of them.

Prepare yourself and be ready, you [Gog, Russia's leader; see Ezekiel 38:2–3] and all your companies that are gathered about you; and be a guard for them.

285

After many days you will be visited. In the latter years you will come into the land of those brought back from the sword and gathered from many people on the mountains of Israel, which had long been desolate; they were brought out of the nations, and now all of them dwell safely.

You will ascend, coming like a storm, covering the land like a cloud, you and all your troops and many peoples with you.

'Thus says the Lord God: "On that day it shall come to pass that thoughts will arise in your mind, and you will make an evil plan:

You will say, 'I will go up against a land of unwalled villages; I will go to a peaceful people, who dwell safely, all of them dwelling without walls, and having neither bars nor gates.'"'

Ezekiel 38:7–11

Then you will come from your place out of the far north, you and many peoples with you, all of them riding on horses, a great company and a mighty army.

You will come up against My people Israel like a cloud, to cover the land. It will be in the latter days that I will bring you against My land, so that the nations may know Me, when I am hallowed in you, O Gog, before their eyes.

Ezekiel 38:15–16

Before entering into the description of the battle itself, I would like to touch on the names of the countries mentioned in Ezekiel's prophecy, which will have a direct relation to this battle that Russia will lead against Israel. I will not dedicate too much to this issue, because the purpose of this section is to emphasize the importance of the battle itself and its consequence for Israel after God's intervention. But let us see what the Scriptures say about the countries that shall comprise the coalition military forces headed by Gog.

Now the word of the Lord came to me, saying,
'Son of man, set your face against *Gog*, of the land of *Magog*, the prince of *rosh*, *Meshech*, and *Tubal*, and prophesy against him, and say, "Thus says the Lord God:

'Behold, I am against you, O Gog, the prince of *rosh*, *Meshech*, and *Tubal*.
I will turn you around, put hooks into your jaws, and lead you out, with all your army, horses, and horsemen, all splendidly clothed, a great company with bucklers and shields, all of them handling swords.
Persia, Ethiopia [Cush], and *Libya [Put]* are with them, all of them with shield and helmet;
Gomer and all its troops; the house of *Togarmah* from the far north and all its troops—many people are with you.""'

Ezekiel 38:1–6

After a deep search, looking for information about these ancient countries through many sources, I conclude that there is not much accuracy about the specific location of some of these countries in our current world.

Let us begin with the phrase, "Gog, of the land of Magog, the prince of rosh, Meshec, and Tubal." Many expositors say that "rosh" refers to Russia, grounding their thinking in the similarity of the two words. I think this is not an accurate basis. Just for reference, I will cite the same phrase from three other Bible versions (see *References*), some of them translated to English:

Gog, in the country of Magog, supreme prince of Meshec and Tubal.—BJ
Gog in the land of Magog, sovereign prince of Meshec and Tubal.—RV60
Gog, the land of Magog, the chief prince of Meshec and Tubal.—KJV

I understand that the best interpretation for *rosh* is any of the words used by these three Bible versions—supreme, sovereign, or chief. So this means that Gog is a leader with authority, able to persuade other nations and make agreements of war with them against Israel.

Therefore, the above-mentioned phrase could be rephrased in this way: *Gog, sovereign prince of Meshec and Tubal in the country of Magog.* According to Russia's history, the word *prince* was used since its inception (AD 800) to designate their rulers (Ref. 18).

Let us see now the sites mentioned in these verses 38:2–6 of Ezekiel. What do the Scriptures say about their roots? What are their possible current locations? Genesis 10:1–6 says,

Now this is the genealogy of the sons of Noah: Shem, Ham, and Japheth. And sons were born to them after the flood.

The sons of Japheth were *Gomer, Magog,* Madai, Javan, *Tubal, Meshech,* and Tiras.

The sons of *Gomer* were Ashkenaz, Riphath, and *Togarmah.*

The sons of Javan were Elishah, Tarshish, Kittim, and Dodanim.

From these the coastland peoples of the Gentiles were separated into their lands, everyone according to his language, according to their families, into their nations.

The sons of Ham were *Cush,* Mizraim, *Put,* and Canaan.

The places where the descendants of Noah's sons moved are of great importance, to at least suggest the possible location of the countries that will be Russia's allies in the battle against Israel.

The Scriptures say that Noah's ark rested on the mountains of Ararat (Gen. 8:4), located in the northeastern part of modern Turkey, Asia Minor. According to Genesis chapter 10, Noah's descendants moved from Ararat to the four corners of this place.

Shem's descendants went toward the mountainous eastern region (Gen. 10:30); Ham's descendants were established in Canaan and nearby areas (southeast); and the Japheth's descendants moved to the west and northern regions of Ararat.

Let us see some of these places in a little more detail. Ezekiel says that Gog, a prince or leader, comes from the land of Magog, located in a "place out of the far north [of Israel]" (v. 38:15). Also, Ezekiel 39:2 says, "bringing you up from the far north."

The countries located to the far north of Israel are Turkey and Russia. According to the available information, Magog is in a region of Russia. Tubal is related to Tobolsk, a city in west-central Siberia, Russia. It lies at the confluence of the Irtysh and Tobol rivers. Meshech is identified with Moscow, Russia's capital.

It is interesting that every time the Scriptures mention the word Tubal, it is found together with his brother Meshech—and even more, Magog, Tubal, and Meshech were all brothers, sons of Japheth, who moved to the same region. So Magog, Tubal, and Meshech refer to sites in Russia (Ref. 19).

Gomer (Japheth's son) is said to be called Gimerrai, located to the west of Ararat, at the eastern part of ancient Anatolia (modern Turkey).

Togarmah, Gomer's son, is believed to be a city in the south-eastern part of Asia Minor (actual Turkey). Ezekiel 38:6 locates Gomer and Togarmah to "the far north" of Israel, that is, Turkey, and identifies them as allies of Gog, leader of Russia.

Ezekiel 38:5 mentions three countries (Persia, Ethiopia, and Libya) which are Gog's allies too. Other Bible versions relate Ethiopia and Libya with the names of Cush and Put (Ham's sons), respectively (see references previously mentioned).

Some historians and expositors identify Cush with Northern Sudan and part of Ethiopia in Africa. Libya is an independent Arab country on the northern coast of Africa. Ancient Persia was a land that included parts of modern Iran and Afghanistan. The Persians called that region the "land of the Aryans," from which came the name of Iran. All these countries will also be allies of Russia.

Summarizing, Russia's leader will have at least the following main allies in the battle against Israel: Turkey, Iran, Ethiopia, and Libya. I understand that other nations not included in this group could also collaborate with Russia.

Let us see now what the prophet Ezekiel says about this great battle. There are some verses or phrases that clearly show that Gog, Russia's leader, will be leading the battle, including its planning. First of all, this prophecy is spoken against the person of Gog himself, as verses 38:2–3 state—as per RV60 (see also v. 39:1):

Son of man, set your face against Gog in the land of Magog, sovereign prince of Meshec and Tubal, and prophesy against him, and say, 'Thus says the Lord God: "Behold, I am against you, O Gog, sovereign prince of Meshech, and Tubal."'

I would like to note two passages of chapter 38 related with the battle, where Russia shall take the first step in the planning and development of this battle:

Prepare yourself and be ready, you and all your companies that are gathered about you; and be a guard for them. Thus says the Lord God: 'On that day it shall come to pass that thoughts will arise in your mind, and you will make an evil plan:

289

> You will say, "I will go up against a land of unwalled villages; ...'"
>
> Ezekiel 38:7, 10–11

Russia's leader will gather a *great company* (multitude—v. 38:4; see also vv. 38:6–7, 9, 15) of military forces which come from many allied nations. The multitude is so great that when God destroys them, the house of Israel will be burying them for seven months (v. 39:12); even the place chosen for their burial is called the valley of Hamon-Gog (v. 39:11), which means "multitude of Gog."

According to God's plan, Russia and all the coalition forces will move and come together to gather on the mountains of Israel. They shall come "like a storm, covering the land like a cloud." Thousands of people will gather with only one thought in their minds—to annihilate all the people of Israel. This has been the plan of many other past leaders and dictators.

God will allow them to come very close to Israel, "and I will turn you around and lead you on, bringing you up from the far north, and bring you against the mountains of Israel" (v. 39:2). God will be angry with these enemies of Israel, and He will be waiting for them on the mountains of Israel. "And it will come to pass at the same time, when Gog comes against the land of Israel, says the Lord God, "that My fury will show in My face"" (v. 38:18).

The direct presence of the Lord will cause a great change in the scenario of that battle. The Scriptures say,

> For in My jealousy and in the fire of My wrath I have spoken: 'Surely in that day there shall be a great earthquake in the land of Israel, so that the fish of the sea, the birds of the heavens, the beasts of the field, all creeping things that creep on the earth, and all men who are on the face of the earth shall shake at My presence. The mountains shall be thrown down, the steep places shall fall, and every wall shall fall to the ground.'
>
> Ezekiel 38:19–20

The troops gathered with Gog on the mountains of Israel shall shake with great frightfulness when these surprising events occur. The "hosts" of creation will now "stand up" to lash out against the evil forces which come into the land to fight the people of God's promise. Verses 38:22–23 say

And I will bring him to judgment with pestilence and bloodshed; I will rain down on him, on his troops, and on the many peoples who are with him, flooding rain, great hailstones, fire, and brimstone.

Thus I will magnify Myself and sanctify Myself, and I will be known in the eyes of many nations. Then they shall know that I am the Lord.

Because chapter 39 describes very clearly what will happen to Russia and the coalition countries which come against Israel, I will include part of it here.

And you, son of man, prophesy against Gog, and say, 'Thus says the Lord God: "Behold, I am against you, O Gog, the prince of rosh, Meshech, and Tubal; and I will turn you around and lead you on, bringing you up from the far north, and bring you against the mountains of Israel.

Then I will knock the bow out of your left hand, and cause the arrows to fall out of your right hand.

You shall fall upon the mountains of Israel, you and all your troops and the peoples who are with you; I will give you to birds of prey of every sort and to the beasts of the field to be devoured.

You shall fall on the open field; for I have spoken," says the Lord God.

"And I will send fire on Magog and on those who live in security in the coastlands. Then they shall know that I am the Lord.

So I will make My holy name known in the midst of My people Israel, and I will not let them profane My holy name anymore. Then the nations shall know that I am the Lord, the Holy One in Israel.'"

Ezekiel 39:1–7

God will do amazing things before the eyes of all the enemy's troops. The Lord will suppress all kinds of military forces, even if they are using the most highly-state-of-the-art weapons. Even the Scriptures show that they will kill themselves. Verses 38:21 and 39:3 say,

> Every man's sword will be against his brother.
> Then I will knock the bow out of your left hand, and cause
> the arrows to fall out of your right hand.

A similar event occurred in the time of Gideon, when the Midianites oppressed the Israelites. An army of only three hundred men was chosen by God, with Gideon as their leader. The enemy's army was huge, comprised of Midianites, Amalekites, and the people of the East. The Scriptures describe how this huge army fell before that small group of three hundred men, because of God's direct intervention.

> And every man stood in his place all around the camp; and
> the whole army ran and cried out and fled.
> When the three hundred blew the trumpets, the Lord set
> every man's sword against his companion throughout the
> whole camp; and the army fled ...
>
> Judges 7:21–22

There is another marvelous work of God registered in 2 Chronicles 20:22–24, which says,

> Now when they began to sing and to praise, the Lord
> set ambushes against the people of Ammon, Moab, and
> Mount Seir, who had come against Judah; and they were
> defeated.
> For the people of Ammon and Moab stood up against the
> inhabitants of Mount Seir to utterly kill and destroy them.
> And when they had made an end of the inhabitants of Seir,
> they helped to destroy one another.
> So when Judah came to a place overlooking the wilderness,
> they looked toward the multitude; and there were their
> dead bodies, fallen on the earth. No one had escaped.

In short, this is the word of God. If God did it in the past, why can He not do it again now?

> You will not need to fight in this battle. Position
> yourselves, stand still and see the salvation of the Lord,
> who is with you, O Judah and Jerusalem! Do not fear or

be dismayed; tomorrow go out against them, for the Lord
is with you.

2 Chronicles 20:17

No matter what the secret plans of Russia's leaders are, or the powerful
weapons they will attempt to use, the God Almighty will annul all their
Machiavellian intentions and efforts. The Scriptures speak about this work
of God; Psalm 33:10–11 says:

The Lord brings the counsel of the nations to nothing; He
makes the plans of the peoples of no effect.
The counsel of the Lord stands forever, the plans of His
heart to all generations.

God will not only attack the troops gathered in the mountains of Israel,
but He will also attack mainland Russia and the territories of her coalition
countries. The statement of Ezekiel 39:6 affirms it: "And I will send fire on
Magog and on those who live in security in the coastlands."
This verse could also suggest that this specific accomplishment could
come through an attack of Israeli military air forces on Russia and the
other allied countries, after God intervention. God shall do this for His
own purpose: "Thus I will magnify Myself and sanctify Myself, and I will
be known in the eyes of many nations. Then they shall know that I am the
Lord" (v. 38:23).
In order to know a little more about this prophetic battle, and how
Russia has been building its military plan and strengthening its relationship
with many, mainly Arab/Islamic nations from the East and Middle East, a
few interesting comments, mainly taken from newspapers and magazine
reports, are included in the following list:

- The countries mentioned in Ezekiel, Russia's allies, are mainly
  comprised of Arab/Islamic people.
- The Russians and Ethiopians have developed good relationships
  since many years ago. For example, the Ethiopians were aided by
  Russian military advisers and equipment in the 1977–80's fighting
  with their neighbor Somalia (Ref. 20).
- Syria is one of Russia's most important partners in the Middle
  East region. The Russian navy is reported to be moving ahead
  with plans to upgrade its Soviet-era naval bases at the Syrian
  port of Tartus and Latakia, which have an open access to the

Mediterranean Sea (Ref. 21). Although Syria is not expressly found in Ezekiel's list, Russia has a special interest in this nation due to its very close location to Israel.

- In April 2008, Vladimir Putin became the first Russian leader in history to visit the Islamic country of Libya, to sign several agreements, including the sale of many kinds of military weapons. Libya is reported to be planning to spend $4.7 billion on upgrading its military forces over the next year. Russia is one of the possible sources to complete this investment (Ref. 22).
- In October 2007, Vladimir Putin became the first Russian leader in history to visit the Islamic country of Iran to establish alliances, including high-tech defense systems sales (Ref. 23).
- A Russian leader recently said that Iran is the "main and strategic partner" of Russia in the Middle East. Russia and Iran have had ties in many energy, military, and other economic sector agreements since many years ago, such as: modern military weapons, including nuclear equipment; agriculture; telecommunications; partnerships involving the refining and export of oil and gas; and collaboration in the fields of rail, road, and sea transportation (Ref. 24).

Now, when shall this first fulfillment of the prophecy take place? The following passage shows that this prophecy will have its first fulfillment before the start of the Great Tribulation.

'Then those who dwell in the cities of Israel will go out and set on fire and burn the weapons, both the shields and bucklers, the bows and arrows, the javelins and spears; and they will make fires with them for **seven years**.
They will not take wood from the field nor cut down any from the forests, because they will make fires with the weapons; and they will plunder those who plundered them, and pillage those who pillaged them,' says the Lord God. 'It will come to pass in that day that I will give Gog a burial place there in Israel, the valley of those who pass by east of the sea; and it will obstruct travelers, because there they will bury Gog and all his multitude. Therefore they will call it the Valley of Hamon Gog.
For **seven months** the house of Israel will be burying them, in order to cleanse the land.'

Ezekiel 39:9–12

After the direct intervention of God to defeat the enemy, Israel will be burning the enemy's weapons and other military equipment for seven years. In addition, they will be burying the dead for seven months.

These two events cannot take place at the end of the Millennium, because the next events to happen after the end of the Millennium are the final judgment and the creation of the new earth. At that point, there will not be a period of seven years or seven months to complete the complex cleaning tasks, as described below. We can, therefore, conclude that this portion of the prophecy will begin to be fulfilled before the Great Tribulation.

Let us look now at an interesting fact. How and why will they take seven years to burn the weapons and military equipment of the enemy? How and why will they take seven months to bury the dead fallen in the battle? Why does verse 39:10 say that "They will not take wood from the field nor cut down any from the forests, because they will make fires with the weapons"?

Burned firewood was used as a source of energy for all types of use, and it seems that this will be replaced by the burning of weapons and military equipment. The only way this can happen is that these weapons have energy themselves—they are nuclear arms (Ref. 25).

This may be one of the reasons the burial of bodies takes so long—seven months. In addition to the fact that the dead will be many thousands, the corpses and weapons could be radioactively contaminated. This will require long and complex cleaning processes (v. 39:12). Verses 39:13–16 describe part of these cleaning processes, including day laborers (perhaps workers expert in that field), use of marks or signs, inspection or recognition of the workspace after seven months, and specific places to bury the corpses.

But when will this prophecy be fulfilled, in relation to the rapture of the church? One thing is certain, there is no sign before the rapture occurs. Also, Jesus said that no one knows the time of His coming.

If this battle against Israel could be before the rapture, it would be a clear sign of Jesus' coming for the church. So I understand that this battle will take place after the rapture, but before the Great Tribulation. In this way this will be the last sign for the people of Israel and all the other nations of the earth before the Great Tribulation begins.

I believe that the Lord will use this battle so that many inhabitants in Israel turn their lives and begin to believe and trust in God. When the people of Israel see the powerful intervention of God in this war, many of them will look to God, so that God's purpose and Ezekiel's prophecy will be fulfilled, as follows:

So the house of Israel shall know that I am the Lord their
God from that day forward.
The Gentiles shall know that the house of Israel went into
captivity for their iniquity; because they were unfaithful
to Me, therefore I hid My face from them. I gave them into
the hand of their enemies, and they all fell by the sword.
According to their uncleanness and according to their
transgressions I have dealt with them, and hidden My face
from them.
Therefore thus says the Lord God: Now I will bring back
the captives of Jacob, and have mercy on the whole house
of Israel; and I will be jealous for My holy name.

Ezekiel 39:22–25

Everything God does is for His glory and honor. In the time of the
faithful servant Moses the name God was glorified through the hardening
of Pharaoh's heart. This was His purpose: glorify His name!

But Pharaoh will not heed you, so that I may lay My hand
on Egypt and bring My armies and My people, the children
of Israel, out of the land of Egypt by great judgments.
And the Egyptians shall know that I am the Lord, when I
stretch out My hand on Egypt and bring out the children
of Israel from among them.

Exodus 7:4–5

If God did it in the past, why can He not do it again now? So the same
purpose will be in the Russia's battle against Israel: to glorify the name of
the Lord. The prophet Ezekiel so affirmed it:

You will come up against My people Israel like a cloud,
to cover the land. It will be in the latter days that I will
bring you against My land, so that the nations may know
Me, when I am hallowed in you, O Gog, before their eyes.
Thus I will magnify Myself and sanctify Myself, and I
will be known in the eyes of many nations. Then they shall
know that I am the Lord.

Ezekiel 38:16, 23

And I will send fire on Magog and on those who live in security in the coastlands. Then they shall know that I am the Lord.

So I will make My holy name known in the midst of My people Israel, and I will not let them profane My holy name anymore. Then the nations shall know that I am the Lord, the Holy One in Israel.

Ezekiel 39:6–7

Let us see another interesting fact. We have already seen that the Israelites will take seven years to "burn" (that is, use energy from) the weapons and military equipment of the invaders. We have also seen that this battle of Gog and Magog will mark the beginning of the seven years of the Great Tribulation.

Do you think that the duration of seven years for these two episodes (the disposal of the military weapons and equipment and the Great Tribulation) is a coincidence? Could it be that both prophecies will be fulfilled at the same time? I think that this is what will happen; God has left us that key in the Book of Ezekiel that we may better understand the chronology of all these events that will soon occur on the earth.

This battle shall be the preamble of the public and direct last dealing of God with Israel and other nations. It will be the last sign before the beginning of the Great Tribulation, which will also be the last chance the Israelites and other people of the earth shall have to recognize and believe that Jesus Christ is the Son of God, the Messiah.

Definitely this battle will open the opportunity of a revival in Israel, in such a way that many will assert their faith and believe in God Almighty.

CHAPTER 7

The Church of the Lord

O h, dear reader, Christ is at the door and comes for His church—the church that He is building at this time. But what is that church and where is it? Who constitutes the church of the Lord? What a great blessing it would be if all groups that gather in Jesus' name could be part of the church of the Lord! That would be wonderful; but we know by the fruits we see that this does not seem to be so.

We do see many people today who have a sincere heart and are willing to seek God. May God allow them to find the Lord that they in turn may be found by Him. God seeks worshippers who worship and serve Him in spirit and truth. Serving God is not merely to gather with others, read the Bible, pray, and try to do good works. That is all good, and those things assure us that we are part of a group with good intentions, but they do not guarantee that we are part of the church of the Lord.

What is the church? Who are her members? What is the purpose of the church in this world? These questions are very important, and we need to answer each, especially since we are in the last times—on the last stretch of the race. Let us see what the Scriptures show us about these questions—and I stress, what the Scriptures show, not what the traditions and opinions of many say.

Many times we follow what others say, simply because they are scholarly people, and considered to be wise and teachers of God's word. I am not in the position to criticize and judge others, nor is that the purpose of this chapter of this book. There is only one judge and that is God; when He judges, He does it with equity, justice, and truth.

Dear reader, consider the content of this chapter in the light of the Scriptures, with a sincere and humble heart before the throne of our Lord and Savior Jesus Christ. All of us need a continuous experience with Christ in the Spirit. We must "walk and live in the Spirit," not just be followers of others.

The church was a mystery before Christ's lifetime. This mystery was revealed by God through the apostles and prophets after the death of Christ.

> For this reason I, Paul, the prisoner of Christ Jesus for you Gentiles—if indeed you have heard of the dispensation of the grace of God which was given to me for you, how that by revelation He made known to me the mystery (as I have briefly written already, by which, when you read, you may understand my knowledge in the mystery of Christ), which in other ages was not made known to the sons of men, as it has now been revealed by the Spirit to His holy apostles and prophets:
> that the Gentiles should be fellow heirs, of the same body, and partakers of His promise in Christ through the gospel.
> and to make all see what is the fellowship of the mystery, which from the beginning of the ages has been hidden in God who created all things through Jesus Christ.
> according to the eternal purpose which He accomplished in Christ Jesus our Lord.
>
> Ephesians 3:1–6, 9, 11

Thank to God it is no longer a mystery; the time to open this treasure and make it known has come.

> Now to Him who is able to establish you according to my gospel and the preaching of Jesus Christ, according to the *revelation of the mystery* kept secret since the world began but now made manifest, and by the prophetic Scriptures made known to all nations, according to the commandment of the everlasting God, *for obedience to the faith.*
>
> Romans 16:25–26

The church is not a simple thing; she is part of God's eternal purpose, she is the house of God, the dwelling place of the Holy Spirit, the wife of the Lord Jesus. It was God who designed and founded her, and also He who builds her, not man.

Therefore, the church must develop and grow in accordance with that divine design, which has nothing to do with the religious system implemented by men through the ages. Within the revelation of the mystery, God included not only His design of what the church is, but also His purpose for her.

Now, it is important to note that when God reveals something, He does not do it simply to fill us with knowledge, but *for obedience to the faith.* We cannot remain with our arms crossed in the presence of a word revealed by God; but we must move immediately, giving ourselves with all diligence to the "work of the ministry" (Eph. 4:12), that is, to act and move as members of the body of Christ.

The church that God designed is to express Christ with all pureness and clearness in this world, and to be the instrument used by God to awaken many people, that they might be saved from this perverted and wicked generation.

> And He put all things under His feet, and gave Him to be head over all things to the church, which is His body, the fullness of Him who fills all in all.
>
> Ephesians 1:22–23

This is a great privilege and honor, but also a great responsibility—to be the fullness of Christ, the expression of His glory and majesty. You can see that the church is not anything. Ephesians and 1 Corinthians describe this kind of church:

> ... just as Christ also loved the church and gave Himself for her, that He might sanctify and cleanse her with the washing of water by the word, that He might present her to Himself a glorious church, not having spot or wrinkle or any such thing, but that she should be holy and without blemish.
>
> Ephesians 5:25–27

> For I am jealous for you with godly jealousy. For I have betrothed you to one husband, that I may present you as a chaste virgin to Christ.
>
> 2 Corinthians 11:2

This is the church that Jesus will take away, one in which her members live in true holiness (not appearance), serving God, and clearly expressing Christ in this world. The members of the church are identified by their fruits of the Spirit, and because they keep the word of God and the testimony of Jesus Christ. They are those who do not play the game of religion, because they are faithful and holy.

What great sadness it brings to see many who profess to be Christian but deny the Lord through their lives! "Not everyone who says to Me, 'Lord, Lord,' shall enter the kingdom of heaven, but he who does the will of My Father in heaven" (Matt. 7:21). The church is not an organization or a social or religious group where many gather to have fun and to entertain themselves talking about God.

I feel hurt to see so many adulteries and fornications in many religious organizations. Many so-called believers have had more than one spouse and then, justifying themselves say that the previous relationship occurred before accepting the Lord, or that they were already divorced. Thus they invalidate the word of God, which establishes that the marital union will last until death separates them (Rom. 7:2–3; see also Luke 16:18 and 1 Corinthians 7:10–11, 39).

Marriage, as an institution established by God, is for a man and a woman, regardless of whether or not they are Christian. When a man and a woman unite and live together, the word of God for a marriage is fulfilled, regardless of whether or not a document of commitment has been signed. This legal document, required by governmental laws (and I encourage compliance), does not marry a couple, nor does the lack of it annul the marriage.

The marriage is consummated when the word of God is fulfilled:

'For this reason a man shall leave his father and mother and be joined to his wife, and the two shall become one flesh'; so then they are no longer two, but one flesh.
Therefore what God has joined together, let not man separate.

Mark 10:7–9

Henceforth, any other relationship outside the first marriage (if the spouse lives) is adultery. Repentance before God brings forgiveness of sins, even for adultery; but repentance and forgiveness do not annul the marital union which was formed with the first spouse. The bond is unbroken unless one of them dies.

On the other hand, we also see how many religious groups have become commercial organizations, treating the church as a place of entertainment or business. The money and other carnal aspects have taken control of many leaders. They do not live to serve the Lord, but for their own personal interests. We see how many, showing themselves as leaders and prophets of God, have taken over crowds of people.

Broadly speaking, it is sad to see how in many places the house of God (the church, not the building) has become a "den of thieves" (Matt. 21:13). Where is the holiness and consecration? Where is the obedience to the word of God? What kind of book is used to instruct the people of God?

The church that Jesus Christ builds is a virgin, holy, without spot or wrinkle, prepared as a bride for her husband. This is the church that will be caught up to heaven by Jesus, not another one, "that He might present her to Himself a glorious church, not having spot or wrinkle or any such thing, but that she should be holy and without blemish."

The church of the Lord has a divine personality. She is an organism where the life of God dwells, and moves and walks under the leading of the Holy Spirit. "For as many as are led by the Spirit of God, these are sons of God" (Rom. 8:14). The church consists of all those who are born again, as Jesus said to Nicodemus, "Most assuredly, I say to you, unless one is born again, he cannot see the kingdom of God" (John 3:3).

To be born again is to receive the Holy Spirit, to then walk in the Spirit. These sons of God are saints who do not hesitate to testify of Christ anywhere, not only with their mouths, but with their lives. The Lord said that by our fruits we will be known, not by the many fine words coming out from our mouths, nor for our knowledge.

The Christians who are true members of the church of the Lord are engaged in what is eternal, and everything that honors and pleases God. As it is stated in Romans 12:1, "I beseech you therefore, brethren, by the mercies of God, that you present your bodies a living sacrifice, holy, acceptable to God, which is your reasonable service."

Definitely, Jesus Christ will not "get married" to any group; His wife must be at the spiritual level of Himself: "till we all come to the unity of the faith and of the knowledge of the Son of God, to a perfect man, to the measure of the stature of the fullness of Christ" (Eph. 4:13). We are His "body" and will be His wife; therefore, God, the Father of the Husband, will not accept any mixture, but only a pure virgin, separated and consecrated unto Him.

Many people think that it is not possible to have these qualities here on earth. They think that those are utopian characteristics, and that God shall complete us in heaven, because we are human and we cannot reach that spiritual standard here on earth. They say that God is merciful and will accept them as they are. All this is a great deception of the devil.

The price that Jesus paid, His sufferings and crucifixion, cannot be in vain. We can never override the word of God and the work of the Holy Spirit. If we try to be what God wants us to be by our own strength, knowledge, and abilities, then we have invalidated the redemptive work of Christ and the power of the Holy Ghost.

Christ came to carry our burdens and sins into Him, to then make us capable of experiencing what God demands from our lives. This is the greatness of God—that He Himself does it in us, as it is well said in Hebrews and Colossians:

> make you complete in every good work to do His will, working in you what is well pleasing in His sight, through Jesus Christ, to whom be glory forever and ever.
>
> Hebrews 13:21

> For in Him dwells all the fullness of the Godhead bodily; and you are complete in Him, who is the head of all principality and power.
>
> Colossians 2:9–10

It is not what I can do, but what He does in me. Hallelujah! The church of the Lord is built on the new covenant of the Spirit, where all the old has been put off from her, and she has

> put on the new man who is renewed in knowledge according to the image of Him who created him, where there is neither Greek nor Jew, circumcised nor uncircumcised, barbarian, Scythian, slave nor free, but Christ is all and in all.
>
> Colossians 3:10–11

What about the relationship between the members of the church? The Scriptures teach us that the members of the church are known by their fruits. The greatest of these fruits is love. Jesus taught that we should love each other as He loved us. The love between the brethren must have the same quality as the love of Jesus for others, who even gave His life for mankind. It cannot be a love subject to circumstances or emotions, or in accordance with a personal judgment. Simply, we must love as Jesus loved.

The Lord speaks about the relationship between us in many parts of the Scriptures. As an example, 1 Corinthians 12:12 says, "For as the body is one and has many members, but all the members of that one body, being many, are one body, so also is Christ."

All members of the church are important and necessary. All are a treasure to God, and the union of all of them constitutes His church, His body. Therefore, it is so important that we treat all the brethren with respect and consideration, because each is part of ourselves, and what unites us is not a doctrine, or the meeting place, or anything else, but the love of God poured out in us by the Holy Spirit.

We are one through the Spirit, hallelujah! So, "let us love one another, for love is of God; and everyone who loves is born of God and knows God" (1 John 4:7).

The Lord Jesus builds His church in His own way. He builds on the fellowship between one another. 1 John 1:1–7 is a great passage that we need to experience in a real way. It shows the foundation of the work of building the church. Fellowship is not merely to be together and share some word of God.

Fellowship speaks about a deep relationship in which the oneness and light (truth) of the Spirit are shown. The passage says that "truly our fellowship is with the Father and with His Son Jesus Christ," so, the presence of the Father and Jesus must be in our relationship with one another. "I in them, and You in Me; that they may be made perfect in one, and that the world may know that You have sent Me, and have loved them as You have loved Me" (John 17:23).

God clearly establishes that fellowship is a spiritual relationship worked out upon our real experience with Him:

> That which was from the beginning, which we have heard, which we have seen with our eyes, which we have looked upon, and our hands have handled, concerning the Word of life—the life was manifested, and we have seen, and bear witness, and declare to you that eternal life which was with the Father and was manifested to us—that which we have seen and heard we declare to you, that you also may have fellowship with us; and truly our fellowship is with the Father and with His Son Jesus Christ.
>
> 1 John 1:1–3

The other part of the foundation of fellowship is to walk in light, or in other words, to walk in truth.

This is the message which we have heard from Him and declare to you, that God is light and in Him is no darkness at all.
If we say that we have fellowship with Him, and walk in darkness, we lie and do not practice the truth.
But if we walk in the light as He is in the light, we have fellowship with one another, and the blood of Jesus Christ His Son cleanses us from all sin.

1 John 1:5–7

The intimate communion of the Lord is with those who fear Him, and He will show them His covenant.

Psalm 25:14—RV60

Why make the word of God so complex, if it is so simple? Yes, it is simple for those who are willing to know and obey His will.

Jesus answered them and said, 'My doctrine is not Mine, but His who sent Me.
If anyone wills to do His will, he shall know concerning the doctrine, whether it is from God or whether I speak on My own authority.'

John 7:16–17

CHAPTER 8

The Rapture of the Church

Although the word "rapture" does not appear in the Scriptures, it is commonly used to identify the greatest event in this world's history—the one that will change the direction of the world at this time. This event is the "snatching up" of the church from this world to heaven, by the Lord Jesus Christ. It is the promise of God for all those winners, who by their faith, love, obedience, and service to God, have been faithful to the Lord. The rapture of the church will occur before the beginning of the Great Tribulation.

> Because you have kept My command to persevere, I also
> will keep you from the hour of trial which shall come upon
> the whole world, to test those who dwell on the earth.
> Behold, I am coming quickly! Hold fast what you have,
> that no one may take your crown.
>
> Revelation 3:10–11

God will not allow the church to pass through the greatest tribulation and suffering ever to come upon the earth. The church will be carried to heaven before the destruction and death on earth come.

In antiquity, there was a man named Enoch, the seventh from Adam, who represents the church and the rapture very well.

> And Enoch walked with God; and he was not, for God
> took him.
>
> Genesis 5:24

By faith Enoch was taken away so that he did not see death, and was not found, because God had taken him; for before he was taken he had this testimony, that he pleased God.

Hebrews 11:5

Enoch was taken alive to heaven before the trial of the flood on the earth came. God saved him from judgment and suffering. For this reason, Enoch is a type of the church, which God will also save from the trial of the Great Tribulation that is to come upon the earth. Like Enoch, the church that will be taken now walks with God and has a testimony that pleases Him. The heaven, and then the new earth, will be her reward.

As we saw in chapter 12 of Revelation, there is a similarity between the event experienced by the prophet Noah and his family, when they were saved by God from the judgment of the flood, and the remnant of Israel that will be separated and saved during the time of the Great Tribulation.

Noah and his family went through the trial, but they came out victorious as they remained within the ark. So Noah and his family represent the remnant of Israel that will be victorious in the Great Tribulation. Enoch represents the church that will be taken victorious to heaven before the Great Tribulation.

The rapture is an event that will happen as quickly as the twinkling of an eye.

Now this I say, brethren, that flesh and blood cannot inherit the kingdom of God; nor does corruption inherit incorruption.
Behold, I tell you a mystery: We shall not all sleep, but we shall all be changed—in a moment, in the twinkling of an eye, at the last trumpet. For the trumpet will sound, and the dead will be raised incorruptible, and we shall be changed.
For this corruptible must put on incorruption, and this mortal must put on immortality.

1 Corinthians 15:50–53

It will happen so quickly that what those who remain on earth will see is the immediate disappearance of the servants of God, as it was also with Enoch. On that day, people will be doing the same daily chores, but when the church disappears, they will be terrified and cry bitterly, especially those who know at least a little about the word of God. They shall run scared, to and fro, without any comfort or control. Everything will be a debacle.

On the other hand, this will be the greatest expected day by all those who love the Lord Jesus. Hallelujah, glory to God!

> But I do not want you to be ignorant, brethren, concerning those who have fallen asleep, lest you sorrow as others who have no hope.
>
> For if we believe that Jesus died and rose again, even so God will bring with Him those who sleep in Jesus.
>
> For this we say to you by the word of the Lord, that we who are alive and remain until the coming of the Lord will by no means precede those who are asleep.
>
> For the Lord Himself will descend from heaven with a shout, with the voice of an archangel, and with the trumpet of God. And the dead in Christ will rise first.
>
> Then we who are alive and remain shall be caught up together with them in the clouds to meet the Lord in the air. And thus we shall always be with the Lord.
>
> 1 Thessalonians 4:13–17

Oh, glory to the Lord Jesus! The injustices against the saints of the Lord are finished. The time has arrived for those who withstood temptation to "fly" to the glory of God and of Christ. This will be the time to experience the salvation of God.

We see in this passage that in the rapture of the church, Jesus will not descend to earth, but He will call and catch up the church to join Him in the air, to continue then to heaven.

The church, represented in the Book of Revelation by the twenty-four elders who are sitting around the throne of God (Rev. 4:4), will remain in that glorious place until she comes down to the new earth, after the Millennium, as the bride of Christ. "Then I, John, saw the holy city, New Jerusalem, coming down out of heaven from God, prepared as a bride adorned for her husband" (Rev. 21:2; see also 21:9–27).

John 14:3 says, "And if I go and prepare a place for you, I will come again and receive you to Myself ..." The church is the only one that can be the abode and holy temple of God (Eph. 2:22). In the rapture, Jesus comes for people in whom His presence dwells, those who express a clear and true spiritual image of Himself.

"If anyone loves Me, he will keep My word; and My Father will love him, and We will come to him and make Our home with him" (John 14:23). Jesus does not come for a church with an appearance of holiness, but one that He may see Himself reflected in her.

The catching up of the church will definitely take many by surprise. There are people who believe that the church will go through the Great Tribulation; others say that the period of the Great Tribulation is the one in which we are currently living; there are even others who believe that the Great Tribulation has already happened. But God's message is clear and unequivocal. The Father has a purpose for the church and He will fulfill it thoroughly.

> He who overcomes, I will make him a pillar in the temple of My God, and he shall go out no more. I will write on him the name of My God and the name of the city of My God, the New Jerusalem, which comes down out of heaven from My God. And I will write on him My new name.
>
> Revelation 3:12

Unlike the rapture, which will happen in a blink of an eye, and in which Christ calls His church from above, in the second coming, Christ will come down to the earth and He will be seen by many. In this second coming, which will occur at the end of the Great Tribulation, Christ will stand on the Mount of Olives in Jerusalem, as prophesied by the prophets of the old covenant and the apostles.

> And in that day His feet will stand on the Mount of Olives, which faces Jerusalem on the east. And the Mount of Olives shall be split in two …
>
> Zechariah 14:4

> Now when He had spoken these things, while they watched, He was taken up, and a cloud received Him out of their sight.
> And while they looked steadfastly toward heaven as He went up, behold, two men stood by them in white apparel, who also said, 'Men of Galilee, why do you stand gazing up into heaven? This same Jesus, who was taken up from

you into heaven, will so come in like manner as you saw
Him go into heaven.'
Then they returned to Jerusalem from the mount called
Olivet, which is near Jerusalem, a Sabbath day's journey.

Acts 1:9–12

Christ will come down, with His angels, to the inhabitants of Israel.
With this second coming of Jesus, the greatest battle in all the history of
the earth will take place, called the Battle of Armageddon, where the entire
army of the enemies of the Lord will be destroyed. The other inhabitants
of the earth who have not believed and served God will be judged and
thrown into hell.

When the Son of Man comes in His glory, and all the
holy angels with Him, then He will sit on the throne of
His glory.
All the nations will be gathered before Him, and He will
separate them one from another, as a shepherd divides his
sheep from the goats.
And He will set the sheep on His right hand, but the goats
on the left.
Then the King will say to those on His right hand, 'Come,
you blessed of My Father, inherit the kingdom prepared
for you from the foundation of the world.
Then He will also say to those on the left hand, 'Depart
from Me, you cursed, into the everlasting fire prepared for
the devil and his angels.'
And these will go away into everlasting punishment, but
the righteous into eternal life.

Matthew 25:31–34, 41, 46

A similar picture is also found in Jude, verses 14–15:

Now Enoch, the seventh from Adam, prophesied about
these men also, saying, 'Behold, the Lord comes with ten
thousands of His saints [angels], to execute judgment on
all, to convict all who are ungodly among them of all their
ungodly deeds which they have committed in an ungodly
way, and of all the harsh things which ungodly sinners
have spoken against Him.'

310

After that trial on earth, Jesus will establish a kingdom of one thousand years. The faithful people who come out of the Great Tribulation will enter the millennial kingdom with their mortal bodies. In contrast, as mentioned before, the bodies of the members of the church will be transformed, receiving immortal and incorruptible bodies. In this way, the church will be snatched up and carried to heaven; she will not stay on earth to partake of the millennial kingdom.

If we had to go through the Great Tribulation, then rather than watch and wait upon the Lord, we would have to watch and wait for the sufferings of the Great Tribulation. This is contrary to the teaching of Christ that encourages us to watch out, because "the day of the Lord so comes as a thief in the night" and to "comfort one another with these words."

Is our glorious hope, mentioned by apostle Paul, to wait for the Great Tribulation? How can you encourage and comfort one another (1 Thess. 4:18; 5:11) if what comes over all is tribulation and anguish, "as labor pains upon a pregnant woman. And they shall not escape" (1 Thess. 5:3)?

The Scriptures teach that the Great Tribulation is a judgment for the unbelievers, not for the faithful people. Judgment of God means wrath of God, and it is prepared for those who displease God and live in disobedience to His word.

> For the wrath of God is revealed from heaven against all ungodliness and unrighteousness of men, who suppress the truth in unrighteousness.
> But we know that the judgment of God is according to truth against those who practice such things.
>
> Romans 1:18; 2:2

We cannot be confused, for the Scriptures are clear: the rapture and the second coming of Christ to the earth are two different events, separated by a period of about seven years.

Let us see this fact through the example of the Feast of Tabernacles, which is one of the three most important national Jewish holidays celebrated since ancient times in Israel, namely: the Passover, Pentecost, and the Tabernacles.

We know that many Jewish events have more than one meaning and fulfillment. For example, the Feast of Passover marked the exit of the Israelites from Egypt and also represented the salvation of God.

God commanded Israel, before the departure from Egypt, to kill a lamb and to eat it, and to put the blood of the lamb on the two doorposts and the lintel of their houses (Ex. 12:1–28). In this way, the plague of death of the firstborn would pass over the people of Israel. This feast was celebrated by God's command on the fourteenth day of the first month (Nisan), according to the Jewish calendar.

On the other hand, Christ was crucified on the same day the Feast of Passover was celebrated, showing thereby that Christ Himself was the true Passover—the true salvation of God.

Like the blood of the lambs which saved the people of Israel from the death of their firstborn, now the blood of Christ makes us free from all sin, and opens the door for the salvation of our souls. Christ was the true Lamb of Passover, who offered Himself in sacrifice for all mankind. This was not a coincidence in history that Jesus was crucified during the Feast of Passover.

Fifty days after the Feast of Passover, the Feast of Pentecost was celebrated, in which the first fruits of the earth were offered to God (Lev. 23:15–21; Deut. 16:9–12). The same day Israel was celebrating the Feast of Pentecost God chose to pour out the Holy Spirit into the disciples of Jesus.

> When the Day of Pentecost had fully come, they were all with one accord in one place.
> And suddenly there came a sound from heaven, as of a rushing mighty wind, and it filled the whole house where they were sitting.
> Then there appeared to them divided tongues, as of fire, and one sat upon each of them.
> And they were all filled with the Holy Spirit and began to speak with other tongues, as the Spirit gave them utterance.
>
> Acts 2:1–4

People from all nations were celebrating this feast in Jerusalem, and all of them witnessed this great event. On the Feast of Pentecost, the people offered to God the best of their crops. On the day of Pentecost, God gave the people the best He had, the Holy Spirit. It was not a mere coincidence that these two events happened on the same day.

As we have seen, both the death of Christ and the coming of the Holy Spirit concurred with the celebration of the feasts of Passover and Pentecost, respectively. So also, the third national Feast of Tabernacles will have a double meaning and fulfillment.

The Feast of Tabernacles began on a Sabbath day and ended on the next Sabbath day. This celebration began on the fifteenth day of the seventh month, according to the Jewish calendar. It commemorates the sojourn of Israel in the desert, after its exodus from Egypt (Lev. 23:34–44; Deut. 16:13–15; John 7:2).

The inhabitants of Israel dwelled in tabernacles (movable booths) for seven days. This feast began after the harvest of the fruits. It represented the victory and final salvation of Israel from the yoke of slavery in Egypt. Two trumpets were sounded to summon the congregation of Israel: one at the beginning of the feast, on the fifteenth day of the seventh month, and the other one at the end of the feast, seven days after the feast started (Num. 10:1–10).

I understand that like the other two national holidays, the Feast of Tabernacles will also have more than one meaning and fulfillment. It will concur with two events of utmost importance—the rapture of the church and the second coming of Christ to the earth. The first trumpet blow represents the convocation of the church to be presented to the Lord Jesus in the air,

with the voice of an archangel, and with the trumpet of God.

1 Thessalonians 4:16

In a moment, in the twinkling of an eye, at the last trumpet. For the trumpet will sound, and the dead will be raised incorruptible, and we shall be changed.

1 Corinthians 15:52

In other words, the first trumpet coincides with the calling of the church in the rapture. The second trumpet blow represents the convening of the believers who are found on the earth at the end of the Great Tribulation. "And He will send His angels with a great sound of a trumpet, and they will gather together His elect from the four winds, from one end of heaven to the other" (Matt. 24:31).

Therefore, this second trumpet represents the second coming of Christ to the earth, when the people who will be saved at the end of the Great Tribulation are gathered before the King and Lord Jesus Christ.

As we have seen, a period of seven days separates the beginning and the end of the Feast of Tabernacles; in the same way, a period of seven years will separate the rapture of the church and the second coming of Christ.

We can also see that the Feast of Tabernacles began on a Sabbath day and ended on the next Sabbath day. Likewise, the day of the rapture is seen as the eternal rest of the church, and the Millennium as the expected rest of the people of God (Israel and the other nations). As stated in Hebrews 4:10, "For he who has entered His rest has himself also ceased from his works as God did from His."

It is great and wonderful to see how God has designed all this so perfectly and how He will fulfill all these promises.

There is a wonderful word in 2 Thessalonians 2:1–12 that clarifies even more regarding the rapture of the church, our meeting with Christ. I will cite part of the passage:

> Now, brethren, concerning the coming of our Lord Jesus Christ and our gathering together to Him, we ask you, not to be soon shaken in mind or troubled, either by spirit or by word or by letter, as if from us, as though the day of Christ had come.
> And now you know what is restraining, that he may be revealed in his own time.
> For the mystery of lawlessness is already at work; only He who now restrains will do so until He is taken out of the way.
> And then the lawless one will be revealed, whom the Lord will consume with the breath of His mouth and destroy with the brightness of His coming.
>
> 2 Thessalonians 2:1–2, 6–8

What does the Lord show us in this passage? It tells us that there is someone who currently stops that evil and wicked one (the Antichrist) from being fully manifested. It also tells us that once that someone is removed, that wicked one will take whole control.

We know that the church is the only one dwelling place of God here on earth. Therefore, the church (of course, the Holy Spirit through the church) is the only one that can stop the devil from being fully manifest on earth.

But when the church is taken away to heaven in the rapture, then the wicked one, the Antichrist, will manifest with all power. This full manifestation will occur at the beginning of the Great Tribulation, when the church is no longer present on the earth.

In 2 Timothy 3:1–5, the Lord, through the apostle Paul, describes the character of men in the last days. The passage says,

But know this, that in the last days perilous times will come:
For men will be lovers of themselves, lovers of money, boasters, proud, blasphemers, disobedient to parents, unthankful, unholy, unloving, unforgiving, slanderers, without self-control, brutal, despisers of good, traitors, headstrong, haughty, lovers of pleasure rather than lovers of God, having a form of godliness but denying its power. And from such people turn away!

We see here the full manifestation of the devil in mankind. How can you expect people to treat you in the latter days, with kindness and gentleness? This passage has the answer. In the last days, people will "eat each other." Selfishness will be the normal attitude among the inhabitants of the earth, even within the most intimate family circle.

But that kind of life can be avoided. Come, love and serve the Lord; He will keep you from all the evil that comes over the entire world.

To conclude this chapter on the rapture, I include here 2 Thessalonians 1:3–12, to encourage you to see the great blessing God has for all those who love and serve Him with all their heart, soul, mind, and strength.

We are bound to thank God always for you, brethren, as it is fitting, because your faith grows exceedingly, and the love of every one of you all abounds toward each other, so that we ourselves boast of you among the churches of God for your patience and faith in all your persecutions and tribulations that you endure, which is manifest evidence of the righteous judgment of God, that you may be counted worthy of the kingdom of God, for which you also suffer; since it is a righteous thing with God to repay with tribulation those who trouble you, and to give you who are troubled rest with us when the Lord Jesus is revealed from heaven with His mighty angels, in flaming fire taking vengeance on those who do not know God, and on those who do not obey the gospel of our Lord Jesus Christ. These shall be punished with everlasting destruction from the presence of the Lord and from the glory of His power, when He comes, in that Day, to be glorified in His saints and to be admired among all those who believe, because our testimony among you was believed.

Therefore we also pray always for you that our God would count you worthy of this calling, and fulfill all the good pleasure of His goodness and the work of faith with power, that the name of our Lord Jesus Christ may be glorified in you, and you in Him, according to the grace of our God and the Lord Jesus Christ.

The snatching up of the church to heaven is an event that we can categorize as imminent; therefore, get ready for your soon encounter with Christ. Now is the time—He comes "as a thief in the night," and He will not delay. Today is the day that you can escape from all the tribulation and anguish that will come over the entire world. Today is the day of salvation.

Dear reader, as a final note, I would like to leave you with this thought: even above all that has been shared so far, regarding what will happen on earth and to all mankind, even if there were no Great Tribulation or hell (although we know there are), we must love and serve God. We cannot love and serve God out of fear or any other temporary reason. Love and serve God for one simple reason—because He is God, yes, and because He is the Lord of our lives. Amen.

"And the Spirit and the bride say, 'Come!'
And let him who hears say, 'Come!'
And let him who thirsts come.
Whoever desires, let him take the water of life freely."

OH, LORD JESUS, RIGHTLY WE LOVE YOU!

References

Bible References:

1. NKJV: New King James (copyright © 1982 by Thomas Nelson, Inc. Used by permission. All rights reserved).
2. NKJV–OL: New King James, online version: http://bible.gospelcom.net or http://www.biblegateway.com
3. RV60: Biblia Reina-Valera 1960™ © Sociedades Bíblicas en América Latina, 1960. Derechos renovados 1988, Sociedades Bíblicas Unidas. Utilizado con permiso.
4. ARV: Antigua Versión de la Biblia Casiodoro de Reina (Old Version of Casiodoro de Reina Bible).
5. KJV: King James Bible, (1979). Holman Bible Publishers.
6. BJ: Biblia de Jerusalén. (1975). Bilbao: Desclee de Brouwer.
7. Darby: Bible edited by J. N. Darby. (1980). Kingston Bible Trust.
8. IGNT: The Interlinear Greek - English New Testament (1976). Alfred Marshall D.Litt. Grand Rapids, Michigan, USA. Zondervan Publishing House.
9. IHB–OL: Hebrew Online Interlinear Bible. http://www.scripture4all.org/OnlineInterlinear/Hebrew_Index.htm.

Other References:

1. Larkin, Clarence. *Dispensational Truth.* (p. 6). Glenside, PA, USA: Rev. Clarence Larkin Est. 1920.
2. *The Roman Empire.* In *The World Book Encyclopedia.* (vol. 16, pp. 382-383). USA: World Book. 1985.
3. Fekete, I. *Cómo y Por Qué del Mercado Común* (How and Why of the Common Market). Barcelona, España: Molino. 1976.

4. "La Torre Louis Weiss el gran parecido con 'la torre de babel'". August 9, 2012. *Noticidiario, Wordpress.com site: http://noticidiario.wordpress.com/2012/08/09/la-torre-louis-weiss-el-gran-parecido-con-la-torre-de-babel.* (Accessed March 7, 2013.)

5. *Apocryphal books: 1 Maccabees Chapter 1, and 2 Maccabees 5:11–26, 6:1–9.* Biblia de Jerusalén. Bilbao: Desclee de Brouwer. 1975.

    Fay, Frederic. L. *Geografía Bíblica* (Biblical Geography). (p. 23). Kansas City, Missouri, USA: Casa Nazarena de Publicaciones. 1974.

6. *Diccionario Ilustrado de la Biblia* (Illustrated Dictionary of the Bible). (pp. 117, 155). Ed. Nelson, W. M. Miami, FL: Caribe. 1974.

7. Pasten, Consuelo; Hernán Grenett. "Vino, fibrinolisis y salud" (Wine, fibrinolysis and health). Revista Médica de Chile: vol. 134, no. 8, pp. 1040–1048. August 2006. *http://dx.doi.org/10.4067/S0034-98872006000800015.* (Accessed March 4, 2013.)

    Drago Serrano, María E.; Marisol López López; Teresita del Rosario Sainz Espuñes. "Componentes Bioactivos de Alimentos Funcionales de Origen Vegetal". Revista Mexicana de Ciencias Farmacéuticas: vol. 37, no. 4, pp. 58–68. October–December 2006. *www.redalyc.org/pdf/579/57937408.pdf.* (Accessed March 4, 2013.)

    Hernando, Esperanza. "Aceite de Olivo" (Olive Oil). Plantas Medicinales. (September 9, 2009). *www.plantas-medicinales.es/red/aceite-de-oliva.* (Accessed December 29, 2012.)

    "Remedios caseros con aceite de oliva." (n.d.). *Sabor artesano. www.sabor-artesano.com/remedios-aceite-oliva.htm.* (Accessed March 4, 2013.)

8. "Midyear 2012 population." U.S. Census Bureau. *www.census.gov/population/international/data/idb/worldpoptotal.php.*

9. Waller, Douglas. *China's Arms Race.* Time Magazine. 153 (4). February 1, 1999.

10. Povoledo, Elisabetta. *Vatican Calls for Oversight of the World's Finances.* The New York Times newspaper. (October 25, 2011).

11. *Tabla de Peso y Medidas* (Table of Weight and Measurements). Biblia Reina-Valera. Sociedades Bíblicas Unidas. 1960.
12. *Roma.* In *Enciclopedia Hispánica.* (vol. 12, p. 386). Encyclopedia Britannica Publishers. 1990.
13. *Inquisición* (Inquisition). In *Enciclopedia Hispánica.* (vol. 8, pp. 194–195). Encyclopedia Britannica Publishers. 1990.
14. Goodstein, Laurie. "An Interview With Pope Francis." September 19, 2013. *The New York Times newspaper. www.nytimes. com/2013/09/20/world/europe/an-interview-with-pope-francis.html?pagewanted=all&_r=0.* (Accessed September 20, 2013.)
    Goodstein, Laurie. "Pope Says Church Is 'Obsessed' With Gays, Abortion and Birth Control." September 19, 2013. *The New York Times newspaper. www.nytimes.com/2013/09/20/world/europe/pope-bluntly-faults-churchs-focus-on-gays-and-abortion.html.* (Accessed September 20, 2013.)
15. Meotti, Giulio. "A Seat for the Pope at King David's Tomb." February 01, 2013. *Arutz Sheva Newspaper. www.israelnationalnews. com/Articles/Article.aspx/12814#.UpUn3J1LR9A.* (Accessed November 26, 2013.)
16. *Tabla de Peso y Medidas* (Table of Weight and Measurements). Biblia Reina-Valera. Sociedades Bíblicas Unidas. 1960.
17. *United States.* In *The World Book Encyclopedia* (vol. 20, p. 43). USA: World Book. 1985.
18. *Russia.* In *The World Book Encyclopedia* (vol. 16, pp. 517–518). USA: World Book. 1985.
19. "Magog." 2011. *Wikipedia – The Free Encyclopedia. http://en.wikipedia.org/w/index.php?title=Magog_(Bible) &oldid=440985391.* (Accessed September 2, 2011.)
    "Mushki." 2011. *Wikipedia – The Free Encyclopedia. http://en.wikipedia.org/w/index.php?title=Mushki& oldid=440099798.* (Accessed September 2, 2011.)
    "Tubal." 2011. *Wikipedia – The Free Encyclopedia. http:// en.wikipedia.org/w/index.php?title=Tubal&oldid=445478838.* (Accessed September 2, 2011.)
    Coleman, Lyman. "The World as known to the Hebrews." 2006. *Wikipedia – The Free Encyclopedia. http://en.wikipedia. org/wiki/File:Noahsworld_map.jpg#filelinks.* (Accessed September 2, 2011.)

20. "Russian & East German Documents on Ethiopia and the Horn of Africa, 1977-78." Soviet Foreign Ministry, Background Report on Soviet-Ethiopian Relations. April 3, 1978. *www.banadir. com/77/36.shtml.* (Accessed February 25, 2013.)

"International Affairs." Federal Democratic Republic of Ethiopia, Ministry of Foreign Affairs Internet site. *www.mfa.gov.et/ BilateralMore.php?pg=25.* (Accessed February 25, 2013.)

21. "Russia eyes Med naval base in Syria." July 21, 2009. *United Press International. www.upi.com/Top_News/Special/2009/07/21/ Russia-eyes-Med-naval-base-in-Syria/UPI-87351248190500.* (Accessed September 2, 2011.)

Safronovv, Ivan. "Russia to defend its principal Middle East ally: Moscow takes Syria under its protection." July 28, 2006. *Global Research. www.globalresearch.ca/russia-to-defend-its-principal-middle-east-ally-moscow-takes-syria-under-its-protection/2847.* (Accessed November 9, 2009.)

"Russia builds key naval HQ in Syria: Missile presence worries Israel." July 30, 2009. *DEBKAfile Newspaper. www.debka.com/ search/?search_string=Russia+builds+key+naval+HQ+in+ Syria&x=36&y=14.* (Accessed November 9, 2009.)

22. "Vladimir Putin." 2012. *Wikipedia – The Free Encyclopedia. http://en.wikipedia.org/w/index.php?title=Vladimir_ Putin&oldid=507164214#Libya.* (Accessed August 14, 2012.)

"Libya plans to spend $4.7B on defense." March 26, 2013. *UPI.com. www.upi.com/Business_News/Security-Industry/2013/03/26/ Libya-plans-to-spend-47B-on-defense/UPI-37951364327364.* (Accessed March 26, 2013.)

23. "Vladimir Putin." 2012. *Wikipedia – The Free Encyclopedia. http://en.wikipedia.org/w/index.php?title=Vladimir_ Putin&oldid=507164214#Libya.* (Accessed August 14, 2012.)

24. "Iran–Russia relations." 2012. *Wikipedia – The Free Encyclopedia. http://en.wikipedia.org/w/index.php?title=Iran%E2%80% 93Russia_relations&oldid=507511670.* (Accessed August 20, 2012.)

25. "The Gog Magog War." 2013. *ProphecyTube.com. www. prophecytube.com/articles/gog.html.* (Accessed March 7, 2013.)